Breaking Through the Wall

How God Communicates with His Lost Creation

by
Keith Clouten

TEACH Services, Inc.
PUBLISHING
www.TEACHServices.com • (800) 367-1844

Copyright © 2018 Keith Clouten

Copyright © 2018 TEACH Services, Inc.

ISBN-13: 978-1-4796-0832-4 (Paperback)

ISBN-13: 978-1-4796-0833-1 (ePub)

ISBN-13: 978-1-4796-0834-8 (Mobi)

Library of Congress Control Number: 2017919080

TEACH Services, Inc.
P U B L I S H I N G
www.TEACHServices.com • (800) 367-1844

"Captivating" might not be a word you associate with reading a manuscript on Biblical inspiration, yet, in THE WALL, Keith Clouten has succeeded in blending extensive scholarly research, humility and personal testimony splendidly. Keith is a retired University Librarian, deeply committed Christian, family man, world traveller, and engaged humanitarian, who seeks to stimulate conversation and share wisdom on the relevant topic of how to embrace the Bible as God's Living Word, while not burying our heads in the sands of conformity and comfort zones. I truly believe you will be blessed by reading of his "journey".

—Ron Sydenham, retired Senior Pastor,
College Heights Church, Alberta

Knowing who God is and how to know His will for our lives is not as easy as it once was assumed. In recent years, many issues and ideas have caused people to wonder how we can know God and what is the role of the Bible in this. Can we trust the Bible? Is it a reliable book? Keith Clouten's book Breaking Through the Wall approaches the subject from his own personal experience and questions he has had in his spiritual journey. The inspiration and reliability of the Bible have become a contentious subject and many readers will appreciate Clouten's approach and answers to some difficult questions. As he wrestled with these ideas he found a way to articulate his confidence in the Bible as God's word using the metaphor of a wall and how God broke through the wall to reach a sinful humanity. Clouten affirms that the Bible is God's inspired message to humankind and it is a reliable source of information about God and His will. The book also discusses various issues regarding the writings of Ellen White whom Seventh-day Adventists consider a messenger from God. Clouten addresses many of the questions raised in relationship to her writings and provides valuable answers. Thoughtful readers will appreciate and be challenged by the contributions this book offers to questions regarding revelation, inspiration and the interpretation of sacred writings.

—Denis Fortin, Professor of Historical Theology,
Andrews University; Co-editor, The Ellen G. White Encyclopedia

I have read a number of books on revelation and inspiration during my journey as a pastor, teacher and youth director. During my professional life I have worked with university student groups as they have grappled with what they have been taught by their professors and struggled to reconcile their education and their faith. Keith's personal, honest struggle will resonate with the journey so many people find themselves having travelled. He has worked through so many of the issues related to this topic and I believe his book will prove to have lasting value to all Christians who have honestly wanted solid answers to their questions. So many thinking, educated Christians have sought answers to help deal with the questions hurled at them from both sides of the issues, from the well meaning critics who contend that every word in scripture was dictated by the Spirit of God and hence must be accepted literally, to those who assert that scripture gives us valuable insights into the spiritual world but should not be held up as having any real or final authority. I believe that this book will become a treasured part of the libraries of both the professional pastor and the serious bible student.

—Barry Gane, Adjunct Professor,
SDA Theological Seminary Andrews University;
Conjoint Senior Lecturer, Faculty of Arts, Nursing and Theology,
Avondale College of Higher Education

Contents

Acknowledgements

I think Rodgers and Hammerstein were right when they said, "Nothing comes from nothing." Academically speaking, I brought almost nothing to an understanding of biblical revelation and inspiration. In prayerful study of the Word of God, though, I discovered everything. By immersing myself in the Scriptures and reading widely from respected scholars of the Word, I sourced what I needed to write this book. I am also grateful for friends and colleagues who took the time to read and react to my sometimes-tentative reflections and ruminations.

Four friends in my home province of Alberta, Canada have given valuable help and encouragement as they evaluated my manuscript. Don Corkum, a retired conference president, has been a valued family friend and counselor ever since our arrival in Canada nearly forty years ago. Ron Sydenham was one of my first student library workers in 1980 and since retired as lead pastor of my home church at Burman University. Ron Bissell has been a pastor and university professor in religious studies and is now a close friend and neighbor in our Lacombe condominium community. Ian Hartley, sporting a South African accent, is a retired Alberta pastor and creative thinker.

In the wider world, I am deeply indebted to three individuals. Denis Fortin, who was another of my student library workers at CUC, is now a professor of historical theology in the SDA Theological Seminary at Andrews University and co-editor of *The Ellen G. White Encyclopedia*. Australian-born Barry Gane earned a doctoral degree in organizational leadership and has served the church in the South Pacific and at Avondale College of Higher Education. Neville Clouten, my brother, has always been my confidant and consultant in a wide range of issues and interests.

Last and best, I owe my deepest gratitude to the precious gift of the Holy Spirit, who has always been "on call" for me. Without that level of guidance, my words amount to precisely nothing.

—Keith Clouten

Why I Wrote This Book

The camp-meeting preacher made his final re-consecration call; dozens moved forward while the congregation sang the final verse of the hymn:

> Just as I am, though tossed about
>
> With many a conflict, many a doubt,
>
> Strivings within and fears without,
>
> O Lamb of God, I come, I come.

However, I did not come. Those words aggravated a raw spot in my soul.

Was I a practicing Seventh-day Adventist? Of course. Did I accept the Bible as the Word of God? Yes—well, I think so. What about the writings of Ellen White? Did I accept her as inspired? I'm sorry, but no, though I did not say that very loudly.

As I write this preface in 2017, I am recalling that camp-meeting of fifty years past in my Australian homeland. That low point in my spiritual experience characterized a period of disillusionment with the role and writings of Ellen G. White. I had grown up with a firm belief that this woman was God's prophetic voice to the Seventh-day Adventist Church as it grew from a small band of Millerites who survived the Great Disappointment of October 1844. I knew instinctively, as a *sine qua non* of an Adventist education, that both the Bible and Ellen White were verbally inspired and infallible. One of my college professors vowed that he would destroy all of Ellen White's books if he found a single error in one of them. And why not? I would certainly do the same.

However, I soon discovered that my beloved prophet was not perfect or infallible. The discovery of some strange utterances in her early writing—like the amalgamation of men with animals and unscientific statements about earthquakes and volcanoes—shook me to the core of my being. I spent some sleepless nights wondering what this meant to my belief in Ellen White, and what I should do about it. Sharing my discoveries with any other Seventh-day Adventist might cost me my church employment. Asking questions was dangerous. Therefore, I locked my churning thoughts in a place where they would never be seen or known.

For twenty-five years, I discarded Ellen White from my reading and serious consideration. They were years of external piety, but inner conflict. The 1967 camp-meeting experience reflected well those doubts and painful thoughts.

Nevertheless, God had not abandoned me. In 1979, our family migrated from Australia to Canada, where I accepted the position of library director at Canadian Union College (now Burman University). I still rejected the inspiration of Ellen White, but now I felt more comfortable having questions for which I had no answers. I held to a core of beliefs that identified me as a Seventh-day Adventist. The Bible was important to me, though the picture of God I sometimes encountered in the Old Testament bothered me.

That was my religious stance in 1982 when the student director of campus ministries came to my office one day, asking if I would write a one-act play for a week-long celebration of Adventist history. I had never written a play, and my knowledge of Adventist history at that time was abysmal, but the idea sounded interesting, so I agreed. The week-long program was so successful that it birthed an annual Adventist Heritage Sabbath at the campus church. I took up the task of writing most of the plays, several of which were later published by the North American Division of the church. All this ignited my interest in Adventist history, but lacking experience in that field, I submitted each play to James Nix, who then directed the Ellen G. White Estate branch office at Loma Linda University. I think Jim's knowledge of Adventist history topped the field in North America at that time. His enthusiasm for the subject inspired me.

When Jim advertised a week-long tour of Adventist history sites in New England following an Adventist librarians' conference in Massachusetts, I signed up. Only five other librarians joined the tour, and I was assigned to travel with Jim in his car.

Something deep and important happened to me during that week. I grew in my understanding of Ellen White's role in the formation of the Seventh-day Adventist Church, and even though I did not yet fully understand the nature of her inspiration, I found a confidence in the leading of God in my church's history. The final day of our tour was Sabbath, and Jim took us to the William Miller farm in upstate New York. The old home was still owned and occupied by an unfriendly farmer, but we worshipped in the nearby chapel. As Jim shared his own life story with our little group, I felt the drawing power of the Holy Spirit, and as we celebrated communion on nearby Ascension Rock, I recommitted my life to God.

My growth in understanding continued. Through reading and study, I grasped a new confidence in the Bible and ministry of Ellen White. That confidence became more firmly rooted as I sought the guidance of the Holy Spirit in my personal study of God's Word.

This book has been born out of my spiritual journey. The journey began with a blind faith that collapsed into a broken faith, but was eventually reborn and grew into the secure and living faith in which I stand today.

I know that my story is not unique. As Adventist Christians, we come from many different backgrounds and perceptions about the Scriptures. The pendulum of our understanding about revelation and inspiration swings all the way from belief in an error-free Bible in one direction, to a rationalistic approach that elevates human experience and logic above biblical authority in the other. A similar, broad spread of viewpoints exists in relation to Ellen White's role and authority within Seventh-day Adventism. Believers on both sides are sometimes perplexed with questions and doubts.

We are broken people, dangling a severed relationship with the One who created and sustains us. Sin has severely damaged our understanding and comprehension of God. False concepts of His nature and character range all the way from a disinterested deity who ignores the things that happen on our planet, to an angry God who tortures sinners in an eternally burning hell. In the pages of this book, using the metaphor of a wall, I will portray the formidable barrier that separates us from God, but then explore the amazing ways in which He breaks through that barrier to show us His great love. Whatever your spiritual experience has been, we may together seek to develop a greater understanding of God's character and deeper relationship with Him.

This book comes with a prayer that you will develop a new confidence in the sacred Scriptures, as well as a better understanding and appreciation for the role of Ellen White as God's messenger for a faith movement in a contemporary time.

Be blessed.

THE WALL—A PROLOGUE

During the summer of 2003, I spent a couple days visiting Berlin, a city reunited after the Cold War. Walking the streets, I was constantly reminded that for nearly thirty years, Berlin was a divided city, symbolic of a divided nation. A heavily fortified wall created a detestable barrier, severing communities and families until it was torn down in 1989.

There is another wall, formidable and ancient, bearing the scars of time, that is part of our existence. However, it is not a popular topic of conversation. Some believe the wall is non-existent, a figment of a diseased imagination. Others ignore it, hoping it will just go away.

Who built the wall? Some say that God built it eons ago, in a far-off time when He spoke the world into existence, but then abandoned us, throwing up this high wall so that we could never see or hear from Him again.

Others, with a kinder view of God, blame the devil for constructing the wall as part of a diabolical plan to forever exclude God from us, thus making Him inaccessible and, hopefully, forgotten.

Both are wrong. The sad reality is that *we* built the wall, and that is precisely where our story begins.

PART ONE:
BREAKTHROUGH

When we look in the direction of God

we see only the wall,

impregnable and offensive,

a sad and somber reality.

Is God lost forever

from our sin-darkened eyes?

Are we abandoned creatures

on a forgotten planet?

In our hopeless state, we can do nothing

to find God,

to communicate with Him,

to hear Him speak to us.

But God has done something!

Something unique and wonderful.

And just for us—a

Breakthrough

Breakthrough

Chapter 1—Relationship

Before we talk more about the wall, we must go back to the beginning—the Bible record as we find it in Genesis: "The Lord God formed a man from the dust of the ground and breathed into his nostrils the breath of life, and the man became a living being" (Gen. 2:7). We know it well, but let's use a little imagination in revisiting the story.

One memorable day, we find God doing something new, unexpected, and quite different from the way everything has been happening during creation week. Myriads of angelic beings have already watched in amazement as God has spoken birds, fish, and animals into existence. "He spoke and it came to be", exclaimed the poet, "by the breath of His mouth" (Ps. 33:9; v. 6).

The angels are still celebrating all those wonders when they see God the Son doing something strange and wonderful. In a forest glade, He is down on hands and knees, taking golden soil and working it with His fingers. The entire universe watches, spellbound, as God forms a completely new creature—a man. When the task is completed, He bends down, kisses the lips, breathes into the nostrils, and watches intently as the eyes open.

The man's first memory of his existence will be looking directly into the smiling eyes of his Maker.

God is still smiling as He draws the man to his feet; a tall, majestic figure, his bronze body a fitting match for the ochre brown of the soil. "I want you to meet Adam," God says, and it seems that the entire universe erupts with shouts of joy and amazement.

The angelic beings have already observed that unlike the other creatures, Adam does not have a mate; but God is not finished. "Watch now." Anticipating that He will take more soil and form a second human, the onlookers are surprised to see that God has a different plan. Bidding Adam lie down in the soft grass, He allows him to sleep. While the man dreams of happiness, God gently removes a small rib from his chest, close to his heart. With deft fingers, He manipulates the small bone and within minutes has formed the body of a beautiful woman. Looking on with admiration and astonishment, the entire universe breaks into galaxies of praise. Today they have witnessed the crowning acts of creation—"while the morning stars sang together and all the angels shouted for joy" (Job 38:7). And even while they sing His praise, the liquid notes of God's voice are heard: "My work of creation is complete. It is all very good."

The Image

Our original parents were a unique creation. God had said, "Let us make human beings in our image, to be like us. They will reign over the fish in the sea, the birds in the sky, the livestock, all the wild animals on the earth, and the small animals that scurry along the ground" (Gen. 1:26, NLT). What did God mean by "in our image"? Perhaps it was intended to indicate a physical likeness to God, though we might not want to carry that too far. I don't believe He created the gorilla in His likeness.

The idea of "image" has much more to do with God-like attributes or qualities. As King David pondered the greatness of the Creator God, he exclaimed, "When I consider your heavens, the work of your fingers, the moon and the stars which you have set in place, what are mere mortals that you are mindful of them, human beings that you care for them? You have made them a little lower than the heavenly beings and crowned them with glory and honor" (Ps. 8:3–5).

God gave so much of Himself when He created humanity. Thinking about "image", we may discover three very significant and unique ways in which the human creature shared God's attributes, and none of them were shared with the animal world. The first embodied *the gift of a mind* with a capacity to love, comprehend, know, analyze, and decide. God gave the human mind the potential for incredible ingenuity and creativity—a tiny piece of God's own creatorship, and because God is love and love cannot be forced, God built *freedom* into the human mind. Isn't it astonishing that God gave men and women the capacity and freedom to reject Him, the very One who created them?

A second aspect of God's image was *consciousness—self-awareness*. It means being cognizant of who we are and where we are in the universe. It means being aware of the mind itself, the presence of God in the universe, and our relationship to Him. Paul recognized this self-awareness when he told the philosophers of Athens that God gives us minds to comprehend Him. "God has done all this," he explained, "so that we will look for him and reach out and find him. He gives us the power to live, to move, and to be who we are" (Acts 17:27, 28, CEV).

The third significant aspect of God's "image" was *management*—to have dominion and "reign over" the created earth. David continued his eulogy by acknowledging, "You made them rulers over the works of your hands" (Ps. 8:6). God delegated authority to Adam and Eve. He gave them responsibility to care for and manage the small planet that He specially created for them. This represented an incredible gift from their Creator. It meant a diminutive relinquishing of His control over a defined part of the universe. He endowed humanity with a freedom to plan and make decisions about their environment. God retained the ownership while giving humans the privilege of management.

In the breathtaking tranquility of a garden, God communicated face to face with His human creatures. Adam and Eve spent their first full day together exploring their garden home in company with their loving Master. It was a special, holy day—the Sabbath, the culmination of God's creation. Their first walk of discovery represented communion, intimate relationship, and joy beyond expression. That garden experience was intended to be the opening chapter of a beautiful story that would go on forever.

Sadly, the journey of happiness came to an abrupt and unanticipated end. One tragic day, it took a spiraling downturn. When the first human couple yielded to the subtle invitation of Satan, masquerading as a serpent in a forbidden tree, the beautiful, direct, face-to-face communication with God was lost. Their disobedience created within them a distrust and fear of God, feelings of shame, and a broken relationship. From that point, men and women began to picture an angry God, ready to pounce and punish.

Sin quickly tarnished the image of God in men and women. The gifted mind, with its capacity to make free choices, was corrupted when Adam and Eve chose to disobey a carefully and lovingly formulated instruction. The first bad choice opened the way for multiple choices in favor of evil, warping their divinely installed minds. In the future, humans would apply their creative genius to hurt and destroy one another. There was hope, though. Paul urged, "Do not conform any longer to the pattern of this world, but be transformed by *the renewing of your mind*" (Rom. 12:2, NIV).

The gift of consciousness was also affected by the first act of sin. Adam and Eve quickly became aware of a changed relationship to their Creator and with each other. They became aware of their nakedness of body and soul and desperate need for covering.

On the third level, humans forfeited their right and ability to manage their beautiful earth. Although God maintained ownership of all creation, Satan quickly usurped man's delegated responsibility for the care of the earth. He claimed and took for himself a senior management position while sin, like a deadly cancer, invaded the world. God's beautiful earth would become an abused planet, asset for greed, and dumping ground for refuse.

The Wall

There was more to come. Distrust, fear, and hatred resulted in a formidable barrier—a wall—that brought separation between God and His created beings. As the years rolled on, people forgot that their Creator had once walked and talked with them. It was centuries later that Isaiah, a spokesman for God, reminded them why the separation had occurred: "Listen! The Lord's arm is not too weak to save you, nor is his ear too deaf to hear you call. It's your sins that have cut you off from God" (Isa. 59:1, 2, NLT).

The wall is with us, formidable and strong, but a God of love and kindness has breached it in several places. Mind you, the breaks are quite small, like holes in a fence, so that our eyes are shielded from the fullness of God's glory. Only with help from the Holy Spirit are we able to peek through the wall and comprehend the magnificence of God's grace. There is life in that look and a revelation of something amazing and beyond ourselves. At its best, though, we are seeing "through a glass, darkly", in the way the Apostle Paul described it. At a future day, though, it will again be "face-to-face" (1 Cor. 13:12).

The ways in which God penetrates the wall to communicate with broken humanity is the theme of this book. We will be talking a lot about the Bible, because it is our clearest window to God. The Holy Scriptures are filled with accounts of God breaking through the wall to His family on earth. I like to imagine that Jeremiah had something like the wall in mind when he wrote, "Is not My word . . . like a hammer that breaks a rock in pieces" (Jer. 23:29)? Certainly the most astonishing way that God breached the wall was by the gift of Himself in Jesus Christ. That event assures us that ultimately the wall will be totally demolished and the lost relationship between humanity and God will be restored.

In our study, we will discover and explore how ancient prophets and apostles received information and messages from God and how they conveyed to us what they saw and heard. We will also meet Ellen White, one of the founders of the Seventh-day Adventist Church, and explore her role as a messen-

We will be talking a lot about the Bible, because it is our clearest window to God.

ger of truth and hope for the times in which we live. We need to determine whether or how she fits into a category with the prophets of old. Dozens of books have been written about her life and ministry.[1] We will seek to understand the nature and interpretation of all inspired writings, acknowledging our human limitations to comprehend the God of the universe. We will pray for the Holy Spirit to be our personal guide and point us in right directions.

In the next six chapters, we will build a foundation for the remainder of the book, exploring the what, why, and how of divine communication. What was God's purpose in communicating with humans? Why was it important? What was it like to be a prophet? How did God communicate with him or her? What exactly do we mean by the terms "revelation" and "inspiration"? How was the coming of Jesus into the world a part of that revelation? What comprises the "canon" of Scripture? Are Ellen White's writings an addition to the sacred canon?

Once we have that background, we will seek prayerful understanding of a variety of topics that relate to biblical revelation and inspiration. How should we respond to the Fundamentalist Movement, which emphasizes verbal inspiration and a Bible without error? Did prophets sometimes include their personal opinions in their writings? How about the common knowledge and beliefs of their times? How should we understand literary dependence in the writings of Ellen White? We will look at how God's purpose is revealed in the history of past events and predictions of future events. What can the Bible say to us about science? Did God inspire Ellen White's health messages? Is the revelation of truth progressive? These are important and relevant questions for us living in the 21st century. Our study will be based firmly on the Bible; all other sources, including Ellen White, will be tested by the Scriptures.

You have already read how for twenty-five years of my life, I had serious questions about the authority of the Bible and rejected Ellen White as an inspired messenger of God. I will share more of my story later in this book, always with a prayer that it will encourage each of us in our faith and personal relationship with the God behind the wall.

To think about:

1. How did the life and teaching of Jesus portray the kind of depth of relationship that must have existed in the Garden of Eden? Consider Christ's words, prayers, and interactions with people.

2. "It is time to destroy all who have caused destruction on the earth" is the announcement of Revelation 11:18. What am I doing to protect the earth and its resources in my area of management responsibility?

References:

[1]   Three biographical sketches of Ellen White that I have read and appreciated are:

Arthur L. White, *Ellen G. White*. Her grandson tells her life story in six readable volumes.

George R. Knight, *Meeting Ellen White*.

Jerry Moon and Denis Kaiser, "For Jesus and Scripture: The Life of Ellen G. White", in *The Ellen G. White Encyclopedia*, 18–111

Chapter 2—Purpose

What was God's purpose in communicating with humanity? Why did He do it? During the long centuries after the fall, sin multiplied as the earth became a hotbed of corruption and crime. The world became a lawless mess as humanity became depraved and deranged. Why did God bother to break through the wall of fear and hatred and attempt to communicate with beings who almost totally disregarded Him? Why did He undertake the task? What information did He want them—and us—to have, and why is it important?

In this chapter, we will consider seven distinct purposes that God has for us in His revealed Word, the Scriptures. We might easily enumerate more than seven, but we will choose seven that have profound importance because of our hopeless condition in a messed-up world. As we do that, we might also ask whether Ellen White wrote with the same purposes.

One: A Way Out

The ultimate end of sin is death—eternal and forever. God spoke clearly to Adam and Eve, "You may freely eat the fruit of every tree in the garden—except the tree of the knowledge of good and evil. If you eat its fruit, you are sure to die" (Gen. 2:17, NLT). Those words were clear and unmistakable, until a silver-tongued serpent contradicted them: "You surely will *not* die." Thus, the fruit was taken.

The change came so quickly. Two naked people shivered in shame and fear, hiding from a God who must certainly kill them for their disobedience; two people with a desperate need for a way out, an escape hatch, a deliverance from the death penalty. Making that possible was the core element in God's reconnection with the broken couple. He instituted an amazing plan to restore what was lost. The details were unclear to Adam and his wife, but the Creator and Sustainer of the universe would come all the way down to our lonely planet to live and die as we do, but then live again, smashing the cruel chains of death to give the hope of life forever. Besides being the story of the New Testament, salvation from sin and death is a recurrent theme throughout the Old Testament, where we discover the predictions, promises, and longings for a Savior.

Writing to his young disciple, Timothy, Paul reminded him of what his mother, Eunice, and his grandmother, Lois, had taught him: "You have been taught the holy Scriptures from childhood, and they have given you the wisdom to receive the salvation that comes by trusting in Christ Jesus" (2 Tim. 3:15, NLT). Timothy, unlike most Jewish young men of his time, had a Greek father, but he was wonderfully blessed because most Jews failed to see that their Scriptures—the Old Testament as we know it today—pointed to Jesus Christ as their Savior. "You study the Scriptures diligently," Jesus reminded some of His listeners, "because you think that in them you possess eternal life." Then He added pointedly, "These are the very Scriptures that testify about me" (John 5:39).

The purpose of the gospel writers was to reveal Jesus as the way to salvation. John said it clearly, "These are written that you may believe that Jesus is the Messiah, the Son of God, and that by believing you may have life in his name." (John 20:31).

Salvation through Jesus was also one of the Ellen White's prominent themes. She once described the sacrifice of Jesus for our sins as "the great truth around which all other truths cluster."[1] In her understanding, "every truth in the Word of God, from Genesis to Revelation, must be studied in the light that streams from the cross of Calvary."[2]

Two: Truth

The God behind the wall wants us to understand the truth about Himself; He wants to counteract the clever lies woven by Satan. Truth comes to us from the Bible as a collection of essential beliefs or doctrines that define and describe God's character. Paul continued his words to Timothy by explaining, "All Scripture is inspired by God and is useful to teach us what is true and to make us realize what is wrong in our lives. It corrects us when we are wrong and teaches us to do what is right" (2 Tim. 3:16, NLT).

In the thinking of most Christians, doctrine is the set of beliefs held by a church. Unfortunately, for many of us, the term has developed a negative connotation. We need to understand, though, that doctrine is also defined as a "teaching," and the important teachings of the church are those that relate to the truth about God and His character of love. The Bible is the source, the only source, of all doctrine regarding the nature and character of God.

The Bible is not a textbook of systematic theology. Nowhere in Scripture is there a list of something like "twenty-eight fundamental beliefs", though we might sometimes wish for that. We must remember that the Bible writings were made by many prophets and apostles over a period of about 1,500 years, and God revealed some truth progressively during that time.

Discovering doctrine involves prayerful, careful study, guided by the Holy Spirit, comparing Scripture with Scripture and seeing how each reveals some aspect of the truth. We may be assured that every Bible truth will be completely consistent with the foundational truth that "God is love" (1 John 4:8).

Ellen White always upheld the Bible as the primary revelation of truth. "The Bible is the only rule of faith and doctrine", she declared.[3] She said many times that her writings were never to be used as the source of doctrinal belief. It comes as a surprise to some Adventists that Ellen White was not the initiator of the church's distinctive doctrines. Her early visions regarding Adventist pillars of faith such as the Sabbath, the unconscious state of the dead, and the pre-Advent judgment, simply confirmed what the pioneer Adventist leaders had already discovered and accepted from their prayerful study of the Scriptures.

Three: Correction and Instruction

Paul explained to Timothy: "All Scripture is inspired by God...It corrects us when we are wrong and teaches us to do what is right" (2 Tim.

3:16, NLT). Paul knew what a course correction meant. For several years, he had harassed and persecuted followers of Jesus because he thought he was doing what God wanted him to do. That changed abruptly one day along the Damascus Road. Now Paul reminds us that the Scriptures point out our flaws of character. Throughout his ministry, Paul found it imperative to reprove newly baptized Christians for their moral failures.

Reproof and correction of behavior, whether individual or corporate, was a significant part of a prophet's role. The prophet Nathan confronted King David after his love affair with Bathsheba and role in the death of her husband, Uriah the Hittite (see 2 Sam. 12). Old Testament prophets spoke forcefully against idolatry and injustice. Jesus often corrected the behavior of His disciples, sometimes their lack of faith, and often their ambitions to greatness. In our time, Ellen White wrote letters to individuals as well as testimonies to the church at large, dealing with the spiritual condition or moral failures of the recipients.

Instruction in right living is the other, positive side of the same coin. Bible versions variously translate Paul's Greek text as "instruction in righteousness" or "training in right living." Throughout the Bible, God gives commands and principles regarding the way we ought to live. A genuine faith in Christ transforms our lives and minds. Scripture is filled with inspired admonition on living according to God's plan, as well as case studies of God's grace at work in the lives of people who failed and repented.

Similarly, Ellen White's writings are filled with biblically based counsels on right living. Some of the most familiar examples are found in *Steps to Christ*, as well as specific instruction in her "Conflict of the Ages" series, starting with *Patriarchs and Prophets* and continuing through *The Great Controversy*. Her writings were intended to lead us back to the Bible as our foundation for godly living.

Four: Hope

Here we have one of God's primary purposes in communicating with us. He wants to give us hope. Paul wrote, "Everything that was written in the past was written to teach us, so that through the endurance taught in the Scriptures and the encouragement they provide, we might have hope" (Rom. 15:4). The Bible is a book of hope, beginning with God's promise to Adam and Eve right after their sin (see Gen. 3:15). Scripture presents multiple illustrations of His grace and forgiveness, as well as hope beyond the grave.

Very soon after the Millerite Disappointment of October 1844, Ellen White received her first vision. It was a motion picture that depicted a narrow, upward pathway to heaven on which the disappointed Adventists were traveling. They had been wrong about the event, but it marked the beginning of a journey of promise that would culminate in the soon return of Jesus. That vision brought hope to many disappointed and disillusioned believers. Hope became a prominent theme throughout her writings.

Five: The Future

God knows the future and understands our need to see light at the end of the sin tunnel. Tied to the topic of hope is the way God provides glimpses into the future. Speaking through the prophet Isaiah, God made clear His intention and ability to predict the future: "I am God, and there is no other; I am God and there is none like me. I make known the end from the beginning, from ancient times, what is still to come" (Isaiah 46:9, 10). Centuries later, Jesus shared with His disciples the upcoming events of His death and resurrection: "I am telling you now before it happens," He said, "so that when it does happen, you will believe that I am who I am" (John 13:19).

Declaring predictions was a role of most prophets. Some, like Jeremiah and Isaiah, were given many visions of future events. Among significant predictions were Jeremiah's prophecy of seventy years of Jewish exile in Babylon (see Jer. 25:11) and those of Daniel and the Apostle John about the end times.

Tied to the topic of hope is the way God provides glimpses into the future.

The Old Testament has many "conditional prophecies" which are often time related, depending for their fulfillment on people responses to God's promises and warnings. Jonah's prediction that Nineveh would be destroyed in forty days did not happen because the people repented. Through Jeremiah, God clearly stated that many of His threats were conditional: "Like clay in the hand of the potter, so are you in my hand, house of Israel. If at any time I announce that a nation or kingdom is to be uprooted, torn down, and destroyed, and if that nation I warned repents of its evil, then I will relent and not inflict on it the disaster I had planned" (Jer. 18:6–8).

Later, we will explore the topic of Bible predictions in greater depth, including the role of Ellen White in end-time predictions.

Six: God in History

The Bible is a book of history, but it is history from a particular viewpoint. The Scriptures uncover the events of history from *a divine perspective*. They reveal God's interaction with the world and its people. We should not think of the Bible as a history textbook or a scholarly history of the ancient world, because accuracy of factual detail is secondary to its purpose of revealing the hand of God in history. Think of it as an interpretation of history. Paul shares one of its purposes: "These things happened to them as examples, and were written down as warnings for us, on whom the fulfillment of the ages has come" (1 Cor. 10:11).

God's hand in history is emphasized several times in the Old Testament. The prophet's role was to interpret history for the people. The Psalmist declared: "I know that the Lord is great, that our Lord is greater than all gods. The Lord does whatever pleases him, in the heavens and on the earth, in the seas and all their depths" (Psalm 135:5, 6). In very clear words, God warned King Nebuchadnezzar of Babylon that he would be driven from his throne and dwell with the beasts of the field "until you acknowledge that the Most High is sovereign over the kingdoms on earth, and gives them to anyone he wishes" (Dan. 4:25).

God reveals to us that history began before creation week. In her book *The Great Controversy*, Ellen White portrays the outworking of the great controversy between Christ and Satan since the beginning of time, but with a special emphasis on the last two thousand years. Her book is not so much a history, but rather an interpretation of historical events through the centuries. She was not an historian and she relied on published histories of Europe and the Protestant Reformation which were sometimes factually inaccurate. In the same way as Scripture, *The Great Controversy* presents history from the divine perspective. The facts of history were subservient to a "proper understanding of their application," she said.[4]

The relationship between the facts of history and God's perspective on events is a large topic, and for some Christians a disturbing one. We will explore this topic in a later chapter.

Seven: Relationship

Finally, we come to one of the key themes in God's inspired Word. We already saw how life on this earth began as a special and intimate relationship between the Creator and humans. That beautiful relationship was lost when the wall of fear and distrust put God at a distance. The restoration of a love relationship is God's ultimate purpose for humanity.

However, the word "relationship" is found nowhere in the Bible. Its meaning is comprehended in a different term—"covenant." In a society steeped in sin, God looked longingly for individuals who were willing to stop what they were doing and listen to Him. In return for their trust and obedience, God provided generous promises and future blessings as part of a covenant relationship. The Old Testament stories tell how God found Noah, Abraham, Jacob, David, Daniel, and many others through whom the world's faithful would be blessed through the coming of Jesus.

The amazing reality is that God took the initiative in reestablishing relationship with sinful humanity. The apostle John expressed it in these simple words: "We love Him *because He first loved us*" (1 John 4:19, NKJV). God's covenant relationship with humanity forms an over-arching theme—a love story if you will—that starts in Genesis and ends in Revelation. David Asscherick of Light Bearers summarizes the entire biblical story with just three words: Creation, Conflict, and Covenant[5].

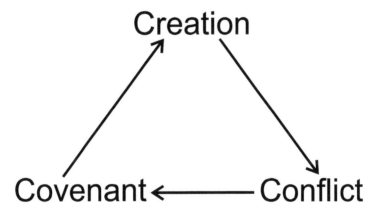

Figure 1: From Genesis to Revelation.

- It begins with **Creation**—a God who made the earth and established a face-to-face relationship with our first parents.
- The story continues with **Conflict**—the arrival of sin on this planet and its results, including the loss of that relationship.
- The good news is about **Covenant**—God working toward restoration of the relationship through the death and resurrection of Jesus; finally we come full circle to a new **Creation.**

Love is the basis of relationship. One great theme in the writings of Ellen White is the love of God. The phrase "God is love" comes as the first words of *Patriarchs and Prophets* and the last words of *The Great Controversy*.

To think about:

1.   Choose Abraham, Joseph, or David. Think of specific ways in which God revealed Himself and developed a relationship with that individual.

2.   The Bible reveals the hand of God in the history of Israel and the lives of individuals like the apostles Peter and Paul. Reflect on times and occasions when you have experienced the hand of God in your own life.

3.   How is the life and death of Jesus a "way out" for you personally?

References:

[1]   Ellen White, Manuscript 70, 1901.

[2]   Ellen White, *Gospel Workers*, 315.

[3]   White, *Fundamentals of Christian Education*, 126.

[4]   White, *Great Controversy*, xi.

[5]   David Asscherick, *What is the Bible?* God? *Episode 1*, Hope Channel, 2013.

Chapter 3—A Prophet's Life

The wall that sin built blocked direct access to God. His face was hidden from humans, but He found a creative way to reveal to us some important things about Himself. He accomplished it by choosing individuals who sought a relationship with Him or whose minds were open to receive and pass on visual images and messages that He gave them. He found men like Enoch, Noah, Abraham, and Moses. We have a term for many of them—prophets. God expected that people would listen to their messages and take them seriously: "I myself will call to account anyone who does not listen to my words that the prophet speaks in my name" (Deut. 18:19).

Have you ever wondered what it would be like to be a prophet? In this chapter, we will look at five different characteristics of a biblical prophet, drawing on what we know from the Scriptures themselves. We will also look at Ellen White's life and work to see if it was similar to the life and work of a biblical prophet.

First, though, we need to make a distinction between the prophets of the Old Testament and the apostles of the New Testament. How were they different? On two occasions, Paul, in his letters, lists a hierarchy of responsibilities in the new Christian churches, and both times he places apostles first, then prophets. "And God has appointed these in the church: first apostles, second prophets, third teachers, after that miracles, then gifts of healings, helps, administrations, varieties of tongues" (1 Cor. 12:28, NKJV). "And He gave some to be apostles, some prophets, some evangelists, and some pastors and teachers" (Eph. 4:11, NKJV).

The word "apostle" means "a sent one". What distinguished an apostle from a prophet was his commissioning by Jesus Christ. Jesus appointed the twelve to "go and make disciples of all nations" (Matt. 28:19). Paul received his apostolic commission from Jesus during his Damascus Road experience (see Acts 9:3–6, 13–16). New Testament scholar Jon Paulien nicely sums up the relationship between the apostle and the prophet: "The apostle is everything the prophet is and more, according to the New Testament. They are equal when it comes to being the objects of direct revelation. But the apostle's authority of office is even greater than the prophet because of the special commission of leadership and the unique relationship in time to the first-century Christ event."[1]

The work of the apostles was primary, but there were also prophets in New Testament times. This came about as a fulfillment of Joel's prediction: "Later, I will give my Spirit to everyone. Your sons and daughters will prophesy. Your old men will have dreams, and your young men will see visions. In those days I will even give my Spirit to my servants, both men and women" (Joel 2:28, 29, CEV; Acts 2:17, 18). Pentecost had come! Through the Book of Acts, Luke tells how men and women became spokespersons for God, bringing edification to the fledgling church as the Holy Spirit inspired them (see Acts 11:27, 28; 13:1, 2; 19:6, 7; 21:10, 11). Remember that the New Testament was not yet written, so the Holy Spirit spoke through dedicated men and women to reveal to new believers, both Jew and Gentile, the truth about Jesus Christ and what it meant for their salvation.

Several of the apostles also functioned in the traditional role of prophets, including John, Peter, and Paul. There were several New Testament individuals separately named as prophets, the best known being John the Baptist. Others included Simeon, Agabus, Philip the Evangelist, and five others named in the Christian community at Antioch (see Acts 13:1, 2).

We will now look at some characteristics of a biblical prophet's life and function. The same characteristics apply to the apostles of the New Testament.

Chosen by God

Prophets are not chosen by other people. God makes the choices, and some of His choices seem strange and inappropriate to our way of thinking. Jonah is a good example. Was he the best of a bad bunch of possibilities? Or did God choose Jonah because the man needed to have a personal makeover? The prophet became very upset when the people of Nineveh repented after listening to his words of warning. I wonder if Jonah ever responded to the question that God put to him in the very last words of his book: "In that city of Nineveh there are more than a hundred twenty thousand people who cannot tell right from wrong, and many cattle are also there. Don't you think I should be concerned about that big city" (Jonah 4:11, CEV)?

How God's call came to the prophet makes interesting reading. Abraham's life in Mesopotamia came to an abrupt end when God asked him to pack up everything, leave family and friends, and head into the great unknown. Amos was a simple Judean sheepherder and cultivator of "poor man's figs", better known as sycamore fruit, when "the Lord took [him] as [he] followed the flock, and the Lord said to [him], 'Go, prophesy to my people, Israel'" (Amos 7:14, 15, NKJV). Philip was in the midst of a very successful program of evangelism and healing in Samaria when God directed him to leave all that and "go south to the road—the desert road—that goes down from Jerusalem to Gaza" (Acts 8:26). Obediently, and without more specific instructions, Philip trekked south into the wild and lonely desert of southern Judea. A result of his journey was that an Ethiopian official learned about Jesus Christ and carried the good news to Africa some time before God stopped Paul in his evil tracks and gave *him* the task of taking the same gospel message into the continent of Europe.

God sometimes chose the prophet before he was born. We read how the young Jeremiah received his call: "The Lord gave me this message: 'I knew you before I formed you in your mother's womb. Before you were born I set you apart and appointed you as my prophet to the nations.'" The surprised teenager responded, "O Sovereign Lord! I can't speak for you. I'm too young" (Jer. 1:4–9, NLT). The Lord did not accept "no" for an answer, but assured Jeremiah that he would be given words to speak. Moses had a call like that while he was keeping sheep in the wilderness. Like Jeremiah, he responded, "Lord, I have never been eloquent. I am slow of speech and tongue" (Exod. 4:10).

In December 1844, just weeks after the Millerite Disappointment, God called a sickly, teenage girl with little formal education to be His messenger to a confused and discouraged people. That seventeen-year-old was Ellen Harmon, and God's call to her came as a vision. She had been very sick in the weeks following the October 22 disappointment, coughing and bleeding from the lungs. A physician diagnosed her case as "dropsical consumption" (tuberculosis). Shortly after her December vision, Ellen received a second one. She was given the task to go and relate to others what God had shown her, but she felt afraid and quite unable to carry out the task. "Death appeared to me preferable to the responsibilities I should have to bear."[2]

Ellen White never identified herself as a prophet, preferring to be known as God's messenger. It is interesting to notice that through the ages, God's canonical-writing prophets were exclusively male—not a surprise, given the status of women throughout Bible times. By contrast, though, on the threshold of our day, God selected a woman to be His messenger.

Imperfect People

The way prophets were called reveals a God who surprises, but it is our turn to be surprised when we look more closely at the people God chose as His communicators. Some of them would not have passed our character test. Consider some of them.

Abraham was the "father of the faithful", but his faith was not perfect. In Egypt, he got into trouble by lying about his wife, Sarah, and failed to learn from the experience when he repeated the same mistake some years later (see Gen. 12 and 20). Today, though, we remember Abraham for his incredible trust when God asked him to sacrifice his son Isaac on a lonely wilderness hilltop. Abraham must have known that the gods of his day celebrated their naked power by requiring the death of firstborn male children. On Mount Moriah, Abraham discovered that Jehovah was not that kind of god. He was a God of love. One day this God would offer Himself as a sacrifice for lost humanity.

Two prophets were guilty of murder. Moses killed an Egyptian in anger and fled to the wilderness where God later called him to lead His people out of Egypt. King David raped Bathsheba and then arranged to have her husband killed. His remorse and deep, heart-felt repentance is also the story of a gracious, forgiving God.

When we review the life of the disciple Peter, we first see a garrulous, impulsive fellow who had a habit of putting his foot in his mouth. On one occasion Jesus called him "Satan" (Matt. 16:23). At Jesus' trial, Peter denied his Master with offensive language. Nevertheless, we see a dramatic change in Peter after the resurrection—an apostle, powerful preacher, miracle worker, and church leader.

Solomon gave excellent advice to men about lusting after women: "The lips of an immoral woman drip honey, and her mouth is smoother than oil; but in the end she is bitter as wormwood. ... Drink water from your own cistern" (Prov. 5:3, 4, 15, NKJV). Somehow, he failed to follow his own counsel: "But King Solomon loved many foreign women, as well as the daughter of Pharaoh ... and he had seven hundred wives, princesses, and three hundred concubines, and his wives turned away his heart" (1 Kings 11:1–3 NKJV).

The Apostle Paul had a sharp disagreement with Barnabas; a sad thing, because when Saul, the infamous torturer of Christians, underwent his conversion, no one trusted him—except Barnabas, a compassionate soul who befriended and supported him at the time of his greatest need (see Acts 15:38–41). Paul was also intolerant of a young and inexperienced worker, John Mark, dropping him from his mission team. However, Paul grew in grace. From his prison cell in Rome, the aged apostle sent this message to Timothy: "Get Mark and bring him with you, because he is helpful to me in my ministry" (2 Tim. 4:11). By that time John Mark was almost certainly writing the gospel that bears his name.

Ellen White was not perfect either. Her limited formal education significantly affected her confidence in her writing ability, so she constantly sought editorial assistance, first from her husband and later from secretarial assistants. She copied from other writers, sometimes without giving them credit, and occasionally claiming their words as her own.[3] Like every one of us, she was human, struggling in her marriage to a "workaholic" husband who suffered several strokes and depression. It took Ellen more than thirty years to personally adopt some of the health practices that she received in vision and urged her readers to follow. Like the prophets of old, she was a sinner in need of salvation. In a letter to her husband James in 1876 she wrote, "I do not claim infallibility, or even perfection of Christian character. I am not free from mistakes and errors in my life. Had I followed my Savior more closely, I should not have to mourn so much my unlikeness to His dear image."[4]

The men and women God chose as His prophets and messengers were imperfect people. If He had waited in the hope of finding a perfect individual to reveal His truth, the Bible would never have been written.

Difficult Assignments

A small boy was asleep on his mat when he awoke, hearing his name called. It happened three times before young Samuel discovered that the God of the universe was speaking to him and giving him a message for the high priest—the kind of message that would frighten any one of us if we were given the task (see 1 Sam. 3). For Samuel, it was just the beginning of a long prophetic ministry characterized by many heavy assignments that included reprimanding the king of Israel for his disobedience.

Elijah, "the prophet of fire", moved like a crackling fireball through the landscape of ancient Israel. Delivering thundering messages from the Almighty, he electrified the heart of King Ahab, met the challenge of insidious Baal worship head-on, performed incredible miracles, and on Mount Carmel brought an entire nation to its knees in a single day of decision. What a prophet! With that said, Elijah was also very human. With a death threat from Queen Jezebel over his head, Elijah ran for his life, ending an exhausting journey in a cave near Mount Horeb. There, in a dramatic replay of his life, the prophet experienced in rapid succession a mighty whirlwind, an earthquake, and a roaring fire, but it was not until all the noise and fury died away that God came to His depressed prophet with "a gentle whisper" (1 Kings 19).

Some prophets, like Isaiah and John the Baptist, were martyrs for Christ, yet God never tested His prophets beyond their endurance. Jeremiah, for his strong denunciation of the king of Judah, suffered beatings, was dropped into a miry pit, and imprisoned, but spoke calmly in the face of a death threat: "Now reform your ways and your actions and obey the Lord your God. . . As for me, I am in your hands; do with me whatever you think is good and right" (Jer. 26:13, 14). The Apostle Paul, appointed by the Lord as a missionary to the Gentile world, suffered multiple hardships, including stoning, floggings, and imprisonment. Writing to Timothy from his prison cell in Rome, Paul recalled "what kinds of things happened to [him] in Antioch, Iconium and Lystra, the persecutions [he] endured. Yet the Lord rescued [him] from all of them" (2 Tim. 3:11).

The prophet Nathan had a potentially perilous assignment when he confronted King David about his love affair with Bathsheba. However, the Holy Spirit gave Nathan great wisdom and the king deep repentance: "I have sinned against the Lord," David confessed. "Cleanse me with hyssop, and I will be clean; wash me, and I will be whiter than snow" (2 Sam. 12:13; Ps. 51:7).

In the course of her ministry, Ellen White was sometimes apprised by the Holy Spirit of immoral behavior of ministers or church leaders. Confronting individuals about these sins was one of her most difficult responsibilities. God gave her the courage and wisdom that she needed.

Some Prophets Used Secretaries

Scribes have a notable history. All ancient people of importance had scribes for the copying and transmission of religious texts, as well as legal documents. We owe very much to scribes for the preservation of the biblical text. Some inspired writers used scribes or secretaries in their work. It is possible that some Old Testament writing prophets were illiterate.

Perhaps the best known Old Testament scribe was "Baruch, the son of Neriah", Jeremiah's loyal friend and scribe. Scholars' interests were aroused by the discoveries of two seals from the seventh century B.C. with the text "Belonging to Berekhyahu [Baruch's Hebrew name], son of Neriyahu [Neriah's Hebrew name], the Scribe".

Figure 2: Seal of Baruch, Son of Neriah.

Jeremiah records a fascinating story which gives insight into the function and importance of the scribe to the prophet (see Jer. 36). During the fourth year of King Jehoiakim's reign in Judah, the Lord told Jeremiah to "take a scroll and write on it all the words I have spoken to you concerning Israel, Judah, and all the other nations from the time I began speaking to you in the reign of Josiah till now." This represented quite an assignment for a prophet who had been receiving revelations from the Lord during a period of several years. "So Jeremiah called Baruch son of Neriah, and while Jeremiah dictated all the words the Lord had spoken to him, Baruch wrote them on the scroll." Those words had a lot to do with the wickedness of King Jehoiakim. The prophet instructed Baruch to take the scroll to the temple and read it aloud to the worshippers and priests. When the scribe read it to the temple officials, they looked at each other in fear and questioned Baruch, "How did you come to write all this? Did Jeremiah dictate it?" They wanted to be sure it was genuine. "Yes," Baruch replied, "he dictated all these words to me, and I wrote them in ink on the scroll."

When the words were read to the king, he took the scroll, cut it in pieces, and threw the pieces into the fire. "So Jeremiah took another scroll and gave it to the scribe Baruch . . . and as Jeremiah dictated, Baruch wrote on it all the words of the scroll that Jehoiakim king of Judah had burned in the fire. And many similar words were added to them" (Jer. 36:32).

During Paul's imprisonment in Rome, he used one or more assistants to transcribe his letters: "I, Tertius, who wrote down this letter, greet you in the Lord" (Rom. 16:22); "I, Paul, write this greeting in my own hand" (1 Cor. 16:21). Peter mentions the assistance of Silas: "With the help of Silas, whom I regard as a faithful brother, I have written to you" (1 Pet. 5:12).

James White assisted Ellen in editing and correcting grammar for her until just before his death in 1881. After that she used several literary assistants in the preparation of her major works. We will study about this in a forthcoming chapter.

God Sometimes Used Pantomime

In the long centuries before printing, when manuscript copies of Scripture were rare and few people could read, God used all sorts of methods to break through the wall and get their attention. People were more inclined to watch what the prophet was doing, rather than listen to what he was saying. Prophets were sometimes asked to do strange and embarrassing things. Often it involved performing a symbolic act in a public place.

Jeremiah was told to buy a new loincloth, wear it around his waist, but then take it off and bury it by a distant river. Later he was told to recover it, but by that time it was soiled and ruined. The prophet had to explain what it meant to the inhabitants of Judah who were soon to be deported to Babylon, land of the two rivers (see Jer. 13:1–11). On another occasion, Jeremiah had to make a yoke for his neck and wear it before the people, again a symbol of their upcoming captivity (see Jer. 27:1–2).

In the public square, Ezekiel took a large clay tablet, drew Jerusalem on it, and then constructed an elaborate model of siege works and ramps all around it. Then, for a specified number of days, the prophet had to lay down beside it (see Ezek. 4 and 5). At another time, Ezekiel had to publicly pack his belongings and set out on a journey (see Ezek. 12:3–7). All this was a vivid demonstration of the approaching siege of Jerusalem by the Babylonians.

Hosea was commanded to marry a prostitute and have children by her, a clear lesson to the people of Israel who were abandoning God, their true lover, for the gods of the Philistines (see Hosea 1:2, 3). People in ancient times sometimes expected their prophets to act in what we consider to be peculiar ways. Isaiah was commanded to "go, and remove the sackcloth from your body, and take your sandals off your feet. And he did so, walking naked and barefoot" (Isa. 20:1–4, NKJV). When King Saul acted the same way, lying naked on the ground, his behavior raised a question in people's minds. "What? Is even Saul a prophet?" they exclaimed (1 Sam. 19:24, NLT).

Sometimes the prophet exhibited physical phenomena during vision. Daniel experienced breathlessness and physical weakness (see Dan. 10:16, 17); Ezekiel lost all strength (see Ezek. 2:1, 2); Balaam's eyes were open during vision (see Num. 24:4, 16).

Early in Ellen White's ministry, God provided physical evidence that her visions were genuine. He sometimes gave her visions during public meetings, in one case interrupting a funeral service. Several eyewitness accounts of Ellen in vision mention supernatural strength, an absence of breathing, and unawareness of her surroundings. On one occasion, while in vision, she held a large Bible high, at arm's length, pointing with her finger to a text she was repeating aloud. These physical phenomena ceased after her prophetic role was generally accepted by the believers.

Through this chapter we saw that a prophet's life was not a bed of roses. It was not a nine-to-five job, five days a week, with a retirement plan. It was a lifetime calling that meant placing oneself in the hands of God and doing His bidding, whatever the cost.

From my study of these prophet characteristics, I learn that God chose and inspired men and women who, like me, were faulty and imperfect, so sometimes their messages come through muddled and messy. Recognizing that, I must come to inspired writings with a humble, teachable spirit and a prayer for the Holy Spirit to show me what I need to know and learn.

To think about:

1. God told Jeremiah that he was chosen to be a prophet before he was born. Does that have implications for human freedom and the power of choice? Is it possible that God had a plan for your life before you were born?

2. It must have sometimes been very hard to be a prophet. Consider the case of Jonah and God's prediction about the destruction of Nineveh. Was God being fair to Jonah?

3. We see that God chose imperfect individuals—sinners, really—to be His prophetic messengers. How does that reality impact your attitude or respect toward Ellen White as God's messenger in modern times?

References:

[1] Jon Paulien, "The Gift of Prophecy in Scripture", in *Understanding Ellen White*, 17.

[2] Ellen White, *Spiritual Gifts*, 2:36.

[3] Robert W. Olson, "Ellen White's Denials", *Ministry*, Feb. 1991.

[4] White, Letter 27, 1876.

Chapter 4—Revelation

The opening sentence in the Book of Hebrews is an important one: "In the past God spoke to our ancestors through the prophets at many times and in various ways, but in these last days He has spoken to us by His Son" (Heb. 1:1).

Did you notice that God spoke "at many times and *in various ways*"? After Adam and Eve were banished from the Garden of Eden, bringing to a close the face-to-face interaction between Creator and creature, God chose some interesting ways to penetrate the wall that divided Him from His people. As we have seen, He had extremely important information to share with them and us. To accomplish those purposes, He selected prophets, and in New Testament times, apostles, to be His mouthpieces to the human race. They were given special messages through what we call **Revelation**.

When you hear something that surprises you about someone or something, you might describe what you heard as a "revelation." More often, though, we associate the word with the Apostle John's Revelation, the last book of the New Testament. In biblical times, God revealed Himself and His messages through dreams, visions, voice, and occasionally an appearance to an individual, but before we talk about that, let's think about something from God that you and I may experience on a daily basis. We call it **General Revelation**.

General Revelation

When I admire and feel inspired by a gorgeous sunset, God may be showing me His love of beauty. As I examine, under a microscope, the intricate design of a leaf or flower, I may reflect on the Creator's artistry. The graceful neck of a giraffe may impress me with the skill of its Designer. In many different ways, I may perceive God through His creation. Job understood that: "Ask the animals, and they will teach you, or the birds in the sky, and they will tell you; or speak to the earth, and it will teach you, or let the fish of the sea inform you. Which of all these does not know that the hand of the Lord has done this" (Job 12:7–9)?

Paul explained the same truth to the believers in Rome: "For ever since the world was created, people have seen the earth and sky. Through everything God made, they can clearly see his invisible qualities—his eternal power and divine nature. So they have no excuse for not knowing God" (Rom. 1:20, NLT). Despite the ravages of sin and time, the world of nature still speaks to us of its Creator.

Jesus is identified as "the true light that gives light to everyone" (John 1:9). Even a blind person, unable to view that gorgeous sunset, receives "light" from God. Each person's conscience comes as an implant from God to guide thoughts and actions (see Rom. 2:15). God has other ways too. Have you ever had an experience that you believed was "providential" or miraculous? Perhaps your guardian angel was protecting you from physical danger, or the Holy Spirit may have been giving you evidence of His presence. Angels have a ministry in helping us find God (see Heb. 1:14).

An illiterate peasant or a spirit-worshiper who has never heard the name of Jesus may nevertheless feel the influence of a loving God yearning for his soul. "Among the heathen," wrote Ellen White, "are those who worship God ignorantly, those to whom the light is never brought by human instrumentality, yet they will not perish. Though ignorant of the written law of God, yet they have heard His voice speaking to them in nature, and have done the things that the law required. Their works are evidence that the Holy Spirit has touched their hearts, and they are recognized as the children of God."[1] The English poet, Francis Thompson, reflected on the Holy Spirit in his life as "the Hound of Heaven", never ceasing in His running, forever in a quest to embrace the fleeing poet with divine grace. Paul talked about that role of the Holy Spirit to the Greek philosophers in Athens when he observed their inscription "To the Unknown God" (Acts 17:25–28).

The Holy Spirit sometimes gives dreams to individuals, perhaps to warn of an impending physical danger to their wellbeing or lead them to a missionary or gospel worker. We have stories of how God gave dreams to Jacob and Joseph, as well as pagan rulers such as King Nebuchadnezzar of Babylon and the Pharaoh of Egypt (see Dan. 2; Gen. 41).

All of this comes under the heading of General Revelation. Think of it as a heart-warming demonstration of a compassionate God who will do almost anything to draw us close, so that we experience His love and saving grace.

Special Revelation

To the Israelites during their wilderness journey, God said, "Listen to my words: 'When there are prophets of the Lord among you, I reveal myself to them in visions, I speak to them in dreams'" (Num. 12:6). We will explore how God communicates with His chosen messengers by dreams and visions. We are now talking about **Special Revelation,** sometimes also described as **Prophetic Revelation**.

Joseph is probably the world's most famous dreamer. "Hey, listen everyone! I had this dream where your sheaves of grain bowed down in front of mine. What can it mean?" Joseph's unwelcome dreams landed him in a deep pit, and then as a slave in Egypt where he earned fame as an interpreter of dreams (see Gen. 40 and 41). His father, Jacob, was also a dreamer. Running from home in fear of his brother, sleeping one night on a stone pillow, Jacob dreamed of a ladder reaching from earth to heaven. It was an assurance of God's presence and a promise that Abraham's blessing would be carried on through him (see Gen. 28:10–12).

The young King Solomon was given a dream I would like to have had. "At Gibeon the Lord appeared to Solomon during the night in a dream, and God said, 'Ask for whatever you want me to give you'" (1 Kings 3:5–10). He could have asked for fame and riches, but Solomon chose the gift of wisdom.

It was to another Joseph, a carpenter in Nazareth, that God gave an important dream. When he discovered that his fiancée, Mary, was pregnant, Joseph had a quiet divorce in mind. "But after he had considered this, an angel of the Lord appeared to him in a dream and said, 'Joseph son of David, do not be afraid to take Mary home as your wife, because what is conceived in her is from the Holy Spirit'" (Matt. 1:20). Joseph trusted and obeyed. Sometime later, when King Herod ordered the death of all boys in Bethlehem who were two years and under, Joseph was again instructed in a dream to take Mary and the child Jesus to Egypt (see Matt. 2:13).

More frequently, perhaps, God gave His prophets visions, sometimes called "waking dreams", because they were typically given in the daytime. The first human to receive a vision from God may have been Enoch, who was shown the second coming and the final judgment (see Jude 14, 15). The first recorded vision in Scripture was given when God made a covenant with Abraham: "After this, the word of the Lord came to Abram in a vision: 'Do not be afraid, Abram, I am your shield, your very great reward'" (Gen. 15:1).

Some prophets had glorious and overwhelming visions of God when they were commissioned. Isaiah reported, "I saw the Lord seated on a throne, high and exalted, and the train of his robe filled the temple." Isaiah's response? "Woe to me! I am ruined" (Isa. 6:1–5)! Ezekiel, at his prophetic calling, had such a vision of God that he could not find the right words to tell us what he had seen (see Ezek. 1). Daniel received a vision of the pre-incarnate Christ one day while he stood with friends on the bank of the Tigris River. "I, Daniel, was the only one who saw the vision; those who were with me did not see it, but such terror overwhelmed them that they fled and hid themselves." The prophet himself lost all strength and fell into a deep sleep on the ground (Dan. 10:4–9).

Many prophets, like Daniel, did not understand the visions they were given, but they reacted in different and sometimes interesting ways. The youthful prophet Zechariah peppered his angel with questions: "What are these, my Lord?" "What are these coming to do?" "Where are you going" (Zech. 1:9, 18; 2:2)? The excited young man even gave the angel instructions during a vision of Joshua the high priest: "I said, 'Put a clean turban on his head.' So they put a clean turban on his head" (Zech. 3:5, NIV). Habakkuk was more impatient with his questions: "How long, Lord, must I call for help?" "Why do you tolerate wrongdoing?" "Why are you silent" (Hab. 1:2, 3, 13)?

Sometimes, in vision, the prophet had the sensation of being transported from one place to another. "The hand of the Lord was on me," said Ezekiel, "and he brought me out by the Spirit of the Lord and set me in the middle of a valley; it was full of bones" (Ezek. 37:1). Paul, too, had a unique experience: "I will go on to visions and revelations from the Lord.

I know a man in Christ who fourteen years ago was caught up to the third heaven. Whether it was in the body or out of the body I do not know" (2 Cor. 12:1, 2).

The Apostle Peter received a life-changing vision at Joppa (see Acts 10:9–18). It changed his attitude toward Gentiles and ultimately cleared the way for the gospel to be taken to all peoples. Paul, at his dramatic vision of Jesus, was directed to go into Damascus and wait for further instructions (see Acts 9:5–9). There God gave Ananias, a disciple, a vision with directions to find Paul at a specific address (see Acts 9:10–15). At Troas in Asia Minor, Paul had a night vision in which a man of Macedonia called for him and his team to cross the sea and take the gospel to Europe (see Acts 16:9, 10).

Their visions convinced and convicted the prophets that they had God's authority to go and tell what they had been shown. They never doubted the source of their messages. To their listeners, they confirmed this with phrases like "This is what the Lord says" and "Thus saith the Lord." Those expressions occur more than four hundred times in the Old Testament.

Sometimes a vision was given for a later time or place. The prophet Habbakuk was upset with God for not sending judgments upon the wicked, but God told him to be patient. "Write down the revelation and make it plain on tablets so that a herald may run with it. For the revelation awaits an appointed time; it speaks of the end and will not prove false. Though it linger, wait for it; it will certainly come and will not delay" (Hab. 2:2, 3).

A more dramatic example comes from Daniel 8, when he was shown what would take place near the end of time. Alarmed by everything he saw and not understanding what it was all about, he wrote, "I, Daniel, was exhausted and sick for days. Then I got up again and carried on the king's business; but I was astounded at the vision" (Dan. 8:27, NASB). Several years passed before an angel came to explain the vision to the distressed prophet (see Dan. 9:20–27).

Special (Prophetic) Revelation is one of the gifts that God placed in His church until the end of time. To the Ephesians, Paul wrote, "Christ himself gave the apostles, the prophets, the evangelists, the pastors and teachers, to equip his people for works of service, so that the body of Christ may be built up until we all reach unity in the faith and in the knowledge of the Son of God and become mature, attaining to the whole measure of the fullness of Christ" (Eph. 4:11–13). These gifts of the Holy Spirit are for the church until the end of time.

During her lifetime, Ellen White received many visions and dreams. Her early visions, soon after the 1844 disappointment, guided in the founding of the Seventh-day Adventist Church. Some notable ones were her December 1844 vision of a pathway to heaven,[2] the "Great Controversy" vision of 1858,[3] and the health reform vision of 1863.[4] We will look in more detail at these visions in later chapters.

Voice

Many times, the prophet heard a voice speaking to him with a message which he then passed on to the people. Ezekiel was instructed, "When I speak to you, I will open your mouth and you shall say to them, 'This is what the Sovereign Lord says'" (Ezek. 3:27).

While herding sheep in the wilderness, Moses heard the voice of God, directing him to go to the Pharaoh of Egypt and deliver divine judgments. However, Moses felt inadequate for the task and complained loudly about his lack of speaking ability. Finally, God arranged for Aaron, Moses' brother, to be his spokesman. I wonder if God was grinning a little when He encouraged Moses with these words: "See, I have made you like God to Pharaoh, and your brother Aaron will be your prophet" (Exod. 7:1).

On a few occasions, God spoke words that were heard, not only by the recipient, but also those standing in the vicinity. Twice during Jesus' earthly ministry, God spoke publicly, the first time being at His baptism in the Jordan River. "As soon as Jesus was baptized, he went up out of the water. At that moment heaven was opened" and John the Baptist "saw the Spirit of God descending like a dove and alighting on him. And a voice from heaven said, 'This is my Son, whom I love; with him I am well pleased'" (Matt. 3:16, 17). The second occasion was Christ's transfiguration on a mountaintop, when Peter, James, and John were present. "While he was still speaking, a bright cloud covered them, and a voice from the cloud said, 'This is my Son, whom I love; with him I am well pleased. Listen to him!' When the disciples heard this, they fell facedown to the ground, terrified" (Matt. 17:5, 6).

The Apostle John tells of another time, during the final Passion Week, when God's voice was heard, speaking encouragement to Jesus. "The crowd that was there and heard it said it had thundered" (John 12:27–29). At Paul's conversion on the Damascus Road, Jesus spoke to him in words he understood, but it was unintelligible to the men who were with him. "The men traveling with Saul stood there speechless; they heard the sound but did not see anyone" (Acts 9:7).

Appearances

On numerous Old Testament occasions, God appeared as "the Angel of the Lord" to one or more individuals. Was it God the Father? Or the pre-Incarnate Christ? How could a sinful human being stand in the presence of God and live? The Scriptures give us some clues.

The Apostle John declares emphatically that "no one has ever seen God, but the one and only Son, who is himself God and is in closest relationship with the Father, has made him known" (John 1:18). He later adds, "Not that anyone has seen the Father, except He who is from God, He has seen the Father" (John 6:46, ESV). Christ identified Himself on earth as the "I AM", the name God used when He appeared to Moses in the wilderness (John 8:56–58; Exod. 3:14).

To the ancient Israelites, God emphasized His oneness. "Hear, O Israel: the Lord our God, the Lord is one" (Deut. 6:4). In a society populated by a plethora of gods, good and bad, the supreme God chose not to disclose His trinitarian nature. It is rare in the Old Testament to find individual members of the Godhead identified. Is it possible to assume that when the Old Testament Scripture talks about "God" making an appearance to humans, it was the pre-incarnate Christ? I think so.

John began his gospel this way: "In the beginning was the Word, and the Word was with God, and the Word was God. He was with God in the beginning" (John 1:1). Why did John describe Christ as "the Word"? It seems a strange way to speak of Christ—until we think about what "words" mean to us. Words are the essence of our communication with each other. Without words, we cannot exchange ideas and information. I

Why did John describe Christ as "the Word"? It seems a strange way to speak of Christ—until we think about what "words" mean to us. Words are the essence of our communication with each other.

need words to tell you what I am thinking. Thus, when sin created the wall of separation between God and us, one member of the Godhead became the "Word", the communication link between heaven and humanity. Ellen White said it beautifully: "He who was one with God has linked Himself with the children of men by ties that are never to be broken."[5] The Son of God has functioned as heaven's emissary to humanity throughout all time, communicating the will of the Godhead to human beings. That's why the Holy Spirit prompted John to describe Christ as the Word, adding that "the Word became flesh and made his dwelling among us" (John 1:14).

When Christ appeared to Abraham, Hagar, Jacob, Gideon, and others, He came either as a "Man" or "the Angel of the Lord" (Gen. 16:6–13; 18:1–33; 22:11–18; 31:10–13; 32:24–30; Judges 6:11–24). When He appeared that way to Moses at the burning bush, the command was given, "Do not come any closer. Take off your sandals, for the place where you are standing is holy ground" (Exod. 3:4–6). Joshua had a similar experience at Gilgal after Israel had crossed the Jordan. While scouting the site of Jericho, Joshua was suddenly confronted by a man with a drawn sword in his hand. Uncertain, Joshua asked, "Are you for us or for our enemies?" "Neither," he replied, "but as commander of the army of the Lord I have now come." Joshua immediately fell face down to the ground, but even that was not enough. "Take off your sandals, for the place where you are standing is holy" (Josh. 5:13–15).

It was Christ who led Israel from Egypt to the Promised Land (see Judges 2:1–4, NKJV). Ellen White understood that Christ proclaimed the Ten Commandments at Mount Sinai.[6] During the Israelite camp at Sinai, He appeared to Moses multiple times. Scripture records this about Moses: "No prophet has risen in Israel like Moses, whom the Lord knew face to face" (Deut. 34:10). God Himself declared, "With him [Moses] I speak face to face, clearly and not in riddles; he sees the form of the Lord" (Num. 12:8). These are amazing statements, but you will notice God *knew Moses* and spoke with him face to face, not the other way around.

Moses was the greatest of the Old Testament prophets. When the two met on the mountain, the Lord had much to share with His servant. They talked there for many days, during which we find this very interesting conversation: "Then Moses said, 'Now show me your glory.' And the Lord said, 'I will cause all my goodness to pass in front of you, and I will proclaim my name, the Lord, in your presence. I will have mercy on whom I will have mercy, and I will have compassion on whom I will have compassion. But', he said, 'you cannot see my face, for no one may see me and live.'" Then, when the Lord passed by, He placed Moses in a cleft in the rock and covered him with His hand until He had gone by. "You will see my back; but my face must not be seen" (Exod. 33:18–22). I wonder if Moses reflected on that experience when he later met with Christ at His transfiguration on a mountain in Galilee (see Matt. 17:1–8).

Writing

God wrote identical words on two separate occasions. The first writing happened as Moses completed forty days with God on the mountain: "When the Lord finished speaking to Moses on Mount Sinai, he gave him the two tablets of the covenant law, the tablets of stone inscribed by the finger of God.…Moses turned and went down the mountain with the two tablets of the covenant law in his hands. They were inscribed on both sides, front and back. The tablets were the work of God; the writing was the writing of God, engraved on the tablets" (Exod. 31:18; 32:15, 16).

However, something happened while Moses spoke with God on the mountain. In the valley below, the unruly crowd of newly liberated slaves figured they were abandoned and forgotten. As Moses descended the mountain, he was shocked to see his people shouting and dancing around their replacement god—a golden calf image. "His anger burned and he threw the tablets out of his hands, breaking them to pieces" (Exod. 32:19).

Forty years later, when a new generation of Israelites gathered at the border of their promised land, Moses told the story of how God wrote His words a second time. "At that time the Lord said to me, 'Chisel out two stone tablets like the first ones and come up to me on the mountain. Also make a wooden ark. I will write on the tablets the words that were on the first tablets, which you broke. Then you are to put them in the ark." Moses did as God directed, chiseling two new tablets and taking them with him up into the mountain. "The Lord wrote on these tablets what he had written before, the Ten Commandments he had proclaimed to you on the mountain…And the Lord gave them to me. Then I came back down the mountain and put the tablets in the ark I had made, as the Lord commanded me, and they are there now" (Deut. 10:1–5).

> *Moses is clear that God wrote the same words each time. Strange, then, that when Moses read the Ten Commandments to the new generation forty years after Sinai, his reading of the fourth and fifth commands differed from the original presentation.*

Moses is clear that God wrote the same words each time. Strange, then, that when Moses read the Ten Commandments to the new generation forty years after Sinai, his reading of the fourth and fifth commands differed from the original presentation (compare Exod. 20 with Deut.5). The fourth commandment in Exodus gives creation week as the basis for Sabbath keeping: "for in six days the Lord made the heavens and the earth" (Exod. 20:11). The same commandment in Deuteronomy supplies a different reason: "Remember that you were slaves in Egypt and that the Lord your God brought you out of there with a mighty hand and an outstretched arm. Therefore the Lord your God has commanded you to observe the Sabbath day" (Deut. 5:15).

Did God change His reason for observing the Sabbath? Or did He inscribe the commandments in fewer words than are given in the Bible? Is it possible that Moses, guided by the Holy Spirit, made some of the commands practical by explaining why they were given, and how they would benefit the people? For example, Moses explained that obeying the fifth commandment to honor parents "as the Lord your God has commanded you" would bring happiness and long life (Exod. 20:12; Deut. 5:16). He gave two different reasons for keeping the Sabbath holy—first, creation, representing the original relationship of God with humanity; and second, the exodus, representing redemption from the slavery of sin.

Study Figure 3 for a moment. Did God inscribe the Ten Commandments on two tablets as we usually picture them—the first four on one tablet, the other six on the other, as in the left illustration? Or did He inscribe two *identical copies* of the entire Ten Commandments, as in the right illustration?

Figure 3: Physical Form of the Decalogue.

Ancient diplomatic treaties or covenants, like one between Pharaoh Ramses II and the Hittite King Hattusilis III (circa 1270 B.C.), were duplicated on stone with a copy for each party. The subordinate party placed their copy in the temple of their god. In the case of Israel, both copies were placed in the Ark of the Covenant in the Most Holy Place of the sanctuary, as God's symbolic dwelling-place with His people. It is meaningful that God followed this protocol of the contemporary culture to emphasize that His moral law was to be regarded as a binding treaty or covenant between Him and Israel, and ultimately us.

Having God Himself write the covenant represented a giant step above other forms of prophetic revelation. The Sabbath commandment goes all the way back to the creation week, when God established a special day to commemorate the creation event. The first thing in the Bible that God made holy was not space, or an object, but time (see Gen. 2:2, 3). It tells me that His holy Sabbath is to be taken seriously.

To think about:

1. Read about God's appearances to Moses (Exod. 3:1–10), Hagar (Gen. 21:14–19), Joshua (Josh. 5:13–6:2), and Gideon (Judges 6:11–16). What do these stories reveal to you about God?

2. Compare some different ways in which God called and commissioned prophets, using the examples of Samuel (1 Sam. 3), Jeremiah (Jer. 1:4–10), Amos (Amos 7:10–15), and Paul (Acts 9:1–19). How were their callings similar or different?

3. Review the first part of the chapter dealing with General Revelation. Reflect on times, places, or ways in which God has shown you His character of love or intervened in your life.

References:

[1] Ellen White, *Desire of Ages*, 638.

[2] White, *Early Writings*, 13–20.

[3] White, *Life Sketches*, 152.

[4] White, *Spiritual Gifts*, v.4, 126–151.

[5] White, *Steps to Christ*, 14.

[6] White, *Desire of Ages*, 307.

Breakthrough

Chapter 5—Inspiration

The prophet has been shown a motion picture or given a message. Now he has to deliver what he saw or received to the right people at the right time and place.

We have talked about revelation, the information that God gives to prophets through visions, dreams, and sometimes voice or appearance. However, revelation is only half the story. The prophet has been shown a motion picture or given a message. Now he has to deliver what he saw or received to the right people at the right time and place. How will he accomplish this? How will he remember all the important information given, especially if there is a time lapse between the receiving and telling, as happened with Jeremiah? Will the message be shared verbally, or is it to be recorded for future generations to read?

How can we be sure that what we read in the Bible is truly the Word of God? "All Scripture is inspired by God" (2 Tim. 3:16, NASB). Those were Paul's words to Timothy, but what do they mean? We need to talk about **Inspiration**.

Inspiration can mean several things. We may feel "inspired" by that beautiful sunset or listening to George Frederick Handel's *Hallelujah Chorus*. An Olympian feat or individual's personal sacrifice for people in need might be an "inspiration" to me. Nevertheless, theologically speaking, inspiration (literally "God-breathed" in the Greek) carries a quite different meaning. **Revelation** is the *content* of God's message—**what** the prophet was shown in a dream or a vision. **Inspiration** is the word we use to describe the *process* by which the prophet receives the message and is enabled to make it known—**how** the prophet's mind is illuminated by the Holy Spirit, directing him to speak or write for God.

Through the process of Inspiration, the prophet is enabled to speak or write, using his own vocabulary and style to present the pictures or thoughts that came through Revelation. The Apostle Peter assures us that "prophecy never had its origin in the human will, but prophets, though human, spoke from God as they were carried along by the Holy Spirit" (2 Peter 1:21). Jeremiah used more colorful language to describe how inspiration worked for him. After receiving a message from God: "If I say, 'I will not mention his word or speak anymore in his name', his word is in my heart like a fire, a fire shut up in my bones. I am weary of holding it in; indeed, I cannot" (Jer. 20:9).

Apart from Jeremiah's colorful words, we have no detailed description of how a biblical prophet was inspired to speak or write. However, in 1860, Ellen White described how her visions were sometimes delivered to those in need of them. "At times I am carried far ahead into the future and shown what is to take place. Then again I am shown things that have occurred in the past. After I come out of vision I do not at once remember all that I have seen, and the matter is not so clear before me until I write, then the scene rises before me as was presented in vision, and I can write with freedom. Sometimes the things which I have seen are hid from me after I come out of vision, and I cannot call them to mind until I am brought before a company where that vision applies, then the things which I have seen come to my mind with force."[1] The Holy Spirit took responsibility to ensure that the information given to her was not lost, but made available at the right time and place.

We get further insight from a letter she wrote to John N. Andrews: "I am just as dependent upon the Spirit of the Lord in relating or writing a vision, as in having the vision. It is impossible for me to call up things which have been shown me unless the Lord brings them before me at the time that He is pleased to have me relate or write them."[2] These experiences of Ellen White may replicate how a biblical prophet received his visions and delivered the messages.

In many cases, the prophet may not have been given a dream or vision, but received **thought inspiration**. What does that mean? While Ellen White was in Europe in 1886, she described the process of thought inspiration this way: "It is not the words of the Bible that are inspired, but the men that were inspired. Inspiration acts not on the man's words or his expressions but on the man himself, who, under the influence of the Holy Ghost, is *imbued with thoughts*. But the words receive the impress of the individual mind. The divine mind is diffused. *The divine mind and will is combined with the human mind and will; thus the utterances of the man are the word of God."*[3] (Italics mine)

In a letter to Stephen Haskell in 1900, she added, "The Creator of all ideas may impress different minds with the same thought, but each may express it in a different way, yet without contradiction. . . . Through the inspiration of His Spirit the Lord gave His apostles truth, to be expressed according to the development of their minds by the Holy Spirit."[4]

Inspiration is a very important and interesting prophetic function. It is also a function that is widely misunderstood among Christians today, including many Seventh-day Adventists, which has unfortunate consequences in the way we read and understand both the Bible and the writings of Ellen White. We will talk a lot more about aspects of inspiration in following chapters.

Poems and Prayers

Biblical understanding and interpretation is complicated by the fact that the Bible is written in many literary styles. Some passages are didactic, prescriptive, and concrete; others are narrative, imaginative, or poetic. Our discussion of revelation and inspiration has focused mainly on the prophetic books of the Bible, but spiritual truths are also revealed through literary devices such as allegory, parable, or metaphor, that were not always intended to be taken literally. How did inspiration function for those who composed poems and songs, wrote historical narratives, and offered prayers recorded in Scripture? What about these difficult words from Psalm 137: "Daughter Babylon…Happy are those who seize your infants and dash them against the rocks" (Ps. 137: 7–9)! Did God inspire those words?

To answer that question, we need to understand that this poem was composed by one of the Judeans taken captive to Babylon following the violent destruction of Jerusalem, which included the separation of families and deaths of loved ones. Listen to the pathos:

> "By the rivers of Babylon we sat and wept
>> when we remembered Zion.
> There on the poplars we hung our harps,
>> for there our captors asked us for songs,
>> our tormenters demanded songs of joy;
>> they said, 'Sing us one of the songs of Zion!'
> How can we sing the songs of the Lord while in a foreign land?
> If I forget you, Jerusalem, may my right hand forget its skill.
> May my tongue cling to the roof of my mouth if
>> I do not remember you. . . .
> Daughter Babylon, doomed to destruction,
> happy are those who repay you according to
>> what you have done to us.
> Happy are those who seize your infants and dash them against
>> the rocks" (Psalm 137)!

Does God listen to our cries of anguish and moments of anger? Certainly. The compiler of the Psalms was inspired to include these outbursts of anger and frustration because we too are prone to the same strong emotions. We need not be afraid to cry out to God, no matter what our feelings and annoyances. God understands and cares, even when He is silent. "My God, I cry out by day, but you do not answer, by night, but I find no rest" (Ps. 22:2).

King David's heartfelt prayer for forgiveness after his adultery with Bathsheba brings hope for every sinner: "Have mercy on me, O God, according to your unfailing love; according to your great compassion blot out my transgressions. Wash away all my iniquity, and cleanse me from my sin" (Ps. 51:1, 2). The books of Job, Proverbs, and Ecclesiastes contain wise sayings based sometimes on extreme life experiences of the writers. Sometimes there is conflicting advice. "Do not answer a fool according to his folly, lest you also be like him." "Answer a fool according to his folly, lest he be wise in his own eyes" (Prov. 26:4, 5).

The Holy Spirit inspired these poets, captives, kings, and wise men to write their songs, prayers, and wisdom for our encouragement and learning. I share the following from Alden Thompson, who has struggled with the way God is sometimes portrayed in the Old Testament: "So now I can open my heart to the Lord even when it is deeply soiled—especially when it is soiled—for He is the only source of my help. My prayers may not be quite so polite now, but I serve Him with a vigor and a joy which was unknown before. I can tell it like it is, for I serve a great God who has given me the privilege of complaining to Him when I feel He has forsaken me."[5]

Stories

The greater part of the Bible consists of stories, which is another way of saying that most of the Bible is history. Think of the historical books of the Old Testament, from Genesis to Chronicles, the New Testament accounts of Jesus' life, death, and resurrection, and the Book of Acts. Are these stories and historical accounts also inspired?

Certainly, all these accounts are inspired, since "all Scripture is given by inspiration of God" (2 Tim. 3:16). However, it is important to understand, and easy to overlook, that throughout Bible times people lived in an oral culture. Even in Paul's day, almost no one owned the Scriptures, because printing was not invented until the 15th century A.D. A Jewish family would be fortunate indeed to possess one or two manuscript pages of Old Testament writings, and even more fortunate to be able to read them. In the main segment of a synagogue service held two or three times each week, portions of the Old Testament, especially the Torah, were publicly read and sometimes interpreted for the listeners. Recall that in the synagogue at Nazareth, Jesus read to the congregation from Isaiah 61, then explained that "today this scripture is fulfilled in your hearing" (Luke 4:18–21).

In the Old Testament era, especially before the time of Moses, there was no inspired Scripture in existence. Instead, the wonderful stories of God's interaction with His faithful ones, all the way from Adam to Noah, and then through the patriarchal age, were passed down orally as families gathered together and repeated these stories together. Our modern culture is defined by written and printed records. We do not need to do much memorization. However, people in ancient times lacked access to recorded information, so they developed powerful memories. As a child, Moses heard the stories of God's leading in Israel's past history, repeated over and over by his parents, Amram and Jochebed. Later, as a brilliant young man educated in the palace of the Pharaoh, he was inspired to write the Book of Genesis.

Ellen White expands on this: "During the first twenty-five hundred years of human history, there was no written revelation. Those who had been taught of God, communicated their knowledge to others, and it was handed down from father to son, through successive generations. The preparation of the written word began in the time of Moses. Inspired revelations were then embodied in an inspired book."[6]

The oral tradition was still alive and active in the later years of the Israelite kingdoms and into New Testament times, but there were now scribes, professional copyists who were responsible for the transmission of the biblical text. Two famous scribes were Baruch, Jeremiah's writing assistant, and Ezra. By the time of Christ, there were also professional memorizers—rabbinic sages known as *tannaim*—who claimed exactness in repeating what they heard from master teachers such as Jesus. These text specialists probably assisted the gospel writers who, inspired by the Holy Spirit, compiled the accounts of Jesus life.

Not every person remembers an event the same way. The gospel writers sometimes differed in their telling of the same event. Both Mark and Luke record the story of Jesus healing a demon-possessed man when He and the disciples arrived by boat on the eastern shore of Galilee (see Mark 5:1–20; Luke 8:26–39). However, Matthew, one of the twelve who was at the scene, says that they met *two* demon-possessed men whom Christ healed (see Matt. 8:28–34). All four gospel writers mentioned that a sign was written and placed on Jesus' cross, but no two of them agree about the exact words that were on the sign. Why did the Holy Spirit not insist that the details of each gospel account be totally accurate? In future chapters, we will give more study to this question.

An Incarnational Model

As we look at how the Bible was inspired, it is helpful to see a parallel with Jesus Christ—the "Word made flesh"—as a divine-human person, truly God and truly man. In His divinity, Jesus was sinless; in his humanity, like us, He experienced hunger, tiredness, gladness, sorrow, was tempted on a daily basis, yet without sin, and dependent on prayer. As Jesus was God in human form, so the Bible is God's Word in human words. The Bible is the Word of God, yet it is also a human document. Ellen White made this same comparison in her introduction to *The Great Controversy* when she penned the original edition in 1888:

"The Bible, with its God-given truths expressed in the language of men, presents a union of the divine and the human. Such a union existed in the nature of Christ, who was the Son of God and the Son of man. Thus it is true of the Bible, as it was of Christ, that 'the Word was made flesh, and dwelt among us' (John 1:14)…God has been pleased to communicate His truth to the world by human agencies…The treasure was entrusted to earthen vessels, yet it is, nonetheless, from Heaven."[7] The earthen vessels, translated in many Bibles as "jars of clay", are fragile and often structurally imperfect, but the Scriptures contain the truth that God placed in them for us (see 2 Cor. 4:7).

Illumination

The Old and New Testaments of the Bible are the product of God's communication with prophets and apostles throughout history. They did their best to write out the messages truthfully, but when we read their words, now translated from Hebrew and Greek, how can we be sure that we are getting the right meaning? Fortunately, God has opened other channels to communicate more directly with us, and that is very good news. In the previous chapter, we looked at General Revelation as one of God's tools in giving us a sense of His presence and character. In upcoming chapters, we will talk about interpretation. We must now talk about **Illumination**.

Illumination is what you and I may experience whenever we prayerfully read inspired writings. The "prayerfully" adverb is critically important. When we open the Bible, humbly seeking the guidance of the Holy Spirit to give us understanding and opening our minds to His will for our lives, we experience illumination. The Psalmist carries this image of illumination when he says, "Your word is a lamp to my feet, and a light for my path" (Ps. 119:105).

My adjoining diagram (figure 4) brings together the three elements of **Prophetic Revelation**, **Inspiration**, and **Illumination**. Notice the key role of the Holy Spirit in all three components. A two-way channel between God and us is essential and always possible through the privilege of prayer. The Holy Spirit is the medium of communication in both directions, presenting our thanks and petitions to God and bringing God's messages or thoughts to us through the Scriptures and general revelation. What a blessing and assurance this is for us!

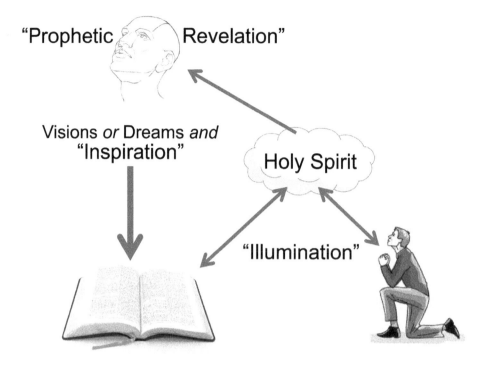

Figure 4: Role of the Holy Spirit.

Thinking about how the Holy Spirit interacts with us personally, we might sometimes wonder about the nature of the Holy Spirit as a member of the Godhead. The Bible has descriptive language for God the Father (see Isa. 6:1; 63:16; Dan. 7:9), and it is easy to picture Jesus because He came to our world as a human, like us in physical appearance. However, the Holy Spirit—or "Holy Ghost" in the King James Version—is more difficult for us to visualize as a person, even though Jesus described Him that way to the disciples. "I will ask the Father, and he will give you another advocate to help you and be with you forever—the Spirit of truth" (John 14:16). "When he, the Spirit of truth, comes, *he will guide you* into all the truth" (John 16:13, 14, italics mine).

It may be helpful to think about the work of a guide. If you have ever been part of a group tour through foreign lands, you have probably discovered the value of a professional and dependable guide. A trustworthy, experienced guide performs a variety of functions—oversight of the travelers' health and safety, sharing information about places to be visited, giving clear directions, interpreting and explaining local customs, and providing emergency assistance if required. Think about the Holy Spirit as your personal Guide—the One who responds to your needs, opens the meaning of the Scriptures to you, listens when you pray, and counsels you in your spiritual journey.

To think about:

1. We have talked about Inspiration and Illumination. What do they have in common? How are they different?

2. Jeremiah 36 tells how Baruch recorded the visions and messages that God had given to the prophet. What insight does the story give us in how Inspiration worked for the prophet?

3. Oral culture, which includes passing on stories from generation to generation, is still practiced in some parts of the world. Does your family have an oral tradition or event that is valued by family members and sometimes repeated or celebrated?

4. Think about the role of the Holy Spirit as your personal Guide— confiding in Him regarding your spiritual concerns, seeking His counsel when facing decisions or direction in your life, requesting His illumination when you open God's Word, and so on.

References:

[1] Ellen White, *Spiritual Gifts*, 2:292.

[2] White, Letter to J.N. Andrews, 1860.

[3] White, Manuscript 24, 1886.

[4] White, Letter 53, 1900.

[5] Alden Thompson, *Who's Afraid of the Old Testament God?*, 127. (1989)

[6] White, *Great Controversy*, v.

[7] *Ibid.*, vi.

Chapter 6—Incarnation

"The Word became a human being and lived here with us. We saw His true glory, the glory of the only Son of the Father" (John 1:14, CEV). We call this the **Incarnation.**

We talked about the prophets of old who were God's special messengers. In most cases, they delivered the messages faithfully and accurately. We also saw that they were human and sinners like the rest of us. Among them were liars, murderers, adulterers, betrayers, backsliders, and lawbreakers. They did not always give a clear picture of God; sometimes they did not understand the words they were asked to say or write. Yet, in spite of all their faults and weaknesses, the Holy Spirit spoke through them, giving the Word of God as our guide to truth and salvation. Through that Word, light penetrates the darkness of sin. "The entrance of your words gives light," wrote the psalmist (Ps. 119:130).

The Bible is a precious source of heaven's communication to humanity, but God had in His arsenal a startling weapon to smash through the wall of sin and distrust. The plan involved something so daring and astonishing that it left the universe spellbound with awe. God would do the unimaginable by becoming a human being, a sacrifice beyond our comprehension. The author of Hebrews explains, "In the past God spoke to our ancestors through the prophets at many times and in various ways, but in these last days he has spoken to us by his Son, whom he appointed heir of all things, and through whom also he made the universe. The Son is the radiance of God's glory and the exact representation of his being, sustaining all things by his powerful word" (Heb. 1:1–3).

The incarnation was to be the ultimate revelation of God's character of love to humanity. Jesus Himself explained it to Nicodemus in these memorable words: "God so loved the world that he gave his one and only Son, that whoever believes in him shall not perish but have eternal life" (John 3:16). The Son of God journeyed all the way from heaven to our lonely planet to become one of us.

Through the ages, there have been many great and amazing journeys taken by humankind—Marco Polo's overland trek from Europe to China; the voyage of Christopher Columbus to the New World; H.M. Stanley's journey into the heart of Africa; Lindbergh's pioneering solo flight across the Atlantic from New York to Paris; man's first space voyage to the moon.

These journeys were great, even incredible, but the greatest journey ever taken happened 2,000 years ago when the Son of God came all the way from heaven to earth to become the Son of Man.

These journeys were great, even incredible, but the greatest journey ever taken happened 2,000 years ago when the Son of God came all the way from heaven to earth to become the Son of Man. It was a journey of immeasurable and unimaginable distance, across the span of the universe, through trillions of light years, to one tiny planet in our solar system. What a journey!

Nevertheless, to contemplate this greatest of all journeys is not to think about distance. True, its length is mind-boggling, but what is incomprehensible is its depth. Paul sought to plumb that depth with these words: "Though he was God, he did not think of equality with God as something to cling to. Instead, he gave up his divine privileges; he took the humble position of a slave and was born as a human being. When he appeared in human form, he humbled Himself in obedience to God and died a criminal's death on a cross" (Phil. 2:5–8, NLT).

The incarnation was not a magic trick to reinstate our relationship with God. It was a carefully formulated plan to reveal the depth of His love for fallen humanity. However, there was risk involved. Ellen White acknowledged that. "Into the world where Satan claimed dominion, God permitted His Son to come, a helpless babe, subject to the weakness of humanity. He permitted Him to meet life's peril in common with every human soul, to fight the battle as every child of humanity must fight it, at the risk of failure and eternal loss."[1] The battle turned out to be all-out warfare between Christ and Satan, who saw this coming of God to earth as his last chance to win the cosmic conflict and maintain the wall of fear and distrust forever.

One thing Satan did well was confusing and mixing up peoples' expectations of the promised Messiah. He ensured that the Jews misunderstood some of the Old Testament prophecies of His coming and ignored others. Thus, the Jews, in the time of Rome, looked for a "royal Messiah", a powerful prince who would overthrow the Roman state and proclaim a political kingdom that would rival the one of King David. They attached to God adjectives like "mighty", "authoritarian", "warlike", and "intolerant" of Gentiles. Even Christ's own disciples misunderstood the nature of God. On the very night before His crucifixion, Jesus was talking about His oneness with His Father when Philip interrupted Him: "Lord, show us the Father and that will be enough for us." Jesus responded, with sadness: "Don't you know me, Philip, even after I have been among you such a long time? Anyone who has seen me has seen the Father. How can you say, 'Show us the Father?' Don't you believe that I am in the Father, and that the Father is in me" (John 14:8–10)?

Even John the Baptist, whose mission was to prepare the way for Jesus and point followers to Him, failed to understand why Jesus came. His preaching about the coming Christ may have scared some of his listeners: "His winnowing fork is in his hand, and he will clear his threshing floor, gathering his wheat into the barn and burning up the chaff with unquenchable fire" (Matt. 3:12). Later, confined in prison, John heard reports about a tender and caring Jesus that did not entirely fit the image he had: "When John, while imprisoned, heard of the works of Christ, he sent word by his disciples, and said to Him, 'Are you the Expected One, or shall we look for someone else'" (Matt. 11:2 ,3, NASB)?

The Messianic Prophecies

To us, looking back, having four gospel accounts portraying the real Jesus, the prophecies of the Old Testament writers fit well with the picture we have of Him. Yet, many Christians in our time reject the miracle of the Incarnation, preferring to believe that Jesus was just a good man who taught moral behavior. Faced with the dozens of fulfilled prophecies about the coming Messiah, they respond by saying that Jesus merely fulfilled them by accident.

Really? The prophets recorded more than four dozen specific predictions about the coming Messiah. What are the chances that one individual could fulfill all of them? Louis Lapides, a Jew and former unbeliever in the Jesus of Christianity, accepted that challenge. He selected just eight of those four dozen predictions and asked a mathematician what the odds were that those eight could be met in one individual. He was dumbfounded at the response—the probability was one chance in a hundred million billion! That number exceeds the total number of people who have ever lived on our planet. No surprise that Louis Lapides is now a Christian pastor and teacher.[2]

I don't know which eight of the prophecies Lapides selected for his probability test, but let's choose eight of them for our own consideration, and see how remarkably each one was fulfilled in Jesus:

1. *He was to come from the tribe of Judah.* Judah was one of Jacob's twelve sons, but not his firstborn. "The scepter will not depart from Judah, nor the ruler's staff from between his feet, until he to whom it belongs shall come, and the obedience of the nations be his" (Gen. 49:10).

    The fulfillment: "Now Jesus himself was about thirty years of age when he began his ministry. He was the son, so it was thought, of Joseph . . . the son of Amminadab, the son of Ram, the son of Hezron, the son of Perez, the son of Judah, the son of Jacob" (Luke 3:23, 33, 34).

2. *He was to be born in Bethlehem in Judea.* "But you, Bethlehem Ephrathah, though you are small among the clans of Judah, out of you will come for me one who will be ruler over Israel, whose origins are from of old, from ancient times" (Micah 5:2).

    The fulfillment: "Joseph also went up from the town of Nazareth in Galilee to Judea, to Bethlehem the town of David, because he belonged to the house and line of David. . . . While they were there, the time came for the baby to be born, and she gave birth to her firstborn, a son" (Luke 2:4–6).

3. *He was to be born of a virgin.* "Therefore the Lord himself will give
    you a sign: the virgin will conceive and give birth to a son, and will
    call him Immanuel" (Isa. 7:14).

    The fulfillment: "This is how the birth of Jesus the Messiah came
    about. His mother Mary was pledged to be married to Joseph, but
    before they came together, she was found to be pregnant through
    the Holy Spirit....And they will call him Immanuel (which means
    'God with us.')" (Matt. 1:18, 22–23).

4. *He would be betrayed for thirty pieces of silver.* "So they paid me
    thirty pieces of silver. And the Lord said to me, 'Throw it to the
    potter'—the handsome price at which they valued me! So I took
    the thirty pieces of silver and threw them to the potter at the
    house of the Lord" (Zech. 11:12–13).

    The fulfillment: "When Judas saw that Jesus was condemned,
    he was seized with remorse and returned the thirty pieces of silver
    to the chief priests and the elders....Judas threw the money into
    the temple and left....The chief priests picked up the coins....They
    decided to use the money to buy the potter's field as a burial place
    for foreigners" (Matt. 27:5, 9–10).

5. *His hands and feet would be pierced, and lots would be cast for his
    clothing.* "They pierce my hands and my feet" (this was written
    hundreds of years before crucifixion was invented) and "they
    divide my clothes among them and cast lots for my garment" (Ps.
    22:16, 18).

    The fulfillment: "They divided up his clothes by casting lots."
    (Luke 23:34) "He said to them, 'Why are you troubled, and why
    do doubts rise in your minds? Look at my hands and my feet. It
    is myself! Touch me and see'...When he had said this, he showed
    them his hands and feet" (Luke 24:38–40).

6. *A special prophet would prepare the way for Him.* "A voice of one
    calling: 'In the wilderness prepare the way for the Lord; make
    straight in the desert a highway for our God....And the glory of
    the Lord will be revealed, and all people will see it together, for
    the mouth of the Lord has spoken" (Isa. 40:3–5).

    The Fulfillment: John the Baptist dressed and lived like a
    desert nomad. "He went into all the country around the Jordan,
    preaching a baptism of repentance for the forgiveness of sins, as

it is written in the book of the words of Isaiah the prophet" (Luke 3:3–6). "After me comes the one more powerful than I...I baptize you with water, but he will baptize you with the Holy Spirit" (Mark 1:7, 8).

7. *He would die in the presence of wicked men, but He would have a rich man's grave.* "He was buried like a criminal. He was put in a rich man's grave" (Isa. 53:9, NLT).

   The fulfillment: "Two rebels were crucified with him, one on his right and one on his left....As evening approached, there came a rich man from Arimathea, named Joseph, who had himself become a disciple of Jesus....Joseph took the body, wrapped it in a clean linen cloth, and placed it in his own new tomb that he had cut out of the rock" (Matt. 27:38, 57–60).

8. *He would be anointed as Messiah [His baptism] in a specified year, and die three-and-a-half years later.* "So you are to know and discern that from the issuing of a decree to restore and rebuild Jerusalem [457 B.C.] until Messiah the Prince there will be seven weeks and sixty-two weeks [483 years, to A.D. 27];...After the sixty-two weeks the Messiah will be cut off and have nothing.... And he will make a firm covenant with the many for one week, but in the middle of the week [A.D. 31] he will put a stop to sacrifice and grain offering" (Dan. 9:25–27, NASB).

   The fulfillment: "In the fifteenth year of the reign of Tiberius Caesar [A.D. 27]—when Pontius Pilate was governor of Judea, Herod tetrarch of Galilee, . . . during the high-priesthood of Annas and Caiaphas, the word of God came to John son of Zechariah in the wilderness...When all the people were being baptized, Jesus was baptized too. And as he was praying, heaven was opened and the Holy Spirit descended on him in bodily form like a dove. And a voice came from heaven: 'You are my Son, whom I love; with you I am well pleased" (Luke 3:1–3, 21–22). Jesus was crucified in the spring of A.D. 31.

The fulfillment of these eight very specific Old Testament prophecies, at odds that are astronomical, lends affirmation to our faith that Jesus Christ was God Incarnate and died for our sins on Calvary 2,000 years ago. It also confirms that the Holy Scriptures embody messages from the God of the universe to the inhabitants of this small planet.

The Resurrection

The claim that Christ resurrected from the dead and lives again is attacked by atheists and even some Christians, more so than any other story from the Bible. Without this belief in a risen Christ, Christianity is a sham and worthless idea. Paul made this clear: "If Christ has not been raised, our preaching is useless and so is your faith" (1 Cor. 15:14).

Lee Strobel, an atheist-turned-Christian and a *New York Times* best-selling author, wrote the story of his personal investigation of the evidence for Jesus in his book *The Case for Christ*.[3] In researching the resurrection story, Strobel conducted tough interviews with four well-recognized authorities on the subject. Nothing can take the place of a full reading of Strobel's book, but what follows is a summary of his significant conclusions about the resurrection of Jesus:

1. The medical evidence based on Roman floggings and crucifixions proves beyond a doubt that Jesus died on the cross. It was a cold, dead body that Joseph of Arimathea placed in his tomb late on Friday afternoon.

2. Early sources provide strong evidence that the tomb was empty on Sunday morning. For example, Paul's first letter to the Corinthians was written in A.D. 55, just twenty-four years after Jesus' crucifixion. Listen to his testimony: "What I received I passed on to you as of first importance: that Christ died for our sins according to the Scriptures, that he was buried, that he was raised on the third day according to the Scriptures, and that he appeared to Cephas, and then to the Twelve. After that, he appeared to more than five hundred of the brothers and sisters at the same time, most of whom are still living, though some have fallen asleep. Then he appeared to James, then to all the apostles, and last of all he appeared to me also, as to one abnormally born" (1 Cor. 15:3–8).

3. The site of Jesus' tomb was known to both Jews and Christians, so it could have been checked by anyone who was skeptical. "In fact, nobody, not even the Roman authorities or Jewish leaders, ever claimed that the tomb still contained Jesus' body. Instead they were forced to invent the absurd story that the disciples, despite having no motive or opportunity, had stolen the body—a theory that not even the most skeptical critic believes today."[4]

4. Jesus was seen alive after His death on the cross. Besides the independent reports of the four gospel writers, Paul, and Luke in the Book of Acts, we have the remarkable evidence that Christianity developed and spread like wildfire immediately after the resurrection of Christ. What kind of movement would spread throughout the world, celebrating a dead man killed on a Roman cross?

5. The disciples went to their deaths proclaiming the resurrected Jesus. Skeptics like James and Paul, who persecuted Christians, were converted and proclaimed the gospel until their deaths. Who would knowingly and willingly die for a lie? Dr. C.F.D. Moule, Professor of Divinity at the University of Cambridge, formulated this question: "If the coming into existence of the Nazarenes [a name used by the early Christians], a phenomenon undeniably attested by the New Testament, rips a great hole in history, a hole of the size and shape of the Resurrection, what does the secular historian propose to stop it up with?"[5]

Jesus' closest followers did not anticipate His death, let alone a resurrection. Several times during His ministry, Jesus tried to prepare His disciples for these events, but they were not listening. "He said to them, 'the Son of Man is going to be delivered over to human hands. He will be killed, and after three days he will rise.' But they did not understand what he meant and were afraid to ask him about it" (Mark 9:31, 32). It is a sad reality that those men hung all their hopes on a political future and kingdom in which they would have prominent places. The idea that their beloved Master would be condemned and consigned to a Roman cross never entered their minds.

Failure to understand Christ's words brought peril to two of the twelve on the night before the crucifixion. Judas saw his grand hopes unravel as Jesus was condemned to death. Hit with the shocking reality of what he had done, and seized with remorse, Judas flung the betrayal money before the temple priests, ran from the court, and hanged himself.

The same night, another disillusioned disciple betrayed his loyalty to the Master. At his third courtyard denial, Peter saw Jesus looking straight at him. Running from the scene, the disciple cried his heart out. Hope died for Peter that night, but God did not forget him. In the darkness of an early Sunday morning, three women were met at the empty tomb by an angel who proclaimed a risen Christ and instructed them, "Go, tell his disciples," adding, "and Peter" (Mark 16:6, 7).

Their discovery of a resurrected Jesus changed everything for eleven confused and disillusioned men. Their powerful testimony of a living Christ turned the world upside down. His resurrection is why we have a New Testament in our Bibles. Paul affirmed it over and over in his writings. "But Christ has indeed been raised from the dead, the first-fruits of those who have fallen asleep." He adds these triumphant words from Isaiah: "Death has been swallowed up in victory" (1 Cor. 15:20, 54; Isa. 25:8). We rejoice in the magnificent hope of resurrection.

Truly, the Incarnation is the most glorious event this planet has ever experienced. The incredible journey undertaken by God 2,000 years ago makes possible the greatest journey that any human being can ever take—a single, faltering step toward Jesus Christ and salvation. Millions have taken that step and experienced forgiveness, acceptance, joy, and a new life.

> *The incredible journey undertaken by God 2,000 years ago makes possible the greatest journey that any human being can ever take—a single, faltering step toward Jesus Christ and salvation.*

To think about:

1. Why do you think so many people reject the New Testament story of Christ's death and resurrection, in spite of all the evidence?

2. John 7 recounts Christ's attendance at the Feast of Tabernacles, where many Jews questioned His authority and ultimately rejected Him because of their false expectations of the Messiah. Read the chapter and ask if it is possible for us to have faulty assumptions about the character of God.

3. Reflect on how the reality of Christ's death and resurrection strengthens your personal assurance of salvation and eternal life.

References:

[1] Ellen White, *Desire of Ages*, 49.

[2] Louis Lapides, quoted by Lee Strobel in *The Case for Christ*, 197, 198.

[3] Lee Strobel, *The Case for Christ*.

[4] *Ibid.*, 283.

[5] C.F.D. Moule, *The Phenomenon of the New Testament*, 3.

Breakthrough

Chapter 7—Canon

The Protestant Bible, made up of an Old Testament and a New Testament, consists of sixty-six books written over a period of approximately 1,500 years by about forty different authors in three different languages. The writers came from many walks of life—kings, shepherds, fishermen, priests, physicians, soldiers, statesmen, tax collectors, and poets. Those facts alone make the Bible a unique and amazing work. The prophet Isaiah affirms this by saying, "The grass withers, the flower fades, but the word of our God stands forever" (Isa. 40:8, NASB). When you add the Christian belief that the Bible is the inspired Word of God and every one of those writers was imbued with the presence of the Holy Spirit who gave them pictures, words, and thoughts, you have a magnificent concept of God piercing many holes in the wall that separated Him from His creation.

We refer to the collection of biblical books as the *Canon*. An affirmed biblical scholar, Bruce Metzger, defines "canon" as "an authoritative collection of books." We use the term to describe the Bible as a collection of divinely inspired books. Nevertheless, questions come into our minds. Were there not some other ancient prophetic writings that were excluded from the canon? Who made the decision to select this one and reject that one? For example, there are at least a half dozen "gospels" claiming to tell about Jesus' life and sayings in addition to Matthew, Mark, Luke, and John. Why were four chosen and the others excluded? We will talk about that, but let's begin with the Old Testament.

The Old Testament

Think of the Old Testament as the Jewish Bible. According to Jewish tradition, a "Great Assembly" of scribes took place in Jerusalem soon after the return of the exiles from Babylon in the sixth century B.C. Not all the exiled families returned to Jerusalem, but among those who did come home were dedicated leaders who sensed that this was a time for reestablishing the faith of their ancestors and making a new, clean start. Ezra the scribe led the way in gathering and preserving the ancient writings that recounted the history of his people, beginning with the books of Moses. Nehemiah tells how all the people came together "in the square before the Water Gate" and heard the law read by Ezra who "stood on a high wooden platform built for the occasion" (Neh. 8:2–4). Ezra was a major player in gathering together the writings of the prophets, and about the same time he probably wrote the Chronicles, which are the last books in the Hebrew Scriptures. All this took place about 400 years before Christ.

By the time of Jesus, the Jewish Scriptures had been translated into the common Greek language of the Roman world. Jesus and the apostles used this translation of the Scriptures, which later became known as the Septuagint or "the seventy", because the work had been accomplished by about seventy Jewish scholars during the second or third centuries before Christ. By that time, the Jewish Scriptures were bundled together in three groupings—the Law, the Prophets, and the Psalms. The groupings may look strange to us today:

- "The LAW": the five books of Moses (Pentateuch, known to Jews as the Torah).
- "The PROPHETS": Joshua, Judges, 1 and 2 Samuel, 1 and 2 Kings (the *Former Prophets*); Isaiah, Jeremiah, Ezekiel, and the twelve minor prophets (the *Latter Prophets*).
- "The PSALMS": Psalms, Proverbs, Job, Song of Solomon, Ruth, Lamentations, Ecclesiastes, Esther, Daniel, Ezra, Nehemiah, 1 and 2 Chronicles.

Jesus made reference to the Scriptures in this fashion when He talked with two disciples as they walked together along the Emmaus road. "He said to them, 'This is what I told you while I was still with you. Everything must be fulfilled that is written about me in the Law of Moses, the Prophets and the Psalms'" (Luke 24:44).

The Jews recognized God's messengers from their past and accepted their writings as inspired by God. At the same time, they rejected writings that did not carry the same authority. Among those were a *Book of the Wars of the Lord* (Num. 21:14, 15) and the *Book of Jasher* (Josh. 10:13). The compiler of Chronicles lists several other works including the *Annals of King David*, the *Chronicles of Samuel the Seer*, the *Chronicles of Nathan the Prophet*, the *Book of the Prophet Iddo*, and the *Words of Shemaiah the Prophet* (1 Chron. 27:24, 29:29; 2 Chron. 12:15, 13:22). None of them exist today.

Soon after the fall of Jerusalem in A.D. 70, Jewish leaders convened at the Council of Jamnia to discuss the canon of the Scriptures. A debate centered around four books considered marginal—Proverbs, Ecclesiastes, Esther, and Song of Solomon—but it was finally decided to include them in the Jewish canon.

Those thirty-nine books of the Jewish Canon became the Scriptures of the early Christian Church. The fact that Jesus quoted and attributed authority to all three sections of the Old Testament and referred to the prophecies concerning Himself (Luke 24:25–27) was very important. A contemporary of Christ, Philo of Alexandria, accepted the Old Testament Canon in the form we have it today.

By the third century A.D., the only issue that remained was the Apocrypha. This is a collection of ancient Jewish books and manuscripts that were composed shortly before the time of Jesus. Several, such as the books of Tobit, Judith, and Maccabees, came into existence between the fourth and second centuries B.C. Hebrew scholars considered most apocryphal books to be useful historical and religious documents, but they were never accepted as authoritative or belonging in the Hebrew Canon. Several were accepted by the Roman Catholic Church and are still included in the Catholic Bible today. However, the apocryphal writings are no longer included in the Protestant Canon. Neither Jesus nor the apostles quoted from them as they did from the Old Testament Scriptures.

The New Testament

The earliest Christians accepted the Jewish Scriptures—the Old Testament—as their Bible, but the emergence of the New Testament Canon took considerable time. There was one question that always demanded an answer: Where was the evidence of divine inspiration?

The apostles Paul and Peter helped provide the answer. In his instructions to Timothy, Paul quoted from Luke, considering his writings to be as authoritative as Moses: "The Scripture says 'Do not muzzle the ox while it is treading out the grain'" (Deut. 25:4); and "'the worker deserves his wages'" (Luke 10:7; 1 Tim. 5:18). Peter clearly recognized Paul's writings as Scripture: "Bear in mind that our Lord's patience means salvation, just as our dear brother Paul wrote you with the wisdom that God gave him. He writes the same way in all his letters, speaking in them of these matters. His letters contain some things that are hard to understand, which ignorant and unstable people distort, as they do the other Scriptures" (2 Peter 3:15, 16).

The movement toward a New Testament Canon began when early Christians began to accept books that had apostolic authority—that is, they were written by the apostles themselves, or by those who were closely associated with the apostles. Using these criteria, they accepted the gospels of disciples Matthew and John, Mark (a follower of Peter), and Luke (an associate of Paul). All the epistles of Paul were accepted, along with 1 Peter and 1 John.

Books of uncertain authorship, such as Hebrews, James, 2 Peter, 2 and 3 John, and Revelation were held in abeyance for some time. Eventually, all those books were accepted because they conformed to the "rule of faith", meaning that their writings harmonized with the teachings of Jesus. Scholars were also able to verify the identity of their authors in most cases. There was an additional problem with the letter of Jude because he quotes from a spurious work known as the *Book of Enoch* (Jude 14, 15), which originated in the third century before Christ, but was purported to have been written by Enoch, before the flood. Eventually, Jude was accepted as inspired. A fifth "gospel" that never qualified for the New Testament Canon was the *Gospel of Thomas*, which has supposed words of Jesus that were completely alien to the four canonical gospels. Some examples: "Split wood. I am there. Lift up a stone, and you will find me there"; "Let Mary go away from us, because women are not worthy of life"; and "every woman who makes herself male will enter the kingdom of heaven."

All twenty-seven New Testament books were affirmed by the Synod of Hippo in A.D. 393. The criteria they used to determine which books should be considered authoritative have ensured that we possess the best records about Jesus. They looked for clear evidence of the Holy Spirit's inspiration and authority. A renowned New Testament scholar, Bruce

Metzger, says that when compared with other ancient documents, there is an unprecedented number of New Testament manuscripts and that they can be dated extremely close to the original writings.[1] Another Bible scholar, Professor F.F. Bruce, expresses the belief that "those early Christians acted by a wisdom higher than their own in this matter, not only in what they accepted, but in what they rejected."[2]

The "Other" Prophets

We must not overlook the fact that throughout history, God spoke through other men and women whose writings did not become part of the biblical Canon. Many were contemporaries of Old Testament authors. Nathan and Gad were prophets during the time of David (2 Sam. 7 and 12; 1 Sam. 22:5) and both were writers (1 Chron. 29:29). Two other prophets, Iddo and Shemaiah, wrote during the reign of Rehoboam (2 Chron. 9:29). Among women who prophesied were Deborah in the time of the Judges (Judges 4:4) and Huldah during King Josiah's reign (2 Kings 22:14). The work of these prophets was similar to that of the Bible writers, but their messages were of a local nature and for a particular situation. They spoke or wrote for their own time and people.

Non-canonical prophets in New Testament times included John the Baptist (Luke 7:28) and Agabus (Acts 21:10). However, there were other early writings in the Christian era that did not make it into the New Testament. There were several spurious "gospels" and other writings about Christ that appeared during the early Christian centuries. The *Apocalypse of Peter* describes horrible things that happen in hell. Those who blaspheme God are hung by their tongue. The *Gospel of Judas* claims to reproduce conversations between Jesus and Judas Iscariot; it was composed in the second or third century by Gnostic Christians. There were also some "infancy gospels" that recounted some strange stories about Jesus as a child.

We may be confident that God oversaw the development of the entire Canon of Scripture. As one writer observed, "Ultimately, it was God who decided what books belonged in the biblical canon. A book of Scripture belonged in the canon from the moment God inspired its writing. It was simply a matter of God's convincing His human followers which books should be included in the Bible."[3] The same Holy Spirit who inspired the writers guided those who in council established the sacred Canon.

The Canon and Translations

The Scriptures come to us either as translations or paraphrases. How are they different?

- A **Translation** works from one language to another. Since the original text of the Bible was written in Hebrew/Aramaic (Old Testament) and Greek (New Testament), we depend upon translations to read and understand the text.
- A **Paraphrase** starts and stays with the same language. It is not a translation, but uses different words to convey the translated text of the Bible. A paraphrase is usually the work of a single individual, so does not usually carry the authority of a translation, though it may have value for devotional reading of Scripture. Among popular paraphrases are *The Living Bible* by Kenneth Taylor, *The Message* by Eugene Peterson, and for some Adventists, *The Clear Word* by Jack Blanco.

For at least two centuries, the King James Version (first published in 1611) was the accepted translation for English readers. It came from a group of translators who worked from the best Greek New Testament manuscripts available at that time. The biblical *Textus Receptus* constituted the translation base for the original German Luther Bible, the translation of the New Testament into English by William Tyndale, and the King James Version. More recent discoveries of ancient manuscripts such as *Codex Sinaiticus* (fourth century A.D.), the *Chester Beatty Papyri* (second and third centuries A.D.) and the *Dead Sea Scrolls* of the Old Testament (first and second centuries B.C.), have led to new translations of the Scriptures. It is noteworthy, however, that scholars found remarkable similarity between the newly discovered manuscripts and those that were used for the King James Version of 1611. Today there are dozens of translations available to us. Most represent the work of teams of Bible scholars who have made the original languages their study. Ellen White used various translations as they became available to her.

A respected Bible scholar, Frederic Kenyon, assures that "the Christian can take the whole Bible in his hand and say without fear of hesitation that he holds in it the true Word of God, handed down without essential loss from generation to generation throughout the centuries."[4] J.B. Phillips gave his testimony: "In translating the Greek of the New Testament into modern English I made every effort to correct any bias of which I was conscious. When I came to compare it with the writings that were excluded from the New Testament by the early 'Fathers', I can only admire their wisdom." He adds, "It was the sustained down-to-earth faith of the New Testament writers which conveyed to me that inexpressible sense of the genuine and the authentic."[5] Bryan Ball, an Adventist Bible scholar, concludes that "we may be quite sure that when we read the Bible today in English, or for that matter in French, Spanish, Portuguese or any other language, we are reading what the original writers meant, and what they wanted their original readers and hearers to understand."[6]

The Canon and Ellen White

Have books been added to the Canon of Scripture? Mormonism claims to have added four books to the biblical canon: the *Book of Mormon*, the *Book of Abraham*, *The Doctrine and Covenants*, and *The Pearl of Great Price*. The Christian Science movement makes a similar claim for *Science and Health* by Mary Baker Eddy. Do any or all of the writings of Ellen G. White belong as additions to the biblical Canon? That question deserves our careful consideration.

We saw that the gift of prophecy was not meant to disappear with the first-century church. Paul tells us that God placed apostles and prophets in the church "for the equipping of the saints for the work of ministry, for the edifying of the body of Christ, till we all come to the unity of the faith and of the knowledge of the Son of God, to a perfect man, to the measure of the stature of the fullness of Christ" (Eph. 4:11, 12, NKJV). Paul also lists the prophetic gift among other spiritual gifts in his first letter to the Corinthians (see 1 Cor. 12:28, 29).

In Revelation, the remnant church in the time of the end is identified as having the "testimony of Jesus" which the angel explains is the "spirit of prophecy" (Rev. 12:17; 19:10). It makes perfect sense that in the aftermath of the 1844 Disappointment, God would raise up a prophet to guide in the development of the church in earth's last days. Seventh-day Adventists believe that this promise was fulfilled in the ministry of Ellen G. White. Like Nathan and Gad in the time of David, Ellen White was called for a specific time and purpose.

The Protestant Canon of sixty-six books is accepted by Seventh-day Adventists, who also affirm that the Bible is a complete revelation of God to humanity, including the truth about Jesus. Writing to new Christians, Jude was confident "about the salvation we all share." Then he adds, "but now I find that I must write about something else, urging you to defend the faith that God has entrusted *once for all time* to his holy people" (Jude

1:3, NLT). Seventh-day Adventists believe and clearly state that the canon of Scripture was closed with the completion of the New Testament. Ellen White's husband, James, concurred: "The Bible is a perfect and complete revelation. It is our only rule of faith and practice."[7]

None of Ellen White's writings constitute part of the Canon of Scripture or additions to it. Her writings are not on the same level as Scripture. "The writings of Ellen White are not a substitute for Scripture. They cannot be placed on the same level. The Holy Scriptures stand alone, the unique standard by which her and all other writings must be judged and to which they must be subject."[8]

We face an interesting situation when we consider the enormous volume of her published writings. Whereas the entire Bible, comprised of sixty-six books and multiple authors, recorded during a period of approximately 1,500 years, totals only about 1,200 pages of print, Ellen White's published books and articles, plus her letters and manuscripts, total approximately 100,000 pages. She is the world's most translated female author. Figure 5 illustrates the comparison.

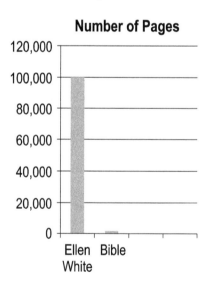

Figure 5: Volume of Ellen White's Writings.

Ellen White never equated her writings with the Bible. At multiple times during her life, she emphasized this fact, reminding her readers that she was not a bearer of new truth. In 1851, twelve years before the founding of the Seventh-day Adventist Church, she wrote, "I recommend to you, dear reader, the Word of God as the rule of your faith and practice.

By that Word we are to be judged. God has, in that Word, promised to give visions in the 'last days', not for a new rule of faith, but for the comfort of His people, and to correct those who err from Bible truth."[9]

Twenty years later, in 1871, she said, "The written testimonies are not to give new light, but to impress vividly upon the heart the truths of

> *Ellen White never equated her writings with the Bible.*

inspiration already revealed."[10] She described her role as that of a "lesser light", drawing attention to the "greater light", the Bible: "The Lord has sent His people much instruction, line upon line, precept upon precept, here and little, and there a little. Little heed is given to the Bible, and the Lord has given a lesser light to lead men and women to the greater light."[11]

From her introduction to *Great Controversy* in 1888: "In His Word God has committed to men the knowledge necessary for salvation. The Holy Scriptures are to be accepted as an authoritative, infallible revelation of His will. They are the standard of character, the revealer of doctrines, and the test of experience….The Spirit was not given—nor can it ever be bestowed—to supersede the Bible; for the Scriptures explicitly state that the Word of God is the standard by which all teaching and experience must be tested."[12]

Again in 1901, she wrote, "When you make the Bible your food, your meat, and your drink, when you make its principles the elements of your character, you will know better how to receive counsel from God. I exalt the precious Word before you today."[13] At one of her last public appearances, in 1909, she lifted the Bible from the pulpit, with hands trembling with age, and said, "Brethren and sisters, I commend unto you this Book."[14]

Using Ellen White's Writings

If Ellen White was inspired in the same way as the biblical prophets were, how was she different? The difference lies in *authority*. She recognized the Bible as her authority: "We are to receive God's Word as supreme authority."[15] The following statement by George Knight captures well the non-canonical nature of Ellen White's writings. "We find a careful balance here. Even though Adventists viewed her inspiration as being equally divine in origin with that of the Bible writers, they did not see her as being the same in authority. Ellen White and her fellow Adventists held that her authority was derived from the Bible and thus could not be equal to it."[16]

Unfortunately, as Knight adds, Adventists have sometimes put Ellen White's writings in a position she never intended them to be placed. Note this statement from the Ellen G. White Estate: "There has been confusion about, as well as abuse and misuse of, Mrs. White's writings. Some members have indeed made a second Bible of them, often seeming to make Mrs. White the more important of the two. Some ministers and teachers have quoted Mrs. White ten or more times for every quotation from Scripture....But we do not make of her writings a second Bible, or even an addition to the sacred canon of God's Word."[17]

James White clearly understood the relation between his wife's writings and Scripture: "Every Christian is therefore in duty bound to take the Bible as a perfect rule of faith and duty....He is not at liberty to turn from them to learn his duty through any of the gifts. We say that the very moment he does, he places the gifts in a wrong place, and takes an extremely dangerous position."[18]

These are bold statements which should help us read and understand Ellen White in the way that God intended. With that said, questions may arise in our minds. Do we interpret the Bible through her writings? Did she experience the same degree of inspiration as that of the biblical authors? We will address these and other important questions in forthcoming chapters.

To think about:

1. Suppose archaeologists unearth manuscripts that they identify as the writings of Nathan the prophet who lived during King David's time. How should we relate to them?

2. In her published writings, Ellen White used the phrase "Bible and the Bible only" forty-five times and "Bible and the Bible alone" forty-seven times. What does this suggest to you about her relationship to the canon of Scripture?

3. We have clear evidence that the canon of Scripture was closed with the completion of the New Testament about nineteen hundred years ago. How should we understand this in the context of prophecy as a spiritual gift in the end of time (consider Rom. 12:4–8, Eph. 4:11–13, and Heb. 1:1, 2)?

References:

[1]   Bruce Metzger, *The Canon of the New Testament*.

[2]   F.F. Bruce, *The Books and the Parchments*, 103.

[3]   S. Michael Houdmann, *Questions About the Bible*, ch. 3: "Questions about the biblical canon".

[4]   Frederic G. Kenyon, *The Bible and Modern Scholarship*, 23.

[5]   J.B. Phillips, *Ring of Truth, a Translator's Testimony*, 95.

[6]   Bryan Ball, *Can We Still Believe the Bible?* 112.

[7]   James White, *A Word to the Little Flock*, 13 (1847).

[8]   Denton Rebok, *Seventh-day Adventists Believe*, 227.

[9]   Ellen White, *Christian Experience and Views*, 64 (1851).

[10]   White, *Testimonies*, 5:605 (1871).

[11]   White, *Review and Herald*, Jan. 20, 1903.

[12]   White, *Great Controversy*, vii.

[13]   White, Manuscript 43, 1901.

[14]   W.A. Spicer, *Certainties of the Advent Movement*, 202.

[15]   White, *Testimonies*, 6:402.

[16]   George Knight, *Reading Ellen White*, 25.

[17]   Coon, Roger W., "Inspiration/Revelation: what it is and how it works".

[18]   James White, *Review and Herald*, Apr. 21, 1851.

PART TWO:
UNDERSTANDING

The great wall that sin built rises before us,

ancient and formidable.

But God has pierced the wall in many places.

He chose a few people—we call them prophets—

to draw us to those breaks in the wall and, peering through,

we catch glimpses of the One who created us

and longs for our companionship.

He sent His Beloved Son, Jesus,

to show us the extent of His Love,

but we crucified Him.

The offer of forgiveness is amazing

and powerful for change.

Thus, we have great hope.

At best, though,

our picture of God through the wall

is distorted and fragmentary.

We need a lens that is corrected

and clear for discerning truth.

That is what the next twelve chapters are about.

We will call it

Understanding

Understanding

Chapter 8—Confusion

Through long centuries, the voice of God was heard through many prophets, but it was the arrival of Jesus on this planet 2,000 years ago that struck a powerful blow to the wall of fear and misunderstanding. You and I were not there, but in the gift of the New Testament, we have a clear picture of an incredibly gracious God. Praise Him, too, that the entire Bible was miraculously preserved for us through the dark centuries.

Then one day, 500 years ago, Galileo looked through his telescope and made some surprising observations. When he published his theory that the earth revolved around the sun, and not the other way around, his life almost came apart. He was tried by the Inquisition, found "vehemently suspect of heresy", forced to recant, and spent the rest of his life under house arrest.[1] Galileo had challenged authority. The Age of Enlightenment had dawned, a precursor of the Scientific Revolution. All authority would now be challenged—God, the church, and Scripture. Reason would be pitted against revelation.

Throughout the 18th and 19th centuries, most Christians still accepted the Bible as the inspired Word of God, in whatever way they understood inspiration. At the same time, however, there were powerful undercurrents of thought that would challenge head-on their historic belief in Scripture. Starting in Europe in the 18th century, scholars began to approach the Bible as ancient literature rather than divine revelation. They posed questions about the biblical text: When and where was it written? By whom? Was it copied from earlier sources? etc. By the time Julius Wellhausen, a German biblical scholar, published his thesis in the 1870s, the Bible was being regarded by many scholars as a human document. Leaders in this "higher criticism" movement asserted that the Bible stories were little more than myths, and miraculous events were denied.

Another significant departure from the long-held belief about the Bible as the source of ultimate truth was the publication in 1859 of Charles Darwin's *On the Origin of Species*. Darwin proposed that all life evolved from more primitive forms through a process of natural selection. His theory presented a direct challenge to the creation story of Genesis. It left little room for divine guidance or design.

Around that same time, some new movements and ideas were shaping biblical thought. During the 19th century in the United States of America, two religiously significant movements were taking place. The Millerite Disappointment of 1844 gave birth to a prophetic voice and a faith movement, the Seventh-day Adventist Church, which believed it had a unique message for the end time. During the later years of the same century, among Protestants in America, there was a growing resistance to the undermining influences of higher criticism and Darwinism. By the 1880s, significant numbers of clergy and Bible students were attending annual Bible conferences held at Niagara-on-the-Lake, Ontario. These and other meetings gave rise to what became known as the Fundamentalist Movement. By 1915, it produced a twelve-volume set of essays defending the traditional view of the Scriptures as God's inspired Word. It defended Scripture against liberal Christianity.[2]

Liberal Christianity

As we saw, this started in the late 18th century, largely influenced by some German scholars, and gradually infiltrated the mainline churches, both Protestant and Catholic. Liberal Christianity is not easy to define, partly because it rejects doctrines and creeds. A correspondent for the *New York Times* highlighted some of its features in 2012:

"What is liberal Christianity? The question is complex, of course. To give a fully adequate answer would demand reference to renewed *confidence in reason*, to a high estimate of the possibilities of *human endeavor*, married to a *downplaying of the doctrine of original sin*" (italics mine).[3]

Followed to its extreme, Christians in the liberal camp rely on the methods of science to interpret the Scriptures. Evolution is embraced and biblical creation denied. They question the authority of Scripture as God-inspired and interpret it in nearly the same way as other ancient writings. The Old Testament is considered a mix of history, myth, metaphor, and poetry. The divinity of Jesus is rejected, including His virgin birth and bodily resurrection. His miracles are downplayed, and in their thinking, Jesus is little more than a good, moral teacher. During the later years of the 20th century, the "Jesus Seminar" originated as an active group of critical scholars who garnered a lot of attention in America by portraying the "historical Jesus" as merely an itinerant Jew and faith-healer who preached a gospel of liberation from injustice.

Many Christians today reject the secular beliefs of liberal Christianity, but hold to a less extreme view: that the inspiration of the biblical prophets was akin to the illumination that any of us may experience through the indwelling of the Holy Spirit. Some use expressions like "divine encounter" to describe this type of experience.

Fundamentalism

Reacting strongly to the claims of liberal Christianity that the Scriptures are a mix of moral codes and myth, some Protestant theologians developed a platform of fundamental teachings of Scripture. In contrast to the liberal rejection of divine inspiration, the fundamentalist theologians formulated the concept of *verbal inspiration*: meaning that the Holy Spirit dictated the Bible to its human authors in its original form, word-for-word. A consensus was reached at the 1895 Niagara Bible Conference, after which a group of Presbyterian theologians at Princeton University hammered out five essential beliefs of Christianity:

1. the inerrancy of Scripture.
2. the virgin birth of Christ.
3. Christ's atonement for our sins on the cross.
4. His bodily resurrection.
5. the objective reality of His miracles.

Seventh-day Adventists have no problem with the last four statements. We accept them as "fundamental" statements of doctrine about

Jesus Christ. Those four statements are clear assertions that answer well the absurd claims of liberal Christianity. However, the first statement—the "inerrancy of Scripture"—appeared as new and potentially controversial. It was another way of saying that everything in the Bible must be absolutely, literally, scientifically and historically as God gave it. The proponents believed that the Bible, in all its detail, is without error. This led directly to the belief in "verbal inspiration"—that every word was dictated by God to the prophet.

We like to use the term "fundamental" when we speak about the foundational doctrines of the Bible, or the core beliefs of Adventism. It is a perfectly good and acceptable word with that meaning. However, the related noun, "fundamentalism", carries with it concepts of fanaticism, extremism, and ultra-conservatism. We associate fundamentalism today with radical religious movements that are intolerant of beliefs that threaten their ideologies. Unfortunately, Christian fundamentalism carries some of that baggage.

James Gray, a respected fundamentalist writer, explained inspiration this way: "When we speak of the Holy Spirit coming upon the men in order to make the composition of the books, it should be further understood that the object is *not the inspiration of the men but the books—not the writers but the writings.* It terminates upon the record, in other words, and not upon the human instrument who made it....The inspiration includes not only all the books of the Bible in general but in detail, the form as well as the substance, the word as well as the thought. *This is sometimes called the verbal theory of inspiration*"[4] (italics mine). Gray is saying that God dictated the words that the prophet wrote down.

If we need anything clearer than that, here is a statement from an 1899 document prepared by an ecumenical group of sixteen Roman Catholic and Southern Baptist theologians: "For Southern Baptists, inerrancy means that the original biblical text was composed precisely as God inspired it and intended it to be because of God's superintendence: *not just the thought comes from God, but every word with every inflection, every verse and line, and every tense of the verb, every number of the noun, and every little particle are regarded as coming from God*"[5] (italics mine).

Opposite Extremes

Look at the adjoining chart (Figure 6) to understand the huge contrast between the view of liberal Christianity (the left column) and the opposing view of the fundamentalists (the far-right column). The *left* column summarizes the liberal view of Scripture:

- A "divine element" perhaps?
- The Bible is basically a human document.
- Many of the Bible stories are fables or myth.
- The Bible is historically and scientifically unreliable.

Now look at the *far-right* column which summarizes the opposing fundamentalist view:

- The Bible is verbally inspired, word by word.
- The Bible is inerrant, that is, without error.
- The Bible is to be read and understood literally, exactly as it is written.
- The Bible is historically and scientifically accurate in all its detail.

Liberal Christianity	Central View	Fundamentalism
"Divine element" perhaps?	Revelation and Thought Inspiration	Verbal (word) Inspiration
Bible is a human document	God's Word in human words and expressions	Inerrant Word of God
Much fable and myth	Much of Scripture is understood literally	Bible is to be understood literally
Historically and Scientifically Unreliable	Historical and Scientific Accuracy is not Bible's Purpose	Historically and Scientifically Accurate in all Detail

Figure 6: Different Understandings of Biblical Inspiration.

As one can clearly see, the left and right columns of the chart reflect two totally opposite and extreme views of the Bible and inspiration. With small modifications, the fundamentalist view is still upheld by many of the evangelical churches in North America today.

This raises some very important questions. Is the Bible inerrant—error-free? Does Scripture reflect science as we understand it in the 21st century? Did God dictate every word to the prophet? Do Seventh-day

Adventists believe in verbal inspiration? In forthcoming chapters, we will address these questions by looking carefully at the biblical record itself.

Did God give Ellen White any light on this question? Yes, and she rejected both extremes. The fundamentalists taught that the Holy Spirit dictated the very words that the prophet wrote. Ellen White rejected that, stating clearly that *the Holy Spirit inspired the prophet with thoughts that he then expressed in his own words and in his own style of writing*. This explains why Paul's epistles, for example, reflect his unique style of logical thinking and writing, and why Jeremiah's writing style is quite different from Isaiah's. The Holy Spirit guides the prophet in choosing "appropriate words with which to express the truth."[6]

Ellen White understood biblical inspiration this way: "*The Bible is written by inspired men, but it is not God's mode of thought and expression. It is that of humanity. God, as a writer, is not represented. Men will often say such an expression is not like God. But God has not put Himself in words, in logic, in rhetoric, on trial in the Bible. The writers of the Bible were God's penmen, not His pen.…It is not the words of the Bible that are inspired, but the men that were inspired. Inspiration acts not on the man's words or his expressions but on the man himself, who, under the influence of the Holy Spirit, is imbued with thoughts.…The divine mind and will is combined with the human mind and will; thus the utterances of the man are the word of God*"[7] (italics mine).

It is interesting that Ellen White penned those words about thought inspiration in 1886, several years before the Fundamentalist Movement came up with its claim that the Bible is inerrant and contains the precise words that God gave to its authors. With her views in mind, look now at the *central* column of Figure 6, reflecting a position midway between the extremes of liberalism and fundamentalism:

- Revelation and thought inspiration.
- The Bible is God's Word, expressed in human words and expressions.
- Much, but not all, of Scripture is to be read and understood literally.
- Complete historical and scientific accuracy is not the Bible's purpose.

Inspiration worked that way for Ellen White. She described in her own words what she saw in vision, or the thoughts that were given her by the Holy Spirit. We should not read her writings as given to her word for word. She never accepted verbal inspiration for her own writings or Scripture, and she was not alone in her central view of Scripture and inspiration. Millions of Christians today reject both liberal views and the fundamentalist concept of inerrancy, yet firmly believe that the Bible is the Word of God. Notice this confirming statement from a mainline Protestant writer:

"God inspired the Bible's human authors to deliver His message to the world, and ensured that they delivered it faithfully. But God left it up to them to express that message in their own words and in literary styles current at the time. He did not give the Bible's authors any supernatural knowledge of future scientific discoveries....The Bible reveals timeless spiritual truths about God, love, salvation, faith, morals and ethics that transcend the realms of science and history."[8]

Observe how prophets expressed God's messages in their own words and literary styles. Amos, for example, was a simple farmer in the rugged hill country of Judea when God called him to present warning messages to the sophisticated people in the northern kingdom of Israel. Therefore, Amos formulated God's messages in words descriptive of the farming background that he knew. Some examples: "Now then, I will crush you as a cart crushes when loaded with grain....As a shepherd saves from the lion's mouth only two leg bones or a piece of an ear, so will the Israelites be saved....Hear this word, you cows of Bashan on Mount Samaria....I will shake the house of Israel among all the nations as grain is shaken in a sieve" (Amos 2:13, 3:12, 4:1, 9:9).

Each Bible writer had his own way of describing what he saw in vision. In Revelation, the Apostle John described how his mind interpreted a vision of the angel sounding the fifth trumpet: "The locusts looked like horses prepared for battle. On their heads they wore something like crowns of gold, and their faces resembled human faces. Their hair was like women's hair, and their teeth were like lions' teeth. They had breastplates like breastplates of iron, and the sound of their wings was like the thundering of many horses and chariots rushing into battle" (Rev. 9:7–9). John's description reflects what he personally saw and experienced.

The heart of the struggle between fundamentalism and Protestant liberalism has centered around the issues of revelation and inspiration. There are significant differences of theological opinion on the topic. During the early years of the 20th century, many Adventists were drawn to the fundamentalist doctrine of inerrancy and verbal inspiration in spite of Ellen White's clear statements that should have kept us away from those errors. Today, a wide variety of positions are held by Seventh-day Adventists, ranging all the way from the liberal "encounter" view to the "verbal inspiration" side of the chart.

The Ellen G. White Estate summarizes the nature of her inspiration this way:[9]

1.   Ellen White never claimed *infallibility* either for herself or for the writers of the Scriptures. "God alone is infallible."

2.   She never claimed *verbal inspiration* either for her own writings or for the Scriptures.

3.   She did claim *thought inspiration* both for her own writings and for the Scriptures.

4.   She did not look upon her writings as comparable to the "commandments of God," but saw them as "reproofs," "counsels," "warnings," "encouragements," "messages," "testimonies," "cautions."

In this chapter, many questions have surfaced. It is crucial for us now to look for answers in the text of the Bible itself and examine the evidence there. In forthcoming chapters, we will address questions such as these: Can the Bible be read and understood literally, exactly as it is written? Did prophets sometimes copy from contemporary sources? How important is context to our interpretation of Scripture? Are some parts of Scripture more inspired than others? Can we treat the Bible—especially the Old Testament—as a textbook of ancient history? Is the Bible up-to-date with modern scientific knowledge? Stay with me as we explore these and other topics prayerfully and thoughtfully.

To think about:

1.   Zechariah and Malachi were minor prophets, contemporary with the Jewish community soon after the return from Babylonian exile. Read the first four chapters of Zechariah, then Malachi's four chapters, observing how each prophet had his own unique style of writing the messages he received. How does this help us understand the freedom the prophet had in responding to divine messages and writing them down?

2.   In the third-to-last paragraph above, we noted that among Adventists, there is a wide diversity of beliefs about biblical inspiration. What implications does this have when we read and discuss inspired writings together?

3.   Think and comment about the fact that Ellen White wrote her insights about thought inspiration several years before the

Fundamentalist Movement developed the concept of verbal inspiration.

4. Prayerfully consider what has been presented in this chapter. What has been your understanding about the nature of the inspiration of the Bible and Ellen White? I can testify, from personal experience, that a change of stance in this area does not come easily.

References:

1   Wikipedia contributors, "Galileo Galilei," *Wikipedia, The Free Encyclopedia*, http://1ref.us/m7 (accessed October 10, 2017).

2   R.A. Torrey, editor, *The Fundamentals: A Testimony to the Truth*.

3   Ross Douthat, *New York Times*, July 16, 2012.

4   James M. Gray, "The Inspiration of the Bible" in *The Fundamentals*, 1917, 138, 141.

5   "Report on Sacred Scripture: Southern Baptist - Roman Catholic Conversation," September 10, 1999.

6   Ellen White, *Selected Messages*, 3:51 (1907).

7   *Ibid.*, 1:21 (1886).

8   Cliff Leitch, "Should the Bible be Interpreted Literally?" http://1ref.us/m6 (accessed October 10, 2017).

9   Denton E. Rebok, *Believe His Prophets*, 202, 203.

Understanding

Chapter 9—A Prophet's Words

God inspired and spoke through men and women who were fallible. They received visual images and concepts which they then expressed in their own words and styles of writing.

Only rarely did God dictate words to the prophet. In most cases, the Holy Spirit gave the prophet dreams, visions, or thoughts. How did those images or thoughts translate into the words of the Bible? How should we understand inspiration as it relates to the words that we read in the Scriptures? We will look at five ways in which the prophet used words to convey what he had been shown or received as thoughts from the Holy Spirit.

Common Knowledge

In communicating truth that he had been shown or given, the prophet drew from his personal knowledge and experience. The prophet belonged to a community and culture in which he lived and worked; he was familiar with the issues and beliefs of his time and place. It was part of his "common knowledge" about the world around him, so his writing reflected this knowledge and experience. We saw how Amos used the farming idiom of his rural occupation when he wrote out the revelations God gave him.

"Common knowledge" is what people believe to be true at a particular time and place. Living in the 21st century, we have views and perceptions about contemporary events in our world, as well as issues that are discussed in our local communities. It is all part of our common knowledge. We must be aware, though, that common knowledge changes whenever we have new information that updates it, or sometimes makes it obsolete. Think about how our knowledge of astronomy has changed during the past hundred years. Common beliefs of people in Bible times were not always accurate by today's knowledge.

The adjacent diagram (Figure 7) is redrawn from *The Ellen G. White Encyclopedia.*[1] Take a few moments to study it carefully. It illustrates how inspired writing comes to us through a combination of the prophet's common knowledge and the revealed truth from the Holy Spirit. It is important to understand that the writings of a prophet reflect a divine message given through vision or thought inspiration (the vertical), but encapsulated in the prophet's own words, drawn from his own culture and local knowledge (the horizontal). The Holy Spirit superintends the whole activity.

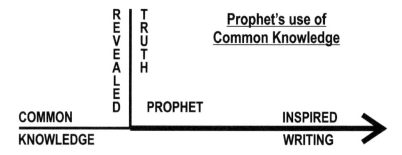

The left end of the baseline = input of common knowledge
The vertical line = descent of revealed truth to the prophet
The right end of the baseline = inspired writing
Note that the communication from the prophet's mind to the
audience combines revealed truth and common knowledge.

Figure 7: Prophet's Use of Common Knowledge.

Introducing his gospel, Luke explained that he set out to write an orderly narrative about the life of Jesus and sought out "eyewitnesses and ministers of the word" to construct the story of Jesus. He explained: "Many have undertaken to draw up an account of the things that have been fulfilled among us, just as they were handed down to us by those who from the first were eyewitnesses and servants of the word. With this in mind, since I myself have carefully investigated everything from the beginning, I too decided to write an orderly account for you, most excellent Theophilus, so that you may know the certainty of the things you have been taught" (Luke 1:1–4). In other words, Luke, a non-Jew by birth, drew from the firsthand knowledge of people who were present in Galilee and Judea during Jesus' life and ministry as he prepared to write his gospel account. Luke was also a close friend of Paul and accompanied him on some of his missionary journeys. In composing his sequel, the Book of Acts, Luke included an amazing amount of detail about places they visited together, including their voyage from Caesarea to Rome. He drew from all he had personally observed and experienced (see Acts 21:1–9; 27:13–41; 28:1–16).

Beginning his first letter to the Corinthians, Paul used some knowledge he received from friends: "My brothers and sisters, some from Chloe's household have informed me that there are quarrels among you" (1 Cor. 1:11). Paul's memory was not always perfect either. Continuing his letter, he writes, "Now I am thankful that I baptized only Crispus and Gaius, so none of you can falsely declare you were baptized in my name. Now wait, as I think about it, I also baptized the household of Stephanas; if there are others in your community whom I baptized, I cannot recall at this moment" (1 Cor. 1:14–16, Voice Bible).

Among Old Testament prophets, Nahum may give us an interesting example of how inspired messages were filtered through personal awareness. Nahum's task was to prophesy against wicked Nineveh and predict the downfall of the cruel Assyrian empire. God may have chosen Nahum for his unique knowledge of Assyrian power and practices. Remembering inscriptions that depicted Ashurbanipal, its king, as a royal lion and a lion hunter, Nahum wrote, "Where now is the lions' den, the place where they fed their young, where the lion and lioness went, and the cubs, with nothing to fear?…the sword will devour your young lions. I will leave you no prey on the earth" (Nahum 2:11, 13). An Old Testament scholar demonstrates that Nahum was familiar with ten curses that Assyria pronounced on its enemies, so he articulated the same ten curses against the Assyrians.[2]

With biblical prophets, we have only what is preserved for us in the Bible. The story is quite different with Ellen White. We have virtually everything she said publicly or wrote—her personal letters, diaries, sermons, and accounts from people who associated with her or her family on a day-to-day basis. Ellen White made much use of common knowledge for which she did not claim inspiration. This included letters to family members, conversations with friends, and discussions with church leaders. In her inspired writings, she also depended on widely accepted sources of knowledge. On one occasion, her casual reading led her to confuse Herod Antipas with Herod Agrippa. She later corrected the error.[3]

In 1909, she wrote to a minister in California who had lost faith in her testimonies because she made reference to Paradise Valley Sanitarium as having forty rooms, when in fact there were only thirty-eight. Responding to Elder Ballenger, she wrote: "The information given concerning the number of rooms in the Paradise Valley Sanitarium was given, not as a revelation from the Lord, but simply as a human opinion. There has never been revealed to me the exact number of rooms in any of our sanitariums, and the knowledge I have obtained of such things I have gained by inquiring of those who were supposed to know."[4]

She further explained, "There are times when common things must be stated, common thoughts must occupy the mind; common letters must be written, and information given that has passed from one to another of the workers. Such words, such information, are not given under the special inspiration of the Spirit of God....We converse about houses and lands, trades to be made, and locations for our institutions, their advantages and disadvantages."[5]

Personal Opinions

Bible writers used human logic in their thinking, just like the rest of us. Sometimes their thinking turned out to be personal opinion rather than inspired counsel.

Nathan gave his personal opinion in support of King David's proposal to build a temple in Jerusalem: "Whatever you have in mind, go ahead and do it, for the Lord is with you." However, that night "the word of the Lord came to Nathan" and he was sent to instruct David that he was *not* to build the temple. Nathan then gave the inspired message: "When your days are over and you rest with your ancestors, I will raise up your offspring to succeed you, who will come from your own body, and I will establish his kingdom. He is the one who will build a house for my Name" (2 Sam. 7:1–5, 12, 13). Nathan's first response to David was his personal opinion.

When God rejected Saul as king of Israel, Samuel was directed to invite Jesse and his sons to a special sacrifice. God had told Samuel that one of Jesse's sons was to be anointed as Israel's next king. As Samuel assessed tall and handsome Eliab, the eldest son, he was ready to take up the anointing oil, but God nudged His prophet: "Do not consider his appearance or his height, for I have rejected him. The Lord does not look at the things human beings look at. People look at the outward appearance, but the Lord looks at the heart" (1 Sam. 16:6, 7). God sometimes had to overrule the opinions of His prophets.

> *Bible writers used human logic in their thinking, just like the rest of us. Sometimes their thinking turned out to be personal opinion rather than inspired counsel.*

On a couple of occasions, the Apostle Paul gave his personal views on divorce and sexuality. He explained this clearly: "To the married I give this command (not I, but the Lord): a wife must not separate from her husband. But if she does, she must remain unmarried or else be reconciled to her husband....*To the rest I say this (I, not the Lord)*: If any brother has a wife who is not a believer and he is willing to live with her, she must not divorce him" (1 Cor. 7:10–12). "Now about virgins, *I have no command from the Lord, but I give judgment* as one who by the Lord's mercy is trustworthy" (1 Cor. 7:25–28, italics mine). In each case, the prophet's counsel was his own, but the Holy Spirit did not counter Paul's thinking, which was firmly based upon his pastoral experience.

In his letter to a missionary, Titus, Paul quoted some rather unkind remarks about the people of Crete, a small island in the eastern Mediterranean, before adding his own low opinion about them: "One of Crete's own prophets has said it: 'Cretans are always liars, evil brutes, lazy gluttons.' He has surely told the truth! Therefore rebuke them sharply, so that they will be sound in the faith" (Titus 1:12, 13). Paul's advice to Titus may not always be a good missionary tactic for us.

Sometimes Ellen White expressed her own opinions based on the best information available. In 1902, when the new southern publishing house in Nashville was losing money, she supported the view of the General Conference president, Arthur G. Daniells, that it should be closed. Later, though, she was shown in vision that the publishing house should not be closed: "During the night following our interview...the Lord instructed me that I had taken a wrong position."[6]

Using Writings of Others

The biblical writers did not limit themselves to what came to them through visions and dreams. They sometimes copied or quoted from other sources, and not all those sources were inspired.

We have already used the example of Luke—a Greek Jew who undertook to write an orderly account of the life of Christ for his "most excellent" friend, Theophilus. Besides using eyewitness accounts of Christ's ministry, Luke appears to have drawn from the gospel account of Mark, as well as interviews with people. Whatever the sources of information that Luke utilized, we may be assured that he wrote his gospel, as well as its sequel (the Book of Acts) with the guidance of the Holy Spirit (Luke 1:1–3, Acts 1:1).

The historians of ancient Israel had access to several extra-biblical sources that were possibly not inspired writings. These included the *Acts of Solomon* (1 Kings 11:41), which may have been written by a prophet named Iddo. The historian of the Book of Kings had access to the now lost *Chronicles of the Kings of Judah* and the *Chronicles of the Kings of Israel*. A typical reference is this one: "As for the other events of Rehoboam's reign, and all he did, are they not written in the book of the annals of the kings of Judah" (1 Kings 14:29)? Other sources are mentioned by the writer of Chronicles: "As for the events of King David's reign, from beginning to end, they are written in the records of Samuel the seer, the records of Nathan the prophet and the records of Gad the seer" (1 Chron. 29:29). The chronicler also identified the records of Ahijah the Shilonite, Iddo the seer, Shemaiah the prophet, and the annals of Jehu son of Anani (1 Chron. 29:29; 2 Chron. 9:29; 12:15, 20:34).

Ellen White sometimes used the writings of others in her books and articles. In expanding the story of the great controversy from creation to the end times in the five-volume *Conflict of the Ages* series, she paraphrased quite extensively from several published commentaries in her personal library. We will study more about this in the next chapter.

Contending with False Prophets

God's true prophets were often confronted by other prophets whose messages contradicted theirs. God told Jeremiah that He would destroy the disobedient Judeans "with the sword, famine and plague." Jeremiah immediately protested, "Ah, Sovereign Lord, the prophets keep telling them 'You will *not* see the sword or suffer famine. Indeed I will give you lasting peace in this place.'" The Lord responded, "The prophets are prophesying lies in my name. I have not sent them or appointed them or spoken to them. They are prophesying to you false visions, divinations, idolatries, and the delusions of their own minds" (Jer. 14:11–15).

False prophets were not always easy to identify. When Hananiah contradicted Jeremiah's prophecy of the coming destruction of Jerusalem and seventy years of captivity in Babylon, he told his listeners that there would be peace. People were happy with his comforting words. Jeremiah responded to Hananiah: "From early times the prophets who preceded you and me have prophesied war, disaster and plague against many countries and great kingdoms. But the prophet who prophesies peace will be recognized as one truly sent by the Lord only if his prediction comes true. . . Listen, Hananiah! The Lord has not sent you, yet you have persuaded this nation to trust in lies" (Jer. 28:8, 9, 15).

Nearing the end of their forty years of wilderness wandering, the Israelites were encroaching upon the plains of Moab east of the Jordan River. Watching them nervously from the heights above, the Moabite king determined to have a curse placed on them, and dispatched messengers to Balaam, a "prophet" who was willing to curse for cash. You likely remember the story of how Balaam's plan to curse was overruled by the Lord, and he blessed Israel instead (see Num. 22–24; Jude 11). It was while the Israelites were gathered there on the threshold of Canaan that Moses warned the people about false prophets who would cause Israel to turn away from the Lord and serve other gods (see Deut. 13:1–3). Balaam's actions fulfilled that warning. He persuaded the Midianites to have their women seduce the Israelite soldiers and lead them away from God (Num. 31:7, 8).

False prophets might sometimes perform wonders and miracles. Moses warned about prophets who made predictions that came to pass, but then instructed the people to follow and worship other gods: "You must not listen to the words of that prophet or dreamer" (Deut. 13:1–4). Jesus warned His listeners, "Watch out for false prophets. They come to you in sheep's clothing, but inwardly they are ferocious wolves. By their fruit you will recognize them." (Matt. 7:15, 16). Paul had similar words: "I urge you, brothers and sisters, to watch out for those who cause divisions and put obstacles in your way that are contrary to the teaching you have learned. Keep away from them" (Rom. 16:17).

Prophetic claims did not end with the time of Paul. Among those claiming prophet status in North America during the past 200 years were Joseph Smith of the Mormon faith and Mary Baker Eddy of Christian Science. Within Adventism there have also been some who claimed to have inspired messages for the church. While Ellen White was in Australia during the 1890s, Anna Phillips Rice believed she had prophetic experiences in Battle Creek, Michigan. When her testimonies were read in public meetings, they created quite a stir. Eventually, Anna gave up her claims and later served the church as a Bible worker. In 1901, Helge Nelson visited Ellen White, claiming he had divine messages for her. Ellen refuted his claims, and at the 1903 General Conference Session, he attempted to assault her physically. Shortly after Ellen White's death in 1915, Margaret Rowen claimed to be Mrs. White's successor, but church leaders discovered a forged document and evidence that she had embezzled a large sum of money.[7] Throughout history, Satan has tried repeatedly to counterfeit the work of God's prophets, creating confusion and conflict.

Change Makers

Change is tough. Just ask a senior if it was easy to downsize and move into assisted living; or ask the Israelites how they adapted to nomadic life in the desert after generations of living in Egypt. "If only we had died by the Lord's hand in Egypt! There we sat around pots of meat and ate all the food we wanted" (Exod. 16:3). Most of us resist change. Even ruts become comfortable places after a while.

After settling in Canaan, the Israelites adopted the ways and worship of the local inhabitants. "They forgot the Lord their God and served the Baals and the Asherahs" (Judges 3:7). Worship of false gods gradually became their culture and they again grew resistant to change. The Lord commented sadly, "When Israel was a child, I loved him, and out of Egypt I called my son. But the more they were called, the more they went away from me" (Hosea 11:1, 2). They ignored or rejected the promises and warnings of a compassionate God.

While false prophets were giving "peace and safety" messages and supporting existing religious practices, the true prophets brought words from God that called for changed behavior. Numerous messages of the prophets were dynamic calls for reformation, repentance, and renewal. Listen to Jeremiah: "Stand at the crossroads and look; ask for the ancient paths, ask where the good way is, and walk in it, and you will find rest for your souls" (Jer. 6:16). Hear Isaiah's conditional promise: "Your people will rebuild the ancient ruins and will raise up the age-old foundations; you will be called Repairer of Broken Walls, Restorer of Streets with Dwellings." The conditional promise included a restoration of the Sabbath (Isa. 58:12, 13).

At the dedication of Solomon's Temple, God made this beautiful plea for change: "If my people, who are called by my name, will humble themselves and pray and seek my face and turn from their wicked ways, then will I hear from heaven and will forgive their sin and will heal their land" (2 Chron. 7:14). Not all of these pleadings for change were ignored. Reformations occurred in the days of David, Hezekiah, and Josiah. Centuries later, John the Baptist preached evangelistic sermons that resulted in baptisms and re-consecration.

Many of God's prophets were given ability to accomplish change through qualities of leadership. Moses was the epitome of superb leadership. For forty long years, he led a complaining and rebellious band of ex-slaves through the desert, giving of himself as he taught them survival skills in an unfriendly environment. Later, Joshua led a new generation across the Jordan to victory and settlement in Canaan. Centuries later, Nehemiah gathered a disheartened bunch of returned exiles and organized them into a willing team that rebuilt the walls of Jerusalem in fifty-two days. Peter preached powerful sermons after Pentecost and guided in the formation and organization of the early Christian Church.

In our time, Ellen White, poorly educated though she was, and in a culture of male dominance, was given this same gift of leadership and became a powerful agent of change in the formative years of the Seventh-day Adventist Church. Her vision and leadership were evident in several aspects of church development—she launched the publishing work, led in the growth of education and schools, pioneered health and medical work, encouraged international missions, and initiated some needed change in church organization. As a rapidly growing denomination with a global presence, we owe much to Ellen White's determination and inspired counsel.

It seems that openness to change may have been among the qualities God looked for in His choice of prophetic messengers. Certainly, change-making was an important facet of a prophet's role.

To think about:

1. Prophets incorporated their personal knowledge, and sometimes personal opinions, into their writing. God did not always correct their words. Should this concern us? Why or why not? Does it teach us anything about God and human freedom?

2. Calling for change is never easy. Consider Moses. Why, after a superior education in the court of Pharaoh, was he resistant to

the call to lead his people out of Egypt (review Exodus 3:1–4:17)? How do I respond to calls for change?

3.   How should the knowledge that Ellen White depended on "common knowledge" of her time guide us in reading and understanding her writings?

References:

[1]   Jud Lake and Jerry Moon, "Current Science and Ellen White", in *The Ellen G. White Encyclopedia*, 216.

[2]   Elias Brasil de Souza, "The Hebrew Prophets and the Literature of the Ancient Near East" in *The Gift of Prophecy in Scripture and History*, 125–127.

[3]   Ellen White, *Spiritual Gifts*, 1:71, and *Spirit of Prophecy*, 3:334.

[4]   White, *Selected Messages*, 1:38.

[5]   *Ibid.*, 39.

[6]   White, Letter to A.G. Daniells, Dec. 26, 1902.

[7]   *The Ellen G. White Encyclopedia*, 475, 495, 503.

Understanding

Chapter 10—Literary Dependence

"There is nothing new under the sun" (Eccles. 1:9). That was the inspired conclusion of one of the wisest men who has ever lived. And you thought you had an original idea!

What do we mean by "literary dependence"? If we view God as the ultimate source of all wisdom and knowledge, then there is indeed nothing new under the sun. The truth of that statement changes, though, when we use words, because the same idea or concept may be expressed in a thousand different ways.

Some Bible authors depended on other writers, sometimes copying from one another or even uninspired sources. Here are a few examples of literary dependence in Scripture.

- Isaiah copies a large section from the writer of the Second Book of Kings—or was it the other way around (compare Isaiah 36–39 with 2 Kings 18–20)?
- Jeremiah 52 is an almost verbatim copy of portions of 2 Kings 24–25 and 2 Chronicles 36.
- The Second Book of Samuel reproduces a poem or song from a collection of nationalistic poems in the now unknown *Book of*

Jashar (see 2 Samuel 1:17–27).

- Almost ninety percent of Mark's gospel appears to have been copied by Matthew and Luke.
- The historians of ancient Israel depended upon several extra-biblical sources that may not have been inspired writings (see 1 Kings 14:19, 29; 1 Chron. 29:29; 2 Chron. 9:29; 12:15, 20:34).
- Luke, under inspiration, compiled his gospel from several sources, including eyewitnesses of Christ's ministry (see Luke 1:1–3).

Scholarly interest in biblical, textual studies has turned up many examples of borrowing from ancient sources. Many are of little significance. Studies of the Book of Proverbs reveal that some of the wisdom in 22:17–23:11 was borrowed from a compilation of thirty chapters of proverbs composed by an ancient Egyptian scribe, Amenemope, as counsel for his son. Egyptian influence was strong in Israel during the time of King Solomon.[1] The final chapter of Proverbs, which celebrates a virtuous woman, is introduced as the words of a wise mother to her son, King Lemuel, a character otherwise unknown to Old Testament scholars. Textual studies reveal that Proverbs is not an isolated case of dependence on ancient near-eastern sources.

There are many examples of literary dependence by biblical authors. We already saw that Moses depended upon stories handed down orally from generation to generation in compiling the Book of Genesis. Ezra and Nehemiah include letters to and from Persian officials and listings of various items. Paul quoted from a secular author: "in Him we live and move and have our being. As some of your own poets have said, 'For we are his offspring'" (Acts 17:28).

Both Jude and John the Revelator quote from the *Book of Enoch*, a pseudonymous Jewish work compiled about 150 years before the time of Christ (see Jude 14, 15; Rev. 14:14–16). Facts such as these should not trouble us. We know that prophets expressed divine inspiration in their own words, sometimes borrowing from the commonly accepted knowledge of their time; but the Holy Spirit guided the prophet's thinking so that he could express God's message faithfully.

Ellen White and Literary Dependence

Ellen White was one of the world's most prolific female authors, generating approximately 100,000 pages of text over a period of about sixty years. It is well known that she used the writings of others fairly extensively in preparing some of her books and articles. Is this a problem for

Seventh-day Adventists? I quote from Jud Lake, a professor at Southern Adventist University in Tennessee, who is also director of the university's Institute for the Study of Ellen White and Adventist Heritage:

"As we recall Ellen White's prophetic ministry a century after she laid down her pen, the old allegation that she plagiarized much of her writing continues unabated. From D.M. Canright's claim that she was a 'great plagiarist' to the contemporary Internet allegations that she copied ninety percent of her material, the charge that Ellen White derived her insights from human authors rather than God persists as the most popular criticism of her prophetic ministry."[2]

Before reviewing some of these allegations, let's summarize a few facts:

1. As Ellen White worked on expanding the story of the great controversy from creation to the end of time in the five-volume *Conflict of the Ages* series, she copied and paraphrased fairly extensively from several devotional books that she had personally collected through the years. During the 1980s, in response to questions and accusations, a General Conference-commissioned study of several chapters of *The Desire of Ages* was conducted by Fred Veltman, a professor of New Testament at Pacific Union College. Veltman's comprehensive study of fifteen randomly selected chapters concluded that she drew from the works of other authors, not for their ideas or theology, but to "enhance her writing."[3]

2. In writing *Great Controversy*, she read extensively from published histories of modern Europe and the Reformation, borrowing and paraphrasing from their works. In her introduction to *The Great Controversy*, she said she accepted "facts of history, well known and universally acknowledged by the Protestant world" for inclusion in her work. These "facts of history" did not come to her by way of revelation, and occasionally some of the facts were inaccurate.[4]

3. For twenty-five years, from 1879 until 1904, Marian Davis was Ellen White's faithful and knowledgeable "bookmaker" in the preparation of major works, including the original edition of *The Great Controversy* (1888) and *Patriarchs and Prophets*. In 1891, Marian accompanied Ellen to Australia, where she played a

major role in the production of *The Desire of Ages*, *Christ's Object Lessons*, *Steps to Christ*, and *Thoughts from the Mount of Blessing*.

Speaking of this help she received, Ellen wrote: "Marian is my bookmaker....She does her work in this way: she takes my articles which are published in the papers, and pastes them in blank books. She also has a copy of all the letters I write. In preparing a chapter for a book, Marian remembers that I have written something on that special point, which may make the matter more forcible. She begins to search for this, and if when she finds it, she sees that it will make the chapter more clear, she adds it. The books are not Marian's productions, but my own, gathered from all my writings."[5]

Ellen White was not unique in getting help with her writing. Bible scholars have concluded that the apostles Paul and Peter used literary assistants in preparing their letters to the various churches. This explains several variations in writing style that we find throughout their epistles. In the last chapter of Romans, we find this: "I, Tertius, who wrote down this letter, greet you in the Lord" (Rom. 16:22). Peter also had this kind of help (see 1 Peter 5:12).

4.   The extent of Ellen White's borrowing from other authors is considerably less than what is alleged by her critics. A documented, ongoing study by the White Estate puts the percentage in the low single digits when compared to her total literary output.[6]

> *Why was Ellen White so dependent on the writings of others? Her lack of formal education severely limited her understanding and ability to express herself well.*

Why was Ellen White so dependent on the writings of others? Her lack of formal education severely limited her understanding and ability to express herself well. She was conscious that she was not highly gifted in literary talent, but she recognized and admired it when she saw it in the writing of others. She read widely and developed a fine personal library that numbered 1,300 volumes at the time of her death. As she contemplated writing about the life of Christ in *The Desire of Ages*, she expressed her feelings in a letter to the General Conference President, O.A. Olsen: "This week I have been enabled to commence writing on the life of Christ. Oh, how inefficient, how incapable I am of expressing the things which burn in my soul in reference to the mission of Christ….I know not how to speak or trace with pen the large subject of the atoning sacrifice. I know not how to present subjects in the living power in which they stand before me. I tremble for fear lest I shall belittle the great plan of salvation by cheap words."[7] That sense of personal inadequacy helps us understand why she utilized the writing style of other devotional authors.

The Question of Inspiration

For a person who believes in verbal inspiration, every word Ellen White wrote must have been inspired by God. Anyone who believes that God dictates the words to the prophet is extremely troubled by the idea of literary dependence, whether by Bible prophets or Ellen White. This was the major question about Ellen White faced by Seventh-day Adventists in her own day and still our time. How should we relate to her use of material from other authors when she claimed divine inspiration?

If we accept that the biblical prophets described in their own words what they had been shown in vision or received through thought inspiration, we cannot require that the prophet use the very words given during a vision. Lengthy periods of time sometimes elapsed between receiving a vision and writing it down (see Jer. 36:1, 2). In response to a question from Dr. J.S. Gibbs about a vision she had received, Ellen White responded, "I cannot write the exact words as He spoke them. I will try my best to give you the import of them."[8] In trying her best, Ellen White sometimes chose another's words to express well the thoughts God wished her to communicate.

A careful examination of the evidence, supported by her own description of how she worked, leads us to conclude that God inspired her with concepts and ideas, and sometimes showed her "motion pictures" of scenes in history to reveal how He was involved in these events. She wrote these in her own words, but sometimes utilized materials from other sources to help her express her thoughts better. In this case, God inspired the person, not the words.

An interesting example of how Ellen White used her source material relates directly to this issue of inspiration. While she was in Europe in 1886, Ellen had access to a book entitled *The Origin and History of the Books of the Bible*. Its author, Calvin Stowe, was somewhat influenced by liberal thinking about inspiration, and his book, published in 1867, was one of the first American publications to examine the Bible from a historical perspective. In his book, Stowe expressed his belief that while the Holy

Spirit spoke to the prophet, neither the prophet's words nor his thoughts were inspired: "Inspiration was not on the man's words, *not on the man's thoughts*, but on the man himself" (italics mine). Believing that the prophet's thoughts were *not inspired*, Stowe was moving towards the "encounter" view of Scripture that we described in an earlier chapter.[9]

Ellen White borrowed some phrases from Stowe's book, but she rejected his thesis that God did not inspire the prophet's thoughts. Notice how her words contradict Stowe's belief: "It is not the words of the Bible that are inspired, *but the men that were inspired....Inspiration acts not on the man's words or his expressions, but on the man himself, who, under the influence of the Holy Ghost, is imbued with thoughts.*"[10] Clearly, Ellen had Stowe's book at her desk when she wrote those words, but she did not mindlessly copy his ideas. Had she done so, she might have adopted a theory of inspiration similar to what liberal theologians were beginning to publish around that time.[11] She continued, *"The divine mind and will is combined with the human mind and will; thus the utterances of the man are the word of God"* [12] (italics mine).

Ellen White's perspective is unique. Her copying and paraphrasing from other writers reflects an overarching view of the conflict between Christ and Satan that is not found in any other author's work. Her changes in wording from other writers often reflect truth inspired by the Holy Spirit.

The Issue of Plagiarism

Plagiarism is the practice of taking someone else's work or ideas and passing them off as one's own. In the case of Ellen White, plagiarism need never have been an issue. Those who have accused her of plagiarism, then and now, subscribe to a belief in verbal inspiration, or are judging her literary borrowing by today's copyright rules that did not exist in her time.

Copyright law in the United States was almost a non-issue until it was updated in 1909, six years before Ellen White's death. Prior to that time, any author who wanted his or her work protected for a period of fourteen years from its first publication had to carefully follow certain registration and deposit formalities and include in the book a printed notice that copyright requirements had been met. Not all authors bothered to take advantage of the opportunity. Throughout the 18th and 19th centuries, there was still a culture of literary ethics from an earlier time that did not discourage authors from freely borrowing from one another without giving credit. The practice was especially common among religious writers who valued the spreading of Christian truth. John Wesley, in the preface to one of his books, chose not to give credit to authors from whom he had borrowed: "I resolved to name none, that nothing might divert the mind of the reader from the point in view."[13]

Because of constant accusations, the General Conference, in 1981, sought an independent legal opinion from an attorney who specialized in intellectual property issues. Attorney Vincent L. Ramik spent more than 300 hours researching relevant cases in American legal history before concluding that "Ellen White was not a plagiarist, and her works did not constitute copyright infringement/piracy."[14]

Changes to copyright law in 1909 coincided with the publishing explosion beginning in America. Accordingly, the 1911 reprinting of *The Great Controversy* corrected some historical information and added statements of credit wherever they were due.

Recently, two Adventist scholars gave this verdict: "Whether Ellen White used Biblical descriptions, assimilated language, adapted gems of thought, or words and phrases absorbed from her use of sources as storyline guides, one thing is certain—her finished product is clearly her own, and she has done her readers a great service in *identifying, improving, and making more memorable* some of the most effective language available for telling the 'story of Jesus' love.'"[15]

Degrees of Inspiration?

Are there degrees of inspiration? That question occupied the minds of many 19th century Adventists who knew about Ellen White's literary borrowing. They believed she was clearly inspired by the Holy Spirit when she wrote testimonies that came from visions and "the Lord has shown me...", but was she less inspired when she wrote books with material borrowed from other writers? Perhaps, too, there were portions of the Bible that were less inspired than other parts. Proverbs, for example?

We saw the evidence that specific portions of Scripture were copied or paraphrased from secular sources. During the 1880s, two Seventh-day Adventist leaders had discussions about inspiration. George I. Butler was president of the General Conference at that time, and Uriah Smith was editor of the *Review and Herald* church paper. Together they advanced the idea that there were degrees of inspiration in the Bible. They considered, for example, the books of Moses to be on a higher planc of inspiration than the Psalms and Proverbs and tried to apply the same concept to Ellen White's writings. They wondered whether all of her testimonies were equally inspired. Their views were published by Butler as a ten-part series in the *Review*.[16]

Ellen White did not share their view: "Both in the Tabernacle and in the college the subject of inspiration has been taught, and finite men have taken it upon themselves to say that some things in the Scriptures were inspired and some were not. I was shown that the Lord did not inspire the articles on inspiration published in the Review."[17] She took the position that there are no degrees of biblical inspiration. The prophet was either inspired by the Holy Spirit or not.

Is there another way of looking at inspired writings? Instead of thinking about *degrees* of inspiration, we might ask whether all inspired writings have the same *purpose*.

We may discern different purposes for many of the books of the Old Testament. Think about the **prophetic books** (Isaiah through Malachi) that reveal Yahweh as God of all peoples; He pleads with wayward Israel to listen and change their behavior, fulfill their mission among the nations, and prepare for a coming Messiah. Then consider the **historical books**. They appear to be inspired for a different purpose—to recount the story of Israel, their exodus from Egypt, victories and defeats, Jehovah's leading throughout their history, and how God cared for His people in spite of their failures. The purpose changes again in **devotional books** like Psalms, Proverbs, and Ecclesiastes, where the writers open their hearts to the reader, sharing personal joys and sorrows, their heartfelt convictions, and what life has taught them.

New Testament writings also reflect different purposes. The gospel writers tell the story of Jesus; Luke gives an account of Paul's missionary journeys; Paul and other apostles write letters of encouragement and reproof to new believers in faraway churches; the Book of Revelation gives us animated pictures of last-day events.

In His great wisdom, God saw that we don't all come to the Scriptures with the same needs and understandings. Our needs are varied and different. Therefore, Jeremiah's message is strikingly different from Solomon's, but one was not more inspired than the other. The same Holy Spirit inspired them both.

Can we apply the same concept in the writings of Ellen White? If inspiration operated with different *purposes* for biblical authors, can the same be true for her writings? Let us look at some comparisons.

The Old Testament books of Joshua, Judges, Samuel, and Kings recount the history of Israel from the occupation of Canaan up until the Babylonian captivity. Later, though, during or after the exile, the author of Chronicles was inspired to present much of the same history for a new generation of Jewish people just released from Babylonian captivity. Chronicles focuses on worship issues and religious life in a new time. The writer omits a lot of the history from the earlier narratives, makes a few factual corrections, and adds some history not previously given, along with new applications. Thus, the chronicler's purpose was different from the earlier Hebrew historians.

Did Ellen White have a purpose similar to the chronicler when she wrote her *Conflict of the Ages* series? In four consecutive books—*Patriarchs and Prophets, Prophets and Kings, The Desire of Ages,* and *The Acts of the Apostles*—she retells the Bible story all the way from creation to Paul's missionary journeys, but with applications for a new generation of Christians in the end time. She omits a lot of detail, but provides homiletical applications for our time and culture. Like the chronicler of the Old Testament, she writes *the same stories with a new purpose.*

Can we also see a parallel between Paul's letters to the early Christian churches and Ellen White's letters and testimonies for the fledgling Adventist church? Paul was given new truth about salvation to share with new Christians in the Roman world, as well as corrective counsel and admonition wherever needed. Ellen White, through her letters and testimonies, brings new understandings about the great controversy to a new generation of end-time believers. Like Paul, she offers reproof and correction when required. The Holy Spirit may have different purposes with inspired messages—purposes to meet needs of time and place. It makes sense to think about *purposeful inspiration.*

Keeping all this in mind, I will read inspired writings in appropriate ways. I won't go to Psalms or Proverbs to confirm a doctrinal point, but when I feel sad or disappointed, the song of a shepherd may restore my soul. When I'm looking for theology, I will probably open the letters of Paul. I will read the Books of Moses to see how Jehovah worked through the lives of ancestors like Abraham and Sarah, Jacob, and Joseph; when I read *Patriarchs and Prophets* I discover that their stories carry some lessons for us "on whom the culmination of the ages has come" (1 Cor. 10:11). The prophetic books of Scripture show me the magnitude of God's grace with the waywardness of ancient Israel. My spiritual enjoyment of *Desire of Ages* is often enhanced by choice phrases and sentences that she carefully selected from other writers of her time. Needing practical counsel for my daily living, I sometimes search appropriate terms in the online database of Ellen White's writings, so that I can understand the context of some of her statements, and apply them appropriately.[18]

Ellen White was not given authority to add or make corrections to the biblical Canon. Her authority was derived from the Bible, but not equal to it. However, her writings provide me with an inspired commentary on Scripture and guide me in ordering my life in harmony with the precious Word of God. As a Seventh-day Adventist Christian, I am doubly blessed.

To think about:

1.   The concept of a prophet's dependence on another's writings worries some Christians. How should we think about the level of God's control and supervision over the inspiration process? Why is that important?

2.   Reflect on Solomon's observation that "there is nothing new under the sun" (Eccles. 1:9). Discuss what that statement implies for the prophet's use of other writers.

3.   How might the concept of "purposeful inspiration" impact the way you read the Bible and the writings of Ellen White?

References:

[1]   James R. Black, *The Instruction of Amenemope*, a critical edition and commentary.

[2]   Jud Lake, "Ellen White's Use of Extrabiblical Sources" in *The Gift of Prophecy in Scripture and History*, 320–336.

[3]   Fred Veltman, Life of Christ Research Project, 1988.

[4]   Ellen White, *Great Controversy*, xi.

[5]   White, *Selected Messages*, 3: 91.

[6]   Tim Poirier, "Ellen White and Sources", in *Understanding Ellen White*, 154.

[7]   White, Letter 49, 1892.

[8]   White, Letter 8, 1888.

[9]   Calvin Stowe, *Origin and History of the Books of the Bible*, 19. (Hartford Publishing, 1867).

[10]   White, *Selected Messages*, 1:21 (1886).

[11]   Denis Fortin, "Plagiarism", in *The Ellen G. White Encyclopedia*, 1034.

[12]   White, *Selected Messages*, 1:21.

[13]   John Wesley, *Explanatory Notes Upon the New Testament:* Preface (1754).

[14]   Fortin, 1029.

15   E.M.A. King and Kevin L. Morgan, quoted in Jud Lake, 335.

16   George I. Butler, *Review and Herald*, 1884.

17   White, *Review and Herald*, January 15, 1884.

18   Ellen G. White Estate, http://1ref.us/m8 (accessed October 10, 2017).

Chapter 11—Interpretation

The message of the Bible—salvation in Jesus—is so simple that a child can understand it, yet the words of Scripture are not always easy to comprehend. Jesus once prayed, "O Father, Lord of heaven and earth, thank you for hiding these things from those who think themselves wise and clever, and for revealing them to the childlike" (Matt. 11:25, NLT). Scholars and theologians spend much time and effort discussing hermeneutics, the science of biblical interpretation. Like the Ethiopian official who was reading from Isaiah on his journey home, we may sometimes need help to find meaning in the Scriptures. "'Do you understand what you are reading?' Philip asked the Ethiopian. 'How can I,' he said, 'unless someone explains it to me?'" (Acts 8:30, 31).

> *The message of the Bible—salvation in Jesus—is so simple that a child can understand it, yet the words of Scripture are not always easy to comprehend.*

Jesus walked the Emmaus road with two discouraged men who wondered why their Lord and Master had been taken from them. Jesus opened ancient prophecies to their understanding: "Then Jesus took them through the writings of Moses and all the prophets, explaining from all the Scriptures the things concerning himself" (Luke 24:27, NLT). If those faithful followers of Jesus needed the Word to be interpreted for them, we certainly need that help too. The Scriptures were written down during a long period of about 1,500 years. During that time, customs and cultures changed many times. Science was not understood the way we know it today. Additionally, ancient poetry and figurative language create barriers to our understanding.

Someone has said, "We don't see things as they are; we see things as we are." When I read Scripture, I see and interpret it through the eyes of my past experience. I make a personal interpretation of what I read, believing my understanding is true and correct. I am prone to take Bible verses and passages out of context and use them as "proof texts" for my particular belief. I may sometimes be guilty of using Scripture the way a drunk uses a lamppost—for support rather than illumination. It's no surprise that critics say, "the Bible can be made to say anything you want it to say."

On the other hand, an authoritarian approach to Scripture assumes that all our thinking has been done for us. God created us with minds to think, question, interpret, and apply what we read. After the 1888 General Conference session in Minneapolis, when the truth of righteousness by faith in Christ was emphasized to the church for the first time, Ellen White spoke repeatedly about the need for believers to study and think for themselves. "If you allow another to do your thinking for you, you will have crippled energies and contracted abilities.... You should wrestle with problems of thought that require the exercise of the best powers of your mind."[1] The Holy Spirit is ready and able to help us interpret Scripture for our personal needs.

Much of the Bible may be read and understood plainly, exactly the way it is written. That is especially true when we are reading Scripture as story, like the narratives of Israel's history, the gospel accounts of Jesus' life, and Paul's missionary journeys. However, even in the narratives, we come upon statements that we are uncomfortable about accepting literally. What about these words of Christ: "If your eye causes you to sin, gouge it out and throw it away. It is better for you to enter life with one eye than to have two eyes and be thrown into the fire of hell" (Matt. 18:9,

NIV)? If we followed that instruction literally, there would be a lot of one-eyed Christians in the world.

The Bible also contains many figures of speech like this one: "Jesus said, 'I am the gate for the sheep'" (John 10:7). It does not mean that Jesus is a literal gate. Scripture contains metaphors, hyperbole, poetic language, and apocalyptic literature that requires interpretation. Solomon's proverbial advice may not apply in every situation: "A gentle answer" may not always "turn away wrath" (Prov. 15:1) and unfortunately it is not always true that if we "train a child in the way he should go…when he is old he will not turn from it" (Prov. 22:6). We should interpret counsel like that to make sense in our situation.

Jesus' disciples were sometimes uncertain about the meaning of what He said. His words didn't always make sense to them. When some Pharisees challenged Jesus on how the Mosaic laws applied to divorce, He presented guidelines that took His disciples by complete surprise. "If this is the situation between a husband and wife," they exclaimed, "it is better not to marry" (Matt. 19:10). During a sermon by the lake, Jesus used several parables in His discourse. The meanings were sometimes lost on the listeners, including the disciples. "With many similar parables Jesus spoke the word to [the people], as much as they could understand. But when he was alone with his own disciples, He explained everything" (Mark 4:33, 34).

Joseph, in an Egyptian prison, gave a good answer to his troubled cell mates when they came to him with their problem: "We both had dreams, but there is no one to interpret them." Joseph responded, "Do not interpretations belong to God? Tell me your dreams" (Gen.40:8). Joseph knew He could rely on the Holy Spirit to reveal truth to him. The same heavenly Counselor whom Jesus promised to His disciples the night before His death can be ours for interpretation and understanding of the Bible. We are to approach God's Word with humility and a sincere desire to know God's will for us and be open to the Holy Spirit speaking to our hearts. God's message for me may not be the same as His message for you.

When Prophets Interpret Each Other

"Above all, you must understand that no prophecy of Scripture came about by the prophet's own interpretation of things. For prophecy never had its origin in the human will, but prophets, though human, spoke from God as they were carried along by the Holy Spirit" (2 Peter 1:20, 21). Peter confirms inspiration as we have come to understand it, but the prophet did not always comprehend what he was being told or shown. His task was to report the message faithfully. He was not sharing his own thoughts or ideas; he was seeing the world through the eyes of God.

Does one prophet interpret the words of another? Yes, sometimes. In his first, Pentecostal sermon after Christ's resurrection, Peter saw the fulfillment of Joel's prophecy about a future day of the Lord: "And afterward, I will pour out my Spirit on all people. Your sons and daughters will prophesy, your old men will dream dreams, your young men will see visions" (Joel 2:28). Standing before the large crowd of curious onlookers, Peter cried out, "Fellow Jews and all of you who live in Jerusalem, let me explain this to you; listen carefully to what I say....This is what was spoken by the prophet Joel: 'In the last days, God says, I will pour out my Spirit on all people" (Acts 2:14–21). However, Peter's interpretation did not limit the fulfillment of Joel's prophecy. Two thousand years later, another inspired writer, Ellen White, saw an application of Joel to the last days of earth's history: "If this prophecy of Joel met a partial fulfillment in the days of the apostles, we are living in a time when it is to be even more evidently manifest to the people of God. He will so bestow His Spirit upon His people that they will become a light amid the moral darkness; and great light will be reflected in all parts of the world."[2] Neither the Apostle Peter nor Ellen White may have exhausted the meaning of the message given to Joel so many centuries earlier.

The Jews of Christ's day, including His own disciples, gravely misunderstood and misinterpreted many Old Testament prophecies that related to the coming Messiah. They looked for a political Messiah to throw off the Roman yoke. With minds made up on that score, they liked these Messianic words from King David: "Ask me, and I will make the nations your inheritance, the ends of the earth your possession. You will break them with a rod of iron; you will dash them to pieces like pottery" (Psalm 2:7–9). At the same time, they overlooked other prophecies like this one: "He grew up before him like a tender shoot, and like a root out of dry ground. He had no beauty or majesty to attract us to him. . . He was despised and rejected by others, a man of suffering and familiar with pain. Like one from whom people hide their faces he was despised, and we held him in low esteem" (Isa. 53:2, 3).

Jesus gave new interpretations of many Old Testament passages. He defined and amplified the meaning of the Ten Commandments, which were originally given in simple words to thousands of abused and dysfunctional slaves. "You shall not murder" includes hatred and anger (Matt. 5:21, 22); "You shall not commit adultery" includes lustful desire (Matt.

5:27, 28). He also clarified the observance of the Sabbath commandment. Responding to a charge of Sabbath-breaking because His disciples picked heads of grain as they walked through the field, Jesus declared, "The Sabbath was made for people, not people for the Sabbath" (Mark 2:27).

Matthew made some interesting applications of Old Testament Scriptures. He quoted from Hosea—"out of Egypt I called my son" (Matt. 2:15)—and applied it to the time when Joseph and Mary took the boy Jesus to Egypt to escape Herod's murder decree. However, Hosea was talking about something quite different—the exodus of Israel from Egypt: "When Israel was a child, I loved him, and out of Egypt I called my son" (Hosea 11:1). Matthew made a new interpretation of Hosea's text, but we cannot impose Matthew's interpretation on Hosea. Hosea's original meaning still stands.

The Apostle Paul also made some new applications of Old Testament Scriptures. For example, he took Moses' concern about animal welfare—"do not muzzle an ox while it is treading out the grain"—and applied it to fair financial support for the ministry: "Is it about oxen that God is concerned?…This is written for us, because when farmers plow and thresh, they should be able to do so in the hope of sharing in the harvest. If we have sown spiritual seed among you, is it too much if we reap a material harvest from you" (Deut. 25:4; 1 Cor. 9:9–12)? Paul's application does not change the original meaning of Moses' text. The same principle applies to interpretations of Scripture made by Ellen White. Her interpretations do not close the biblical text from further study and interpretation.

Methods of Interpretation

There are two quite different ways of approaching the words of Scripture: Homiletics and Exegesis. We must distinguish between these two methods.

Homiletics is what preachers usually do when they stand in the pulpit and deliver sermons. They are seeking to enrich our souls with spiritual applications for our daily living. Think of it as a **Devotional** approach to our Bible reading. When I do this, I am leaning on the Holy Spirit to show me the meaning of the text for my personal needs and spiritual growth.

Exegesis is the scholarly approach to the text, to discover the meaning of the writer. When I seek a critical interpretation of the text—to understand the meaning of the writer—I am making an exegetical approach. For that level of understanding, I may utilize various aids to my Bible study—Bible commentaries, biblical handbooks and encyclopedias, and "study" Bibles.

With the promised help of the Holy Spirit the entire Bible, from the first verse of Genesis to the last verse of Revelation, is wide open for our exploration and study. But there is something important to understand. The apostle Peter explains, "Above all, you must understand that no prophecy of Scripture came about by the prophet's own interpretation of things. For prophecy never had its origin in the human will, but prophets, though human, spoke from God as they were carried along by the Holy Spirit" (2 Peter 1:20, 21). Peter confirms inspiration as we have come to understand it. But the prophet did not always comprehend what he was being told or shown. His task was to report the message faithfully. He was not sharing his own ideas; he was seeing truth through the eyes of God.

Scripture interprets Scripture. We are admonished to become students of the Word and compare Scripture with Scripture. Ellen White emphasized this: "The Bible is its own best interpreter and when studied as a whole it depicts a consistent, harmonious truth."[3]

There are some simple steps to follow when we seek to interpret and understand a biblical text using the method of hermeneutics or exegesis. It involves, first, discovering what the passage meant in the day and age of the writer. Then we look for its application to us in our world. We will look at four steps in interpreting a passage; then we will make a practical application by using those four steps for a particular verse of Scripture. Remember always to pray for the Spirit's guidance before you begin.

1. Observation: Who wrote the passage and to whom was it addressed? What does the passage say? Are there words or phrases that need to have their meaning made clear?

2. Interpretation: What did the author mean in his own historical setting? What is the historic and cultural background? We must look at the literary context of the verse or passage—not just the preceding verses, but the broader context within the chapter and the book.

3. Evaluation: What does this passage mean in today's culture? Can I apply it to my world and culture?

4. Application: What does this passage mean to me personally? How can I apply what I have learned to how I live my life?

Now let's apply those four steps to a text of Scripture. This interesting one is found in the Gospel of Luke: "It is easier for a camel to go through the eye of a needle than for the rich to enter the kingdom of God" (Luke 18:25).

1.   Observation: Jesus made the statement one day to his listeners. The words seem very clear. Everyone has seen a camel, and even a small child tries to pass a slender cotton thread through the tiny eye of a needle. Jesus makes an impossible statement, an example of hyperbole. There is no way that you could pass a camel through the eye of a needle. Some of Christ's listeners must have interpreted His words literally, because they shook their heads and asked, "Who then can be saved" (Luke 18:26)?

2.   Interpretation: There is an old legend that the "eye of a needle" was a small gate in the city of Jerusalem which a camel could pass through only on its knees. Unfortunately, it is only a legend. The Persians expressed a similar concept of the impossible by saying it is easier to pass an elephant through the eye of a needle.[4]

     Let's look at the context. Starting back from the 18th verse of the same chapter, we read how "a certain ruler" came to Jesus, asking what he should do to inherit eternal life. By comparing the same story in Matthew and Mark, we discover that this man was young, rich, powerful, and confident that by keeping the commandments he qualified for eternal life (Matt. 19:16–22; Mark 10:17–22; Luke 18:18–27). When Jesus advised him to distribute his wealth to the poor, he "became very sad, because he was very wealthy." Jesus commented to those around Him: "How hard it is for the rich to enter the kingdom of God." Then follows the text we are studying.

3.   Evaluation: Jesus was *not* saying that wealthy people do not qualify for salvation. Recall that it was a wealthy Pharisee who gave up his family tomb for the body of Jesus after His death on the cross (see Matt. 27:57–59). No, it seems Jesus was trying to tell His listeners that it is impossible for a *selfish*, wealthy person to be saved.

4.   Application: When I contrast my pride and selfishness with the life of Jesus, who exchanged His heavenly glory for death on a cruel cross, just so that I can have eternal life, I know what I must do.

This four-step model is a very practical one for serious Bible study. We will apply it again when we talk about contextual understanding of inspired writing in the next chapter.

Ellen White and Biblical Interpretation

The writings of Ellen White, particularly her books and articles, lend themselves readily to a devotional or homiletic approach. These books are Bible-based and filled with spiritual applications and understandings for our time in earth's history. Her testimonies fulfill a similar purpose, pointing us toward Jesus as our Savior.

However, we must see Ellen White in a different light when it comes to the *interpretation* of Scriptures. Exegesis was not a significant part of her role. She consistently pointed away from herself to the Bible as our source of truth. She emphasized that "the Bible is its own interpreter", and we should "compare scripture with scripture." "If there is a point of truth that you do not understand, upon which you do not agree, investigate, compare scripture with scripture, sink the shaft of truth down deep into the mine of God's word. You must lay yourselves and your opinions on the altar of God, put away your preconceived ideas, and let the Spirit of Heaven guide you into all truth."[5]

It is a key understanding that interpretations and applications of the Scriptures do not have the same *authority* as the original Scriptures themselves. We saw that the sacred Canon of Scripture was closed with the inclusion of the twenty-seven books comprising the New Testament. "The canon is both complete and sufficient in itself. It offers the complete source of doctrinal beliefs, and it is possible for an individual to find Jesus Christ, to obtain salvation and eternal life, without ever having heard of Ellen White or ever having read one word of her writings."[6]

Robert Olson, who was the director of the White Estate, said it this way: "To give an individual complete interpretative control over the Bible would, in effect, elevate that person above the Bible. It would be a mistake to allow even the Apostle Paul to exercise interpretative control over all other Bible writers. In such a case, Paul, and not the whole Bible, would be one's final authority."[7]

We Seventh-day Adventists are prone to study and interpret the Bible through the eyes of Ellen White and make her our authority for understanding Scripture. However, she made it very clear that her writings should not be used to settle issues of interpretation of Scripture. "Go to the Bible and get the Scripture evidence", she insisted.[8] George Knight, who taught denominational history at the Seventh-day Adventist Theological Seminary for many years, warns us not to impose an Ellen White interpretation on the Bible. "Some Adventists have seen Ellen White as an infallible Bible commentator in the sense that we should use her writings to settle the meaning of Scripture," he says. "While Ellen White claimed that she wrote from the vantage point of one enlightened by the Holy Spirit, she did not claim that we should take her writings as the final word on the meaning of Scripture."[9] Every inspired passage of Scripture should remain open for fresh insight and application.

In 1983, the Biblical Research Institute of the Adventist Church published several statements to guide us in understanding the role of Ellen White in relation to the Bible. Here are some of them:

- "We believe that Scripture is the foundation of faith and the final authority in all matters of doctrine and practice.
- We do not believe that the writings of Ellen White function as the foundation and final authority of Christian faith as does Scripture.
- We do not believe that the writings of Ellen White may be used as the basis of doctrine.
- We do not believe that Scripture can be understood only through the writings of Ellen G. White.
- We do not believe that her writings exhaust the meaning of Scripture."[10]

During Ellen White's lifetime, Adventist leaders and pastors frequently looked to her to settle controversial issues about biblical interpretation. How did she relate to these demands?

The "law" in the third chapter of Galatians (was it moral or ceremonial?) was an issue at the 1888 General Conference session. Ellen had written her view on the subject in a letter back in the 1850s, but she could not find the letter, and "for the life of me I cannot remember that which I have been shown in reference to the two laws."[11] She refused to let her opinion on the matter settle the debate. Settling matters of biblical interpretation was not how she saw her ministry. The issue needed to be settled by prayerful Bible study. "Let all prove their positions from the Scriptures and substantiate every point they claim as truth from the revealed Word of God."[12]

Twenty years after 1888, Ellen White took a similar position regarding the identity of the "daily" in Daniel 8. Some Adventists found a statement she made about it in 1850[13] and insisted that her interpretation should settle the matter, but Ellen White was equally insistent that her writings should not be used for that purpose. "I cannot consent that any of my writings be taken as settling this matter....I now ask that my ministering brethren shall not make use of my writings in their arguments regarding this question."[14]

I think it is interesting that although Ellen White had almost no formal education and never studied theology, she followed the Protestant Reformation principle of *Sola scriptura*—that the Bible is the supreme authority in all matters of doctrine and practice, and is its own interpreter. She refused to function as an infallible interpreter of Scripture. A respected Adventist theologian, Raoul Dederen, comments: "As interpreter of the Bible, Ellen White's most characteristic role was that of an evangelist—not an exegete, nor a theologian, as such, but a preacher and an evangelist....to give God's people a clearer understanding of the Bible, urging them back to God's Word."[15]

The lesson for me in all this is clear and simple. The Bible is my spiritual textbook. I must study it well. Although I have no authority for interpreting Scripture, I have complete confidence that the Holy Spirit can open its meaning for my life.

To think about:

1. Just how much of the Bible should be interpreted literally is one of the hottest debates within Christianity today. According to a Gallup survey in 2011, three in ten Americans interpret the Bible literally, believing it contains the actual words of God. The dictionary meaning of "literal" is "taking words in their usual or most basic sense without metaphor or allegory." Think about how you read the Bible. How do you draw the line for yourself between literal and interpretive reading?

2. Christ's disciples misinterpreted some Old Testament prophecies about the nature and purpose of the Messiah. Are we susceptible to misunderstanding prophecies about end-time events?

3. Apply the four steps of hermeneutics to discover the meaning and application of the following passage of Scripture: "'For I know the plans I have for you,' declares the Lord, 'plans to prosper you and not to harm you, plans to give you hope and a future'" (Jer. 29:11). Does your hermeneutical interpretation prevent others from using it homiletically—applying it to God's plans for their personal lives?

References:

[1]   Ellen White, "Christ Should Be Our Counselor", *Review and Herald*, April 16, 1889.

[2]   *Seventh-day Adventist Bible Commentary*, 4:1175 (Ellen White Comments).

[3]   White, *Great Controversy*, v, vi. (1888).

[4]   *NIV Cultural Backgrounds Study Bible*, Notes on Luke 18:25.

[5]   White, *Review and Herald*, February 18, 1890.

[6]   Roger W. Coon, *Inspiration/Revelation: what it is and how it works*, 73.

[7]   Robert W. Olson, *One Hundred and One Questions on the Sanctuary and on Ellen White*, 41. (1981).

[8]   White, Manuscript 11, 1910.

[9]   George W. Knight, *Reading Ellen White*, 25, 26.

[10]   Biblical Research Institute, "The Inspiration and Authority of the Ellen G. White Writings." *Ministry*, February 1983.

[11]   White, Letter 5, Apr. 13, 1887.

[12]   White, Letter 12, 1890; also, *Evangelism*, 256.

[13]   White, *Early Writings*, 74, 75.

[14]   White, *Selected Messages*, 1:164.

[15]   Raoul Dederen, "Ellen White's Doctrine of Scripture", *Ministry* supplement, July 1977.

Chapter 12—Context

What do we understand by the word "context", and why is it important to our interpretation of the Bible and Ellen White? "Context" is simply defined as the words that come immediately before or after a particular phrase and help explain its meaning. We use the expression "out of context" when we ignore part of what was written or said. When we do that, the meaning may be lost or distorted, and the results can be serious. A politician may try to misrepresent the position of an opponent by taking his or her remarks out of context. "You have misinterpreted what I said because you took it out of context."

> *We use the expression "out of context" when we ignore part of what was written or said. When we do that, the meaning may be lost or distorted, and the results can be serious.*

In the same way, we may easily misunderstand a Bible text or passage if we ignore its context. Awareness of the context is particularly important when we seek to correctly interpret or exegete a passage of Scripture. Paul advised Timothy, in his preaching, to "carefully handle the word of truth" (2 Tim. 2:15).

When I read the Bible, I need to think about context in two different ways. I should think first about **literary context**, which fits our definition above. Here we are talking about the parts of a Bible passage that precede or follow a specific word or phrase that I am studying. Reading the literary context may alter the meaning of what I have read. In the previous chapter, we saw how literary context was important when we applied it to a statement about riches that Jesus made.

When I read ancient writings like the Scriptures, I must also think about **historical context**—how the meaning of a biblical passage is shaped by the times and culture in which it was written. While a literal reading of a Bible text or passage may very often give me the clear meaning, there are times when I miss the intended meaning of a word or text because life and language has changed so much. I must ask when and why the text was written. We will look at some examples where a literal reading may be wrong or confusing.

Literary Context

"Beware of dogs" was Paul's admonition to the Philippian believers, but reading the rest of the verse helps us understand that Paul was warning Gentile believers about Jews who wanted to circumcise them: "Watch out for those dogs, those evildoers, those mutilators of the flesh" (Phil. 3:2).

Knowing the context of a Bible verse sometimes yields a surprising result. Conversing with His disciples, Jesus made this familiar statement: "For where two or three are gathered together in my name, I am there in the midst of them" (Matt. 18:20, NKJV). At face value, this verse suggests that when two or three believers (or a small number) gather to pray or worship, God will be present with them. And while that certainly is true— God will never forsake even one of us when we seek Him—the context of Jesus' remark is the procedure we should follow when a member is found in sin. "If your brother sins against you, go and tell him his fault between you and him alone. If he hears you, you have gained your brother. But if he will not hear, take with you one or two more" (Matt. 18:15, 16, NKJV). It is when dealing with this kind of sensitive situation that Jesus gave the assurance that He will be present with the little group to convict and guide. There is something beautiful about resolving disputes together well.

We might also keep in mind that Bible versions differ in the way an original text is translated. Paul's admonition in Philippians 4:6:—"Be careful for nothing" (KJV)—is more correctly understood with contemporary translations: "Do not be anxious about anything" (NIV).

Historical Context

Historical context of Scripture has to do with the culture of the times in which it was written. Hear this statement by a contemporary Christian writer. "The biblical world and the modern (especially Western) world are literally 'worlds apart.' They are separated by differences in language, culture, values, and circumstances. In order to understand the Bible properly today, we first need to journey back to this ancient world, seeking as best we can to hear the Scriptures through the ears of their first readers. Then we are prepared to carry the message of Scripture back into our world."[1]

Ellen White understood our need to do that. "An understanding of the customs of those who lived in Bible times, of the location and time of events, is practical knowledge; for it aids in making clear the figures of the Bible, and in bringing out the force of Christ's lessons."[2]

John Walton, introducing the Old Testament portion of the *NIV Cultural Backgrounds Study Bible*, seeks to help us by using the metaphor of a cultural river that flowed through the societies and thought beliefs of the ancient world. "Israel was immersed in that cultural river," he says. "Sometimes God gave revelation that drew them out, as Moses from the Nile, and distinguished them, but we should generally think of them in this cultural river. Sometimes they were simply floating on its currents; sometimes they veered out of the currents and stood apart. At other times they swam resolutely upstream against those currents." The "cultural river" metaphor is fascinating, but "as modern readers, we have no familiarity with that river at all. Our cultural river is very different. Whether Israel was floating or swimming, as we read through the Old Testament we must recognize that they were in a different river than we are. To interpret the Old Testament well, we must try to dip into their cultural river."[3]

As we try to dip into their cultural river, we find statements that at first glance do not make sense. We must translate culture as well as language to fully understand the text. By doing that we can ignore, for example, the law that forbids shaving: "You shall not shave around the sides of your head, nor shall you disfigure the edges of your beard" (Lev. 19:27, NKJV), but we have no hesitation in obeying the instruction two verses later: "Do not degrade your daughter by making her a prostitute" (Lev. 19:29).

Even during those distant times, the writings of Moses sometimes had to be explained to the people. When the walls of Jerusalem were rebuilt after the Babylonian captivity, the Levites "read from the Book of the Law of God, making it clear and giving the meaning so that the people understood what was being read" (Neh. 8:8).

The culture of New Testament times may also require us to consider context. Here are two examples: "Every woman who prays or prophesies with her head uncovered dishonors her head—it is the same as having her head shaved" (1 Cor. 11:5). Paul admonishes believers to "greet one another with a holy kiss" (Rom. 16:16).

The leaders of the infant Christian Church were faced with some difficult decisions as they considered how they should apply the Mosaic laws to the lives of new Gentile converts. Paul was present for a vote by the Jerusalem Council that the rite of circumcision should not be imposed on Gentile converts (see Acts 15:5). The same Council voted to instruct Gentile believers that "you are to abstain from food sacrificed to idols" (Acts 15:29). Does that contradict what Paul later wrote to the Colossian converts: "Do not let anyone judge you by what you eat or drink" (Col. 2:16)? When Jesus clearly stated, "I was sent only to the lost sheep of Israel" (Matt. 15:24), did He really mean that? In each case, studying the context is important.

Then again, biblical language is sometimes metaphorical rather than literal, and much of the Old Testament is poetic. These picturesque words were sung by Moses and Miriam after Israel miraculously crossed the Red Sea: "With the blast of your nostrils the waters were gathered together; the floods stood upright like a heap" (Exod. 15:8, NKJV).

Context and Ellen White

Cultures and mores still change with the passage of time. This has been especially true during the last two centuries of rapid and revolutionary social change on a global scale. It is now more than 100 years since the death of Ellen White, and we are even further removed from the years when she did most of her writing. The cultural river has changed its course and character since her time. As time goes by, we can benefit more by understanding her 19th-century environment. A contextual approach to her writing becomes increasingly relevant and important as time passes. Our reading of her testimonies to individuals and the church at large will be enhanced and better understood if we know the context—the people and events about which they were written.

Literary Context

Compare these two Ellen White statements:

- *"Those who accept the Savior,* however sincere their conversion, *should never be taught to say or to feel that they are saved."*[4]
- "Each one of you may know for yourself that you have a living Savior, that He is your helper and your God. *You need not stand where you say, 'I do not know whether I am saved.' Do you believe in Christ as your personal Savior? If you do, then rejoice"*[5] (italics mine in both quotes).

There is an apparent contradiction here, until we look at the literary context of the first statement. In this quote from *Christ's Object Lessons*, Ellen White is talking about Peter's failure after he asserted that he would never deny his Lord. Here she is warning us against self-confidence and trusting in ourselves when faced with temptations: "Even when we give ourselves to Christ and know that He accepts us, we are not beyond the reach of temptation. Those who accept the Savior, however sincere their conversion, should never be taught to say or to feel that they are saved.... Those who accept Christ, and in their first confidence say, I am saved, are in danger of trusting to themselves." Now I can better understand and rejoice with Ellen in her second statement of confidence when I accept Jesus as my personal Savior.

Anyone who believes that every word from Ellen White is inspired will not consider the context to be important. Whatever she wrote, no matter the circumstances, is considered the "last word" on that topic. Ellen was well aware of this practice and warned about the dangers of taking a paragraph or segment from her writings or the Bible, and building a doctrine upon it. "Many study the Scriptures for the purpose of proving their own ideas to be correct. They change the meaning of God's Word to suit their own opinions. And thus they do also with the testimonies that He sends. They quote half a sentence, leaving out the other half, which, if quoted, would show their reasoning to be false. God has a controversy with those who wrest the Scriptures, making them conform to their preconceived ideas."[6] On another occasion she wrote, "God wants us all to have common sense, and he wants us to reason from common sense. Circumstances alter conditions. Circumstances change the relation of things."[7]

Historical Context

How does a knowledge of historical context help me to understand Ellen White? As a girl, she was raised as a strict Methodist when Methodism was the largest denomination in America. Its conservative culture and lifestyle was reflected in the religious publications of the time, including Ellen White's own writings. This knowledge helps us understand her perspective towards popular entertainment, dancing, sports and games, fiction, wearing of jewelry, and sex. These were the hot topics of behavior for Christians during much of the 19th century. Missing, of course, were issues that affect us very much today—motion pictures, multimedia violence, night clubs, nudity, social media, gay marriage, internet pornography, and the list goes on. It is imperative for us to look for the principles that guided her remarks and apply them to our time and culture.

Ellen White spent nine years of her life in Australia (1891 to 1900) and guided in the founding of the Avondale school in 1897. On the second anniversary of the school's establishment, faculty and students organized a school picnic, with games of cricket and tennis. On the following day, Ellen White rebuked school leaders for encouraging "a species of idolatry" where "God was dishonored."[8] Some Australians who were unfamiliar with Ellen White's religious background in America felt that she had acted unfairly and misunderstood the innocent purpose of the celebration.

Context and Interpretation

In the previous chapter we introduced a four-step hermeneutical process in interpreting a biblical passage. These were the four steps:

1. Observation: What are the basic facts of the passage, such as the meaning of the words?

2. Interpretation: What did the author mean in his own historical setting?

3. Evaluation: What does this passage mean in today's culture?

4. Application: How can I apply what I have learned to my own life?

Let's apply this four-step process in understanding context, first to a passage from Scripture, and then to a topic from Ellen White's writings.

Should Women Speak in Church? What did Paul say?

"Women should remain silent in the churches. They are not allowed to speak, but must be in submission, as the law says. If they want to inquire about something, they should ask their own husbands at home; for it is disgraceful for a woman to speak in the church" (1 Cor. 14:34–35).

What provoked this forthright statement from Paul? Open your Bible with me to 1 Corinthians as we examine its broad context.

Observation: Whichever way you read this passage, Paul's words are clear. Women, it seems, have no speaking role in the church—not teaching, preaching, or even discussing the Sabbath School lesson.

Interpretation: For starters, note that the word "speak" (Greek *laleo*) in these verses does not necessarily mean a formal role in the pulpit; it can also be translated simply as "talk." Also, the reference to "law" in verse 34 might be to a Roman law that restricted a woman's role in pagan worship. Women occupied a low status in Roman society. Judaism did not share such an extreme view.

By reading the preceding chapters of Paul's letter to the Corinthians, we find that the early Corinthian believers were sometimes unruly and disorganized when they met for worship (11:17, 18). In Paul's time, it was quite customary for Greek men to marry girls in their teens; Paul's words may have been influenced by this and his knowledge that Greek men who valued older traditions resented a woman speaking in public where men other than her husband were present.[9] Poorly educated young women may have been interrupting with unlearned questions that wasted congregational time. Paul had appropriate advice for them: "If they want to inquire about something, they should ask their own husbands at home" (14:35).

The church at Corinth was sometimes a babble of voices, some of it in foreign languages, and Paul had some strong words to say about it. Hear what he said about their practice of the Lord's Supper: "In the following directives I have no praise for you, for your meetings do more harm than good....When you come together, it is not the Lord's Supper you eat, for when you are eating, some of you go ahead with your own private suppers. As a result, one person remains hungry and another gets drunk....What shall I say to you? Shall I praise you? Certainly not in this matter" (1 Cor. 11:17–22)!

Paul zeroed in on their chaotic worship services, especially when several were speaking in tongues at the same time. Paul saw tongues as one of the less significant gifts, so he set some rules for how they should be used in the service:

- limit to two or three speakers (14:27)
- they should speak one at a time (14:27)
- there should be interpretation (14:27, 28)
- other worshippers, of *both* sexes, should "keep silent" (14:28, 30)

- the same procedure to be followed by those prophesying (14:29)

Evaluation: It was in this context of disorderly worship services at Corinth that Paul included his counsel for young women. "God is not a God of disorder but of peace—as in all the congregations of the Lord's people....Everything should be done in a fitting and orderly way" (14:33, 40). Church order is a universal principle.

Application: The gifts of the Holy Spirit are given to both men and women and are to be used in an orderly way for the edification of the worshippers.

Did Ellen White Condemn Fiction?

The question of fiction is a disturbing one for many Seventh-day Adventists. Understandably so, when we come across emphatic statements like these:

- "Parents had much better burn the idle tales of the day, and the novels as they come into their houses."[10] (1863)
- "Some [novels] are immoral, low, and vulgar; others are clothed with more refinement; but all are pernicious in their influence."[11] (1869)
- "Novel and storybook reading are the greatest evils in which youth can indulge."[12] (1872)
- "The indulgence of light reading and tales of fiction produces a false, unhealthy excitement of the mind, and unfits it for any spiritual exercise."[13] (1880)
- "Novel readers are mental inebriates."[14] (1883)

Observation: First, we note that almost all of Ellen White's references to "novels", "storybook" reading, and "fiction" were recorded between 1855 and 1890; notice the publication dates above. After 1890, her few original statements about fiction relate to the choice of reading matter for youth in church schools, with a new emphasis about "infidel authors."

Interpretation: To understand what initiated those forthright statements, we need to study their historical context. Education in America was mostly in private schools until the 1840s, when there began a rapid expansion of free public schools. This created a large population of literate and reading-hungry young people. Starting in the 1860s, this hunger for reading matter led to an avalanche of cheap literature—sentimental love stories for girls and sensational "dime novels" with wild west themes for boys. One author wrote more than fifty novels for girls, and most of them sold in the six figures. And "literally millions of boys collected whole libraries of dime novels."[15]

American society reacted strongly to these reading trends. Ellen White's dire warnings about the effects of this literature on young people were echoed by educators and public librarians of the period. Here are some examples from secular authors:

"There is a vast range of ephemeral literature, exciting and fascinating, that is responsible for an immense amount of mental disease and moral irregularities in modern society."[16]

"The librarian who should allow an immoral novel in his library for circulation would be as culpable as the manager of a picture gallery who should hang an indecent picture on his walls."[17]

"Do novels teach them [young women] contentment with their lowly but honest occupations? The factory girl, as she tends the loom or her spinning jenny, turns over in her thoughts the fortunes of the heroine of the last novel she has read, raised by impossible suppositious incidents from humble life to princely fortune, and she pines for a lover to so lift her into notoriety."[18] It is interesting to place that quote alongside this one from Ellen White: "I am acquainted with a number of women who have thought their marriage a misfortune. They have read novels until their imaginations have become diseased, and they live in a world of their own creating....From what the Lord has shown me, the women of this class have had their imaginations perverted by novel reading, day dreaming, and castle building, living in an imaginary world."[19]

"In the department of murder, the instruction given by the dime-novel is all that could be desired. There is not a possible method of murder that is not fully described. Our boys are taught how to kill."[20]

"The boy reads of equally false deeds of daring—fortunes made by unjust dealings, glossed over as to half conceal their iniquity—and his bewildered mind is unfitted for the hard duties of life."[21]

Evaluation: Ellen White reacted to this flood of sensational novels for young people during the 1860s through the 1880s with strongly worded counsel for Adventist parents and youth. These early statements about fiction were specifically directed against the trashy novels that were popular among the youth of her day. As we saw, novel reading was also of concern to thinkers and educators of that time.[22]

Application: Yesterday's sensational love stories for girls and dime novels for boys have metamorphosed into today's powerful multimedia—movies, TV, video and role-playing games, social media, the occult, and all kinds of material posted on the Internet. Today's young people constitute a viewing/listening rather than a reading public. We must look for the moral principles that guided Ellen White in her 19th-century counsels about fiction and apply them to the media of today, both print and electronic. The advice of Paul to the Philippians applies to all times and cultures: "Finally, brothers and sisters, whatever is true, whatever is noble, whatever is right, whatever is pure, whatever is lovely, whatever is admirable—if anything is excellent or praiseworthy—think about such things" (Phil. 4:8).

For a broader understanding of how and why Ellen White utilized fiction in her writing, see the summary article "Literature and Reading" in *The Ellen G. White Encyclopedia*, pages 943–946.

Summing Up

From the examples above, we see that context is important to our correct understanding of inspired writings. In my Bible study, I need to look at what precedes and follows the passage I am reading. Grasping the historical context—dipping into the ancient cultural river—is challenging for most of us who are unacquainted with biblical languages or ancient cultures; but help is available from a broad selection of Bible commentaries.

Our study of Ellen White is complicated by the sheer volume of her writings, and especially counsels and testimonies that were addressed to special situations and times. The Ellen G. White Estate has begun the publication of a new series: *The Ellen G. White Letters and Manuscripts with Annotations.* As this series moves toward completion, it will be a valuable resource for the serious study and understanding of her writings.

To think about:

1. Submission of wives to husbands is clear counsel of Paul and Peter (see Eph. 5:22, Col. 3:18, 1 Peter 3:1). Use the four steps of hermeneutics to interpret the historical/cultural context of these passages and determine their application today.

2. Successful foreign missionaries must learn the culture, language, and worldview of the people they are trying to reach. How is this a rationale for the way we should study and teach the Bible?

3. "Confidence in Ellen White is essential, but blind confidence should not be substituted for careful thinking when it comes to what she means today" (Herbert Douglass). In the light of that

statement, discuss this one by Ellen White: "The money expended in bicycles and other needless things must be accounted for."[23]

References:

1. Richard Schultz, *Out of Context*, 30.
2. Ellen White, *Counsels to Teachers*, 518.
3. *NIV Cultural Backgrounds Study Bible*, xlix.
4. White, *Christ's Object Lessons*, 155.
5. *General Conference Bulletin*, Apr.10, 1901.
6. White, *Selected Messages*, 3:82. (1890)
7. *Ibid.*, 217. (1904)
8. Arthur L. White, *Ellen G. White: The Australian Years*, 442–446.
9. *NIV Cultural Backgrounds Study Bible,* notes on 1 Cor.14:35.
10. White, *Review and Herald*, Jan.13, 1863.
11. White, *Testimonies*, 2:236. (1869)
12. White, *Testimonies*, 3:152. (1872)
13. White, *Signs of the Times*, Feb.1880.
14. White, *Review and Herald*, Oct. 1883.
15. John Wood, "The Trashy Novel Revisited: Popular Fiction in the Age of Ellen White", *Spectrum* 7, (April 1976), 16–21.
16. Boston Public Library, *Report of the Examining Committee*, (1875).
17. William F. Poole, *Library Journal* 1:2 (1876), 50.
18. William Kite, *Library Journal* 1:8 (1876), 278.
19. White, *Testimonies*, 2:462. (1871)
20. Anthony Comstock, *Traps for the Young* (1883).
21. Kite, *op.cit.*
22. Keith Clouten, "Ellen White and Fiction, a Closer Look", *Journal of Adventist Education*, 76:4 (2014), 10–14.
23. Ellen G. White, 1888 Materials.

Understanding

Chapter 13—History

It was Marcus Garvey, a Jamaican political leader, who said, "A people without the knowledge of their past history is like a tree without roots." In the historical books of the Old Testament, we find the roots of a people chosen by the Lord to convey His truth to the world. Then in the New Testament, we come face to face with something—Someone—that binds the roots together. Jesus Christ is the focal point of the Scriptures from creation to redemption.

However, there is something else about the Bible. There is an overarching theme or meta-narrative that begins somewhere before the creation of earth and time and continues beyond the glorious second coming in Revelation. We are talking about the existence of a cosmic conflict; a relentless combat between the forces of good and evil; a sweeping spectacle in which Jesus Christ becomes the central figure. The conflict is as wide as the universe, but staged on our small planet. It makes its first appearance in what is perhaps the most ancient book of Scripture—the story of Job—where Satan comes to challenge the justice of God. It forms a backdrop to our understanding of the entire Old Testament. It rears its ugly head in the ministry and death of Jesus Christ. The Apostle Paul recognized its existence: "For we do not wrestle against flesh and blood, but against principalities, against powers, against spiritual hosts of wickedness in the heavenly places" (Eph. 6:12, NKJV). Nevertheless, the conflict finds its most comprehensive portrayal in the last book of the Bible, the Apostle John's Revelation. Seventh-day Adventists know this cosmic drama as the "Great Controversy between Christ and Satan."

In March 1858, James and Ellen White were conducting a funeral service in the small community of Lovett's Grove, Ohio. Suddenly, while Ellen was speaking words of comfort, she was taken off in a vision that lasted for two hours. The small group of mourners understood that you cannot program the Holy Spirit, so they quietly waited while Ellen received an important revelation from the Lord. Describing it later, she said, "In the vision at Lovett's Grove, most of the matter which I had seen ten years before concerning the great controversy of the ages between Christ and Satan, was repeated, and I was instructed to write it out. I was shown that while I should have to contend with the powers of darkness, for Satan would make strong efforts to hinder me, yet I must put my trust in God, and angels would not leave me in the conflict."[1]

Conflict there was, and it happened quickly. On their journey home to Battle Creek, James and Ellen visited friends in Jackson, Michigan. There, Ellen experienced something akin to a severe stroke, including paralysis of her entire left side and an inability to talk or write. It was several days before she recovered sufficiently to be able to write out what she had seen in the Lovett's Grove vision. Later, she was shown that "in the sudden attack at Jackson, Satan intended to take my life, in order to hinder the work I was about to write; but angels of God were sent to my rescue."[2] From that time, the great controversy was a prominent theme in her books and articles.

God and History

In ancient Babylon, King Nebuchadnezzar learned something important about the role of God in world history. His spectacular dream of a great image with a head of gold and feet of iron mixed with clay displayed both God's foreknowledge and macro-involvement in the politics of our world. Down through the long corridors of history, we see people using and abusing their God-given independence and ambition to control affairs on this planet. Satan is blatantly active in all of this, but behind the curtain God is also at work. Jacques Ellul understood it this way: "Man can create new situations which God did not will. And since the Lord does not give up, . . . He changes His plans, He accepts the new situation and enters into it, and He draws from it certain consequences which man certainly did not expect or foresee but which will finally work for the actualizing of God's love."[3]

Therefore, the Bible is a book of history, but it is history from God's point of view. It reveals God's interaction with the world and its people. It is not a history textbook, nor is it concerned with all the factual details of history. It purposes to show God's involvement in the affairs of people and nations. God warned and demonstrated to King Nebuchadnezzar that he would forfeit his kingship "until you acknowledge that the Most High is sovereign over the kingdoms of earth and gives them to anyone he wishes" (Dan. 4:25). King David testified, "The Lord does whatever pleases him, in the heavens and on the earth" (Ps. 135:6).

Ellen White expressed the same concept: "In the annals of human history the growth of nations, the rise and fall of empires, appear as dependent on the will and prowess of man....But in the word of God the curtain is drawn aside, and we behold, behind, above, and through all the play and counter play of human interests and power and passions, the agencies of the all-merciful One, silently, patiently working out the counsels of His own will."[4]

Hence, we must think of the Bible as an interpretation of history. It is not a scholarly history of the ancient world, because that is not its purpose. Accuracy of some factual detail is secondary to its purpose of revealing the hand of God in events. Paul understood that purpose when he wrote about Old Testament events: "These things happened to them as examples, and were written down as warnings for us, on whom the culmination of the ages has come" (1 Cor. 10:11).

One author says, "Historians find the Bible to be an accurate record of many ancient events, more reliable than other ancient writings. But its standard of accuracy is looser than the expectations of modern science and history."[5] We err when we try to impose our values and ways of thinking on the cultures of ancient times. The Bible writers were not concerned about precise accuracy. It is only in recent times that historiography—the writing of history, based on the critical use of sources—has developed in a significant and scientific way.

Everett Harrison expands this concept: "The scientific age in which we live has put a premium upon precise accuracy. Must we impose our standard on an ancient book? We think we know what truth is. The chances are we are thinking in Hellenistic terms, identifying truth with what corresponds to reality. But the writers of the Scriptures were not as greatly influenced by this conception of truth as by the Hebrew conception which identifies as truth what corresponds with the nature and purpose of God."[6]

Having this awareness of biblical history does not lessen its importance for us. We may wisely apply Moses' admonition to the Israelites on the borders of Canaan to our own relationship with the past. "Watch out!" he said. "Be careful never to forget what you yourselves have seen. Do not let these memories escape from your mind as long as you live! And be sure to pass them on to your children and grandchildren" (Deut. 4:9, NLT). Ellen White gave the same advice in 1893 with these words: "We have nothing to fear for the future, except as we shall forget the way the Lord has led us, and his teaching in our past history."[7]

History as Inspired Writing

When a prophet received a revelation from God through vision or thought inspiration, he had the task, in most cases, of writing in his own words what he saw or received. Sometimes the writing did not take place right away, as with Jeremiah in Old Testament times (Jer. 36:1, 2) and Ellen White in the case of her great controversy vision. Prophets had no training in the use and evaluation of sources, so they utilized the common knowledge and writing styles of their time in recording the messages from God. Review the diagram in chapter 9 to visualize how the prophet's writing combined inspired thoughts with his work-a-day knowledge.

A prophet's inspired messages met God's purpose of revealing His activity in the affairs of peoples and nations. The Holy Spirit ensured that the prophet's writings fulfilled that purpose. It did not, however, ensure total accuracy of historical details that were not relevant to the divine purpose. The same was true of Ellen White's writing. While guided by the Holy Spirit, she was sometimes inaccurate with historical and scientific information. She was not a historian and relied on published histories of Europe and the Protestant Reformation. Sometimes her sources were inaccurate, or her casual reading of them led to mistakes. When writing about the French Revolution, she copied some from Uriah Smith, who was likewise not a historian, so errors were reproduced.[8] Her purpose in *Great Controversy* was to portray the outworking of the conflict between Christ and Satan during the last two thousand years. As with Bible prophets, her purpose was an *interpretation* of historical events through the centuries. It presents history from the divine perspective. She said the facts of history were subservient to a "proper understanding of their application."[9]

Many historical errors were corrected with her approval in the revised 1911 edition of *The Great Controversy.* The fact that corrections were necessary and undertaken troubled some believers at the time. Responding to one individual who thought Ellen White was verbally inspired, her son, W.C. White, wrote that *The Great Controversy* was not to be treated as an authority on history: "Regarding mother's writings and their use as an authority on points of history and chronology, mother has never wished our brethren to treat them as authority regarding details of history or historical dates....When *Controversy* was written, mother never thought that the readers would take it as authority on historical dates or use it to settle controversy regarding details of history, and she does not now feel that it should be used in that way....If it had been essential to the salvation of men that he should have a clear and harmonious understanding of the chronology of the world, the Lord would not have permitted the disagreements and discrepancies which we find in the writings of the Bible historians, and it seems to me that in these last days there ought not to be so much controversy regarding dates."[10]

In that letter, Elder White alluded to "disagreements and discrepancies" in biblical history. In the Scriptures, we find such discrepancies. When Matthew quoted Zechariah's prediction that Jesus would be sold for thirty pieces of silver, he confused Zechariah with Jeremiah (compare Matt. 27:9 and Zech. 11:12, 13). King Jehoiachin was eighteen years old when he began to reign, according to 2 Kings 24:8, but the writer of Chronicles puts his age at eight years (see 2 Chron. 36:9). According to 1 Kings 4:26, Solomon had forty thousand stalls of horses for his chariots—clearly an excessive number—but someone caught the error and gave the more believable number of four thousand stalls when history was retold in Chronicles (see 2 Chron.9:25). Even though scribes were professional and careful in copying biblical manuscripts, errors were made. Ellen White acknowledged the issue of scribal mistakes when she wrote, "Some look to us gravely and say, 'Don't you think there might have been some mistake in the copyist or in the translators?' This is all probable." Then she added, "All the mistakes will not cause trouble to one soul, or cause any feet to stumble, that would not manufacture difficulties from the plainest revealed truth."[11]

The New Testament's four gospel writers tell the story of Jesus, each presenting His life and teachings from a different perspective. We should not be surprised by some factual differences in the telling of the stories. George Rice, an Adventist Bible teacher, made a comprehensive study of dozens of apparent conflicts in the three synoptic gospels.[12] Matthew and Luke have a different order for the three temptations of Christ (see Matt. 4:5–9; Luke 4:5–12) and record the beatitudes quite differently (see Matt.5:3–12; Luke 6:20–26). The same two writers also present differing accounts of the healing of the centurion's servant at Capernaum (see Matt. 8:5–13; Luke 7:1–10). The gospel writers give us four differing versions of the inscription placed on Jesus' cross:

"This is Jesus, the King of the Jews" (Matt. 27:37).

"The King of the Jews" (Mark 15:26).

"This is the King of the Jews" (Luke 23:38).

"Jesus of Nazareth, the King of the Jews" (John 19:19).

We could list many more examples of factual differences in the gospels. None conflict with the essential purpose and truth of our Savior's mission on this earth. The Holy Spirit ensured that would be the case.

Old Testament Numbers

The Old Testament presents a greater challenge because it was written over such a long period of time, from Moses to Malachi. During that time, there were many changes in cultural practices and the way language was used. In studying these writings, we are attempting to dive into a "cultural river" that flowed through ancient civilizations, including Israel. Thankfully, we get help from ancient inscriptions as well as archaeological findings. From those sources, we learn important things about community living practices, their heavy dependence on agriculture, religious practices, and the population densities of towns and cities.

These sources also help us understand the seemingly inflated numbers in many Old Testament stories. Ancient peoples tended to exaggerate in relating the numbers of soldiers mustered, enemies killed, and towns overthrown (Incidentally, that still happens in today's world). Notice this report on Joab's numbering of the fighting men of Israel: "In all Israel there were one million one hundred thousand [1,100,000] men who could handle a sword, including four hundred and seventy thousand [470,000] in Judah" (1 Chron. 21:5). These figures are greatly inflated when put beside archaeological findings that show Israel's population in the time of King David to have been around 250,000. The population of the Holy Land never exceeded one million until the 20th century.

Here is another example of inflated numbers: "On the seventh day the battle was joined. The Israelites inflicted a hundred thousand [100,000] casualties on the Aramean foot-soldiers in one day. The rest of them escaped to the city of Aphek, where the wall collapsed on twenty-seven thousand [27,000] of them" (1 Kings 20:29, 30).

Complicating the problem of big numbers is a Hebrew word *eleph,* used in many Old Testament numerical accounts. We know that *eleph* conveyed several different numerical values, depending on how, when, and where it was used. One popular meaning for *eleph* is "thousand", but it does not make sense to apply it that way everywhere. Some Bible students have tried to apply that meaning to the number of Hebrews at the exodus from Egypt, with strange results.

One early meaning for *eleph* is a "family" or "clan". Gideon used it in that way when he was challenged by the Lord to save Israel from the Midianites: "'Pardon me, my Lord', Gideon replied, 'but how can I save Israel? My clan *(eleph)* is the weakest in Manasseh, and I am the least in my family'" (Judges 6:15). Other apparent meanings for the word in various Old Testament passages include "head of family", "chief", "tribal unit", "military unit", and "armed men". In the story of Joshua's capture of the small city of Ai (Josh. 8), one historian equates *eleph* with a squad of perhaps 200 armed men.[13]

These multiple and often disputed meanings of a single word create a lot of uncertainty for scholars and translators working from the original Hebrew text. Such irregularities should encourage us to focus on the broad picture and overall meaning of what we are reading, not on tangential details. We recognize that there are sometimes troublesome numbers or variations in details, but these should not distract us from the points or lessons that God intended with the story. The Bible is the inspired Word of God, authoritative and reliable in matters of faith and doctrine, worship, morals, and ethics. We can rely on the historical truth of events such as creation and the resurrection of Jesus, yet our faith does not require that we accept every numerical detail as precise.

The Exodus Problem

The biblical story of the exodus from Egypt illustrates well the problem we have with numerical data in the Old Testament. It centers on the huge number of people given in the biblical record. The Book of Numbers gets its title from the numbering of Israelites counted in a military census of fighting-age adults who left Egypt. Remembering how ancient peoples consistently exaggerated their military strength, we should not be astonished to read that "all the Israelites twenty years old or older who were able to serve in Israel's army were counted according to their families. The total number was 603,550 (see Num. 1:45, 46). Based on that figure, when all the women, children, and older men are added, the number of Israelites who left Egypt would have totaled at least 2.5 million. Add a large number of non-Israelites (a "mixed multitude") who also joined the exodus: "Many other people went up with them, and also large droves of livestock, both flocks and herds" (Exod. 12:38). The migrants also took with them carts or wagons, along with flocks, herds, and oxen (see Num. 7:4–7).

As faithful readers of Scripture, we have often taken those exodus numbers at face value. Some commentators go to great length to work out the mathematical possibilities of these numbers in terms of birthrate statistics, the logistics of crossing the Red Sea in one night, dwelling in the desert, getting water from a single spring, marching in order of the tribes, massing on the eastern shore of the Jordan River, and conquering the Promised Land. Without denying that God performed many wonderful miracles during the exodus, like the crossing of the Red Sea and the supply of food and water for a multitude of people, the huge numbers raise perplexing questions.

We saw that the Hebrew word *eleph* carries several possible meanings. We do not know how to apply a numerical value to the Hebrew manuscripts for the exodus numbers, or to the tribal census reports, but we have evidence from the Bible itself and historians of the ancient world that the actual numbers were considerably less than those given in the Book of Numbers. We will briefly summarize some of that evidence.

From the Bible

- The descendants of Jacob in Egypt numbered seventy persons, plus Joseph's family (see Exod. 1:5). There were three generations between Jacob's son, Levi, and Moses (see Exod. 6:16–20; 1 Chron. 6:1–3), but perhaps some generations were omitted, since 1 Chronicles 7:22–27 gives ten generations from one of Joseph's sons, Ephraim, to Joshua. Assuming there were ten generations, not three, and that the population doubled every thirty years, we may estimate a population of about 72,000 men, women, and children at the time of the Exodus.
- According to Numbers 3:42–43, the number of firstborn males,

from a month old, at the exodus, was 22,273. To accept that figure, one Bible scholar estimates that each family must have had an average of 80 children.[14]

- It appears there were just two midwives for all Israelite births when Moses was born (see Exod. 1:15–19).
- On one hand, "the Israelites were exceedingly fruitful; they multiplied greatly, increased in numbers and became so numerous that the land was filled with them" (Exod. 1:7), but how many baby boys were drowned in the river by Pharaoh's decree (see Exod. 1:22)?
- Soon after leaving Egypt, the Israelites came in contact with the Amalekite army (see Exod. 17:8–11). Amalek was a grandson of Esau, and little is known of this small nomadic tribe that was able to defeat Israel's army while Moses' hands were not lifted.
- After arriving at Sinai, "the next day Moses took his seat to serve as judge for the people, and they stood around him from morning till evening" (Exod. 18:13, 14).
- In preparing for entry into Canaan, Moses told the Israelites, "The Lord did not set his affection on you and choose you because you were more numerous than other peoples, for you were the fewest of all peoples" (Deut. 7:7). God also warned them of "seven nations larger and stronger than you" (Deut. 7:1). Among the seven "nations" that Moses identified were the Jebusites, Perizzites, and Gergashites, small tribal groups occupying very small territories, each with maximum populations numbering a few hundred, according to archaeological findings.
- God told Moses that He would drive out the Canaanites, "but I will not drive them out in a single year, because the land would become desolate and the wild animals too numerous for you" (Exod. 23:29). In the face of two million people, the wild animals would not have had a chance.
- Ten spies reported, "We can't attack those people. They are stronger than we are" (Num. 13:31).
- According to Joshua's account, about 40,000 Israelite men crossed over the Jordan "to the plains of Jericho for war" (Josh. 4:13).

From Non-Biblical Sources
- Egyptologists tell us that the total population of Egypt around the time of the exodus was between three and five million.

- Archaeological and inscription evidence suggests that the total population of Canaan around the time of Israel's entry was between 50,000 and 100,000 persons.[15]
- If we take the exodus figures at face value, the Israelite march, with wagons and livestock, traveling several abreast, is conservatively calculated to have been at least 300 miles in length; but the road distance from Cairo to Sinai is only 274 miles.[16]
- According to the Quartermaster General of the Israeli Army, the *daily* requirements for two million campers, not including needs of livestock, would be:

     1,500 tons of food

     4,000 tons of wood as fuel

     Eleven million gallons of water

     Plus latrine problems

     A camp of this size would be approximately five miles by five miles square, assuming only 1,000 square feet per family. Someone living in the center of the camp would require a hike of two and a half miles to use the latrine outside the camp, and then walk back.[17]
- Typical size of armies in ancient times:

     Alexander the Great: 90,000 to 100,000.

     Hannibal of Carthage: 20,000 soldiers besieged Rome.

     Egyptian Empire: approximately 20,000.
- Kadesh-Barnea was the chief encampment site for the Israelites during their thirty-eight years of wandering in the wilderness (see Deut.1:46). Many events occurred there (see Num. 13, 14, and 20). A population of two million should have left some remains, but nothing of significance from the Exodus period has been found, despite thorough excavation of the site and surveys of the area.
- The Israelites marched around the walled city of Jericho, which was reckoned among the mightiest cities of the conquest, yet it occupied a site smaller than two average city blocks, with a population considerably less than 2,000 people, from archaeological evidence.

Clearly, even the biblical evidence sits uncomfortably with a picture of more than two million people traversing the desert from Egypt to Canaan. This suggests that we should be careful about placing too much reliance on numbers and genealogies. "Avoid foolish controversies and genealogies," Paul advised Titus (Titus 3:9). Thinking people question the intelligence of Christians who insist on exodus numbers exceeding a million, even when the biblical evidence suggests otherwise. "When studying passages that do not lend themselves to a clear interpretation, we do not need to question the fact that it was inspired by God."[18]

God performed many miracles during the exodus and throughout Israel's pilgrimage to the Promised Land. Remembering that the Old Testament was not given as a textbook of history or science, but to reveal God's purpose and direction in the course of Israel's history, we may accept uncertainty about some details without losing sight of God's overriding providence in the rescue of His chosen people from slavery in Egypt and leading them through to the Promised Land. At their departure from Egypt, Moses instructed the people, "Commemorate this day, the day you came out of Egypt, out of the land of slavery, because the Lord brought you out of it with a mighty hand" (Exod. 13:3). Throughout their history, the Jews celebrated that event in song and at the annual Passover.

> "Marvelous things He did in the sight of their fathers,
> in the land of Egypt.
> He divided the sea and caused them to pass through;
> and He made the waters stand up like a heap.
> In the daytime also He led them with the cloud,
> and all the night with a light of fire.
> He split the rocks in the wilderness,
> and gave them drink in abundance.
> He also brought streams out of the rock,
> and caused waters to run down like rivers.
> [He] had rained down manna on them to eat,
> and given them of the bread of heaven" (Ps. 78:12–16, 24, NKJV).

Summing Up

We began this chapter by introducing the great controversy between Christ and Satan as an overarching theme of history. When we accept that cosmic reality, we have to admit that no human person can truly write history. We simply lack access to extra-biblical sources. Only the Bible writers had access to some of that information.

Therefore, we can read the Bible in one of two ways. If we approach it as secular history, we will quickly conclude that it is untrustworthy and unreliable. Or we can read the Bible as a divine-human record in which a lot is happening beyond the confines of our world. We will catch glimpses of Satan manipulating people for his diabolical purposes, but we will also watch God at His patient work of bringing divine plans to fruition.

Think about it. Could the Holy Spirit have given accurate numbers in the Exodus account? Certainly. Could God have given Ellen White accurate historical data when she wrote *The Great Controversy*? Of course. However, God's purposes are at a higher level than ours are. The prophet's task is to convey ultimate truth about God. Nothing must divert attention away from the great themes of Scripture—the love and justice of God, the outworking of the great controversy in the lives of people, God's overruling providence throughout history, and salvation in Jesus.

> *Therefore, we can read the Bible in one of two ways. If we approach it as secular history, we will quickly conclude that it is untrustworthy and unreliable. Or we can read the Bible as a divine-human record in which a lot is happening beyond the confines of our world.*

Ellen White reminds us, "Those who take only a surface view of the Scriptures will . . . talk of the contradictions of the Bible, and question the authority of the Scriptures. But those whose hearts are in harmony with truth and duty will search the Scriptures with a heart prepared to receive divine impressions. The illuminated soul sees a spiritual unity, one grand golden thread running through the whole."[19] "The treasure was entrusted to earthen vessels, yet it is, nonetheless, from heaven."[20]

To think about:

1. The history of Israel was extremely important for them in establishing their identity, who they were as a people. How does Adventist history help in establishing our identity as a people?

2. "We have nothing to fear for the future, except as we shall forget the way the Lord has led us" (Ellen White, *Life Sketches*, p.196). Reflect on how the Lord has led in your own life.

3. Inspired writing reveals God's hand in history. How does that inform the way you read biblical history and Ellen White's historical books?

References:

[1] Ellen White, *Life Sketches*, 162.

[2] *Ibid.*, 163.

[3] Jacques Ellul, *The Politics of God and the Politics of Man*, 17.

[4] White, *Education*, 173.

[5] Michael Morrison, "The Purpose and Authority of the Bible."

[6] Everett Harrison, "The Phenomena of Scripture" in *Revelation and the Bible*, edited by C.F.H. Henry, 239.

[7] *General Conference Daily Bulletin*, Jan. 29, 1893; reprinted in *Life Sketches*, 196.

[8] Don McAdams, "Shifting Views on Inspiration", *Spectrum*, 10:4, 30, 31.

[9] White, *Great Controversy*, xi.

[10] W.C. White, Letter to W.W. Eastman, November 4, 1912.

[11] White, *Selected Messages*, 1:15.

[12] George E. Rice, *Luke, a Plagiarist?*

[13] Peter Briggs, "Testing the factuality of the conquest of Ai narrative in the Book of Joshua". Associates for Biblical Research. http://1ref.us/mi (accessed October 17, 2017).

[14] Alden Thompson, *Inspiration*, Rev. ed., 268 (2016).

[15] "The Exodus and Ancient Egyptian Records" in *Jewish Action*, Spring 1995.

[16] "The God who provides: Logistics of the Exodus." http://1ref.us/m9 (accessed October 10, 2017).

[17] Benner, Jeff A., "How many came out of the exodus of Egypt". Ancient Hebrew Research Center.

[18] Angel Rodriguez, "Revelation, Inspiration and the Witness of Scripture" in *The Gift of Prophecy in Scripture and History*, 101.

[19] White, *Selected Messages*, 1:20.

[20] White, *Great Controversy*, vi.

Understanding

Chapter 14—Prediction

"Abandon hope all you who enter here." The entrance gate to hell is supposed to carry those famous words, according to Dante Alighieri in his equally famous *Divine Comedy*. One might imagine similar words greeting Adam and Eve on the day of their departure from the Garden of Eden: "Abandon hope as you leave this place"; but praise God, it wasn't like that.

The fallen, distressed couple received God's first message of hope, with a promise, at the very time He found them hiding in the garden. That first promise was also the first prophecy of a future event. Addressing Satan in their presence, God said, "I will cause hostility between you and the woman, and between your offspring and her offspring. He will strike your head, and you will strike his heel" (Gen. 3:15, NLT). A desperate need for hope was met with a gracious promise. When Eve gave birth to her first child, Cain, she thought he might be their promised Redeemer.[1]

The Bible is full of promises of a future filled with hope. Whenever the future looked dark with despair, whenever the great wall of fear and distrust loomed high, shutting out the light of love, God came through with words of hope. When unfaithful Israel faced the terrifying certainty of a long captivity in Babylon, as well as destruction of their city and temple, the word of the Lord came to them through Jeremiah: "When seventy years are completed for Babylon, I will come to you and fulfill my good promise to bring you back to this place. For I know the plans I have for you, declares the Lord, plans to prosper you and not to harm you, plans to give you hope and a future" (Jer. 29:10, 11).

Future Prediction

One facet of God's nature is His omniscience, which encompasses a knowledge of the future. During a time when Israel hankered after Canaanite gods, Isaiah proclaimed this truth: "I am God, and there is no other; I am God, and there is none like me; I make known the end from the beginning, from ancient times, what is still to come. I say: my purpose will stand, and I will do all that I please" (Isa. 46:9, 10). "See, the former things have taken place, and new things I declare; before they spring into being, I announce them to you" (Isa. 42:9).

Challenging the gods of wood and stone that the Israelites worshipped, the Lord declared, "I am the first and I am the last; apart from me there is no God. Who then is like me? Let them proclaim it. Let them declare and lay out before me what has happened since I established my ancient people, and what is yet to come—yes, let them foretell what will come" (Isa. 44:6, 7).

Through prophets, God has always disclosed His plans. When He sent Amos to the idol-worshiping Israelites of the northern kingdom, the people did not want to listen to the prophet's warnings about coming retribution, so they questioned his authority. Amos had this answer for them: "Surely the Sovereign Lord does nothing without revealing his plan to his servants the prophets. The lion has roared—who will not fear? The Sovereign Lord has spoken—who can but prophesy" (Amos 3:7, 8)?

Making predictions about the future was a recurrent feature of the prophet's activity. A few, like Daniel and the Apostle John, were given spectacular images of future events. One Bible student counted 1,239 prophecies in the Old Testament and 578 in the New Testament, totaling more than 1,800.

Witnessing the fulfillment of prophecies is one of the ways we may test whether a prophet is genuine. Moses gave this clear instruction to the wilderness wanderers: "You may say to yourselves, 'How can we know when a message has not been spoken by the Lord?' If what a prophet proclaims in the name of the Lord does not take place or come true, that is a message the Lord has not spoken. That prophet has spoken presumptuously. No one should be alarmed" (Deut. 18:21, 22).

That makes sense, but is the reverse also true? If a prophet's prediction comes to pass, does it prove he is genuine? Not always. Moses had a warning about that too. "If a prophet, or one who fore-tells by dreams, appears among you and announces to you a sign or wonder, and if the sign or wonder spoken of takes place, and the prophet says, 'Let us follow other gods…and let us worship them', you must not listen to the words of that prophet or dreamer" (Deut. 13:1–3).

> *Witnessing the fulfillment of prophecies is one of the ways we may test whether a prophet is genuine.*

Satan, the archdeceiver, has chalked up a lot of experience in reading and plotting the future. He has his chessmen, powerful leaders whom he inspires to make diabolical plans resulting in terror and destruction. He has a field day with false prophets and even leaders of major religions. He leads them to foretell events, knowing that he can almost certainly make them happen. Jesus warned us about the perilous times in which we live. "False messiahs and false prophets will appear and perform signs and wonders to deceive, if possible, even the elect" (Mark 13:22). In our time, God is allowing Satan his last opportunity to show the universe what evil can do if left unchecked.

Understanding Prophecies

The prophetic books of the Old Testament are not always easy to understand. Skeptics point to some prophetic revelations that don't make sense to them. Even Martin Luther found the prophets difficult to under-stand: "They have a queer way of talking, like people who, instead of pro-ceeding in an orderly manner, ramble off from one thing to the next so that you cannot make heads or tails of them or see what they are getting at."[2]

We need help to comprehend the meaning of some prophetic mes-sages and predictions. Here is an example: "Damascus will no longer be a city but will become a heap of ruins," said Isaiah (Isa. 17:1), yet Damas-cus has been the Syrian capital for thousands of years. Isaiah made other predictions of that nature. It is helpful to understand that while there are hundreds of prophetic statements in the Old Testament, only about one percent point to fulfillment in our time. When prophets like Isaiah announced the future, it was usually the *immediate* future for Israel and Judah. It was a time when the people were worshipping false gods and needed the threats and promises that God gave them. Understand Isaiah's statements, like the one quoted above, within the context of the times. In ancient cultures, warlike predictions were often bold and irrational. Isaiah was not immune from that culture.

Another problem for us is that more than half of the prophetic writings are in poetic form, which sometimes makes literal reading of them inappropriate or misleading. Hebrew poetry is characterized by figurative language—simile, metaphor, personification, and often hyperbole, which comes through to us as exaggeration. When the people were not listening, the prophet tried to get their attention and stir their emotions with vivid mental images. God wanted the leaders of Israel and Judah to understand that they must not seek treaties and alliances with surrounding nations, no matter how powerful those nations appeared to be. The time was coming when those nations would be destroyed. God determined whether the destruction was to come sooner or later.

We must also realize that many Old Testament prophecies were conditional in nature. Conditional prophecies were often time-related, or dependent for their fulfillment on people's responses to God's promises and warnings. Notice this prophecy of Amos: "I will plant Israel in their own land, never again to be uprooted from the land I have given them" (Amos 9:15); or this one from Ezekiel: "No longer will the people of Israel have malicious neighbors who are painful briers and sharp thorns" (Ezek. 28:24). These predictions were never fulfilled. Their fulfillment depended on how Israel responded to God's warnings and promises.

God explained to Jeremiah why many prophecies were conditional: "Like clay in the hand of the potter, so are you in my hand, house of Israel. If at any time I announce that a nation or kingdom is to be uprooted, torn down and destroyed, and if that nation I warned repents of its evil, then I will relent and not inflict on it the disaster I had planned. And if at another time I announce that a nation or kingdom is to be built up and planted, and if it does evil in my sight and does not obey me, then I will reconsider the good I had intended to do for it" (Jer. 18:7–10). Joel expressed the same concept in these beautiful words of invitation: "Return to the Lord your God, for he is gracious and compassionate, slow to anger and abounding in love, and he relents from sending calamity. Who knows? He may turn and relent, and leave behind a blessing" (Joel 2:13, 14).

There are many Old Testament examples of conditional prophecies. During the reign of King Hezekiah, the prophet Micah announced the imminent destruction of Jerusalem: "Mount Zion will be plowed like an open field; Jerusalem will be reduced to ruins! A thicket will grow on the heights where the temple now stands" (Micah 3:12, NLT). However, the destruction did not happen at that time. Two centuries later, though, Jeremiah predicted Jerusalem's destruction, followed by seventy years of captivity. As some of the temple elders were listening, they recalled Micah's earlier prophecy: "Did not Hezekiah fear the Lord and seek his favor? And did not the Lord relent, so that he did not bring the disaster he pronounced against them" (JER. 26:19)? Jonah's prediction that Nineveh would be destroyed in forty days is another prime example of how God works. The destruction was waived because the people repented.

The free will of man may also cause a divine prediction to go unfulfilled. King Hezekiah presents an example of this. "In those days Hezekiah became ill and was at the point of death. The prophet Isaiah went to him and said, 'This

> *The free will of man may also cause a divine prediction to go unfulfilled.*

is what the Lord says: Put your house in order, because you are going to die; you will not recover.' Hezekiah turned his face to the wall and prayed to the Lord....And Hezekiah wept bitterly. Before Isaiah had left the middle court, the word of the Lord came to him: 'Go back and tell Hezekiah, the leader of my people....I have heard your prayer and seen your tears. I will heal you'" (2 Kings 20:1–5). We see the same graciousness of God through Israel's troublesome journey to the Promised Land. God repeatedly withdrew threatened punishments when Moses interceded for the rebellious Israelites.

God's graciousness is one reason why a prophecy's fulfillment may be delayed. He wants to save as many as possible. Peter acknowledged, "The Lord is not slow in keeping his promise, as some understand slowness. Instead he is patient with you, not wanting anyone to perish, but everyone to come to repentance" (2 Peter 3:9). Ellen White expressed the same thing about the second coming: "The long night of gloom is trying, but the morning is deferred in mercy, because if the Master should come, so many would be found unready. God's unwillingness to have his people perish, has been the reason of so long delay."[3]

Of course, not all prophecies are conditional ones. Apocalyptic prophecies, such as the notable time prophecies of Daniel 8 and 9 and in Revelation are not conditional in the ways we have discussed. Jesus came "in the fullness of time" (Gal. 4:4). We can be equally certain that

His second coming will take place during a specified, prophetic period of time—defined as "the time of the end." The parameters have been set, the promise is secure, and our hope is firm.

Predictions of Ellen White

Throughout her life, Ellen White preferred to identify herself as God's messenger rather than a prophet. Less than two percent of her writings deal with future predictions. Several of them are found in *The Great Controversy* which presents, not a theology of eschatology, but a guidebook to help us discern the times and prepare for the great finale.

Nevertheless, she *did* make some dramatic predictions, many of which have seen fulfillment.[4] One of them was her vision at the Parkville, Michigan, church on January 12, 1861, predicting the American Civil War, when almost no one believed the war would take place. She was shown that there would be a terrible loss of life, and some Parkville Adventist families would lose husbands and sons in the war.[5] The war broke out three months later, and events transpired just as she had been shown.

Among other prophecies was Ellen's 1848 prediction that the single issue of *Present Truth* that her husband was instructed to publish would be "small at first", but would become "streams of light" all around the world.[6] That seemed unrealistic for a small group of poverty-stricken believers. Today, Adventist publications are distributed in over 230 languages throughout more than 200 countries.

In 1901, she was shown that the Review and Herald publishing house in Battle Creek would be destroyed if the management continued to take commercial jobs instead of focusing on church material. "I have been almost afraid to open the *Review*, fearing to see that God has cleansed the publishing house by fire."[7] Thirteen months later, fire completely destroyed the building.

In 1848, Leah, Margaret, and Kate Fox were living in a house at Hydesville, New York, with their parents, when they reported hearing strange rappings which they said were made by the spirit of a man who had been murdered five years earlier and was buried in their cellar. That same year, Ellen White was shown that the rappings heard by the Fox sisters were the first indications of the revival of spiritualism in modern times. "I saw that the mysterious knocking in New York and other places was the power of Satan, and that such things would be more and more common, clothed in a religious garb so as to lull the deceived to greater security."[8] Spiritualism has since become a worldwide reality.

Ellen White recorded most of her last-day predictions during the middle years of the 19th century, when Seventh-day Adventism was still a small, American church. She predicted that the United States of America would become a world superpower.[9] Believers at that time anticipated an imminent second advent. They watched unfolding events in the United States with interest and concern as Protestant America accepted increasing numbers of Catholic immigrants, Sunday laws became an ominous threat, and spiritualism began influencing religious practices. Uriah Smith busied himself with in-depth studies of the prophecies of Daniel and Revelation, interpreting them according to contemporary religio-political trends and events affecting America. Ellen White's predictions echoed some of Uriah Smith's interpretations of Revelation.[10]

Were any of Ellen White's predictions conditional in nature? Yes. In 1856, she recorded these words about a conference of believers conducted in Battle Creek, Michigan: "I was shown the company present at the Conference. Said the angel: 'Some food for worms, some subjects of the seven last plagues, some will be alive and remain upon the earth to be translated at the coming of Jesus.'"[11] Among the young people in attendance that day was a four-year-old boy sitting on his mother's lap. His name was John Harvey Kellogg. When he died in 1943 at the age of ninety-one, the Lord had not yet come. Some Adventists had been checking off the names as, one by one, they passed to their rest, and wondered about her prophetic statement of 1856.

Living in the End Time

Ever since Jesus ascended to heaven from the Mount of Olives 2,000 years ago, believers have expected His soon return. Paul thought it would happen in his lifetime (see 1 Thess. 4:13–18). Almost two millennia later, the Millerites expected Jesus in 1844, and after their disappointment, the early Adventists anticipated it would happen very soon. Ellen White penned the following words forty years after the "Food for Worms" meeting in the Battle Creek church: "The angels of God in their messages to men represent time as very short. Thus it has always been presented to me. It is true that time has continued longer than we expected in the early days of this message. Our Savior did not appear as soon as we hoped. But has the Word of the Lord failed? Never! It should be remembered that the promises and the threatenings of God are alike conditional."[12]

Did you notice that last sentence? What does it mean for us in the 21st-century? The promise of Jesus' return is secure—Jesus himself emphasized its certainty, though not its timing—but how are we supposed to relate to the many specific predictions about the end time? How are we to live and act in expectation of His return? Today, only four percent of Seventh-day Adventists reside in the United States. Many of our fellow believers on other continents have already experienced violence, persecution, and ongoing "times of trouble." As the years march on, we wonder about Ellen White's interpretation and chronology of last-day events. We wonder if there is indeed a conditional quality to some of her end-time predictions. At the same time, we are busy counting down the predicted events found in *The Great Controversy*. We are sign-watchers, believing that Jesus must come soon, and sometimes tempted to interpret every religious event or political speech as part of a conspiracy for papal control of the world. All the while, we continue to preach the nearness of Jesus' return in glory. How should we relate to its imminence?

On May 19, 1780, people in northeastern America awoke to find a murky haze drifting over the morning sun. An early twilight descended over the next few hours, and by noon, the skies had turned as black as midnight. Night birds sang and confused chickens retired to their roosts. People lit candles to see. Americans feared that nothing less than the biblical Judgment Day was at hand, when "the sun will be turned to darkness and the moon to blood" (Joel 2:31).

A particularly famous scene unfolded in the Connecticut Governor's Council. Shaken by the unnatural darkness, some of the politicians suggested ending their meeting. Councilman Abraham Davenport, a Connecticut militia colonel, spoke up. "I am against adjournment," he said. "The day of judgment is either approaching, or it is not. If it is not, there is no cause of an adjournment; if it is the day of judgment, I choose to be found doing my duty."[13]

Many years ago, in an upper room in Jerusalem on Passover eve, twelve men still had it in their heads that Jesus would somehow metamorphose into a political Messiah. Jesus knew that their long-held expectations were about to be shattered. He sensed how frightening the next twenty-four hours would be for them. Reminding them once more of what was about to transpire, He added gently, "I am telling you now before it happens, so that when it does happen you will believe that I am he" (John 13:19). It was not until after that weekend's events that they truly comprehended the ancient prophet's portrayal of One "despised and rejected of men" (Isa. 53:3) and caught the meaning of the psalmist's words—"They pierce my hands and my feet" (Ps. 22:6).

Like those disciples, we have expectations of an event that even Enoch predicted long ago (see Jude 14). However, it may not happen exactly when and how we expect. Answering a question from His disciples about when they could expect Him to return, Jesus responded, "No one knows the day or hour when these things will happen, not even the angels in heaven or the Son himself. Only the Father knows" (Matt. 24:36, NLT). We serve a God who sometimes surprises. "So you also must be ready, because the Son of Man will come at an hour when you do not expect him" (Matt. 24:44). God is eternal, and all of human history is but a drop in an astronomical bucket. We are impatient, of course, waiting for the fulfillment of Jesus' wonderful promise. "When everything is ready, I will come and get you, so that you will always be with me" (John 14:2, 3, NLT).

One day, Jesus told His listeners a parable about a boss who went away and left his ten employees with work to do. He gave each of them some money so that they could do the job (see Luke 19:11-13). The boss never told them how long he'd be away or when he was coming back.

> *God is eternal, and all of human history is but a drop in an astronomical bucket.*

The story has an important lesson for us. There is work to be done. When Jesus went away to heaven, he gave us a job to do and the Holy Spirit to enable us to accomplish the task. Instead of standing at the window, skygazing or spending my time pondering the predictions of His return, I am admonished to be faithful in doing my duty. "Put this money to work", He said, "until I come back" (Luke 19:13).

To think about:

1. If you had been one of Christ's disciples before His betrayal and death, which of the following Old Testament passages would you likely have not recognized as predictions about Him (Isa. 7:14; 50:6; 53:9; Micah 5:2; Zech. 11:12–13; 12:10)? Does this teach us anything about our understanding of end-time prophecies?

2. Consider how the conditionality of some of God's predictions might affect the life and credibility of a prophet. Contemplate the cases of Jeremiah, Jonah, and Ellen White.

3.   Matthew 24 and 25 include several parables of Jesus that relate to how we should prepare and work in anticipation of the second coming. How do these parables help us in our expectation and preparation for the soon coming of Jesus?

References:

[1]   Ellen White, *Desire of Ages*, 31.

[2]   Cited by Gerhard von Rad, *Old Testament Theology*, vol. 2, 233.

[3]   White, *Testimonies*, 2:194.

[4]   Herbert Douglass, *Dramatic Prophecies of Ellen White*.

[5]   White, *Testimonies*, 1:253–258.

[6]   White, *Life Sketches*, 125.

[7]   White, *Testimonies*, 8:91–96.

[8]   White, *Early Writings*, 43.

[9]   White, *Testimonies*, 6:14–22.

[10] For a summary of her predictions, see Herbert Douglass, "Predictions of Ellen G. White" in *The Ellen G. White Encyclopedia*, 1049–1052.

[11] White, *Spiritual Gifts,* vol. 4b, 18 (1864).

[12] White, *Review and Herald*, Oct. 6, 1896.

[13] Evan Andrews, "Remembering New England's Dark Day". http://1ref.us/ma (accessed October 10, 2017).

Understanding

Chapter 15—Progressive Revelation

The wall of fear and distrust hides much more of God than His face. We have also lost so much knowledge about His nature and character.

Think about all the knowledge that humanity has accumulated since time began. How does the sum total of it compare with how much God knows? Speaking through the prophet Isaiah, God declares, "My thoughts are nothing like your thoughts. . . and my ways are far beyond anything you could imagine. For just as the heavens are higher than the earth, so my ways are higher than your ways and my thoughts higher than your thoughts" (Isa. 55:8, 9, NLT). Writing to the Roman believers, Paul concluded his complex theological arguments by exclaiming, "Oh, the depth of the riches of the wisdom and knowledge of God! How unsearchable his judgments, and his paths beyond tracing out! Who has known the mind of the Lord? Or who has been his counselor" (Rom. 11:33, 34)? Zophar, one of Job's comforters, challenged his suffering friend with a question: "Can you fathom the mysteries of God? Can you probe the limits of the Almighty" (Job 11:7)? Later, God Himself challenged Job: "Brace yourself like a man, because I have some questions for you, and you must answer them. Where were you when I laid the foundations of the earth?

Tell me, if you know so much" (Job 38:3, 4, NLT). In total humility, Job responded, "Surely I spoke of things I did not understand, things too wonderful for me to know" (Job 42:3).

How can I, a sin-damaged human, comprehend important truths about the God of the universe? Not very well. Yet, my understanding of some truth is possible, and even necessary, through my prayerful reading of the Word and the illumination of the Holy Spirit. However, when I think about Job's humble response to his Maker, a follow-up question comes to me: How much understanding do I really have about the character of God, whose very nature is love?

On a different level, how could I, an educated adult, explain everything that I know to a two-year-old? Timothy Johnson, a prominent physician, made this comment after a lifetime of questions: "I have much less confidence in the human mind to figure out the mind of God than I did forty years ago and much more confidence in the mercy of God to tolerate our human explorations on these matters—maybe even to smile with satisfaction as would any good parent watching a child trying to figure it all out."[1]

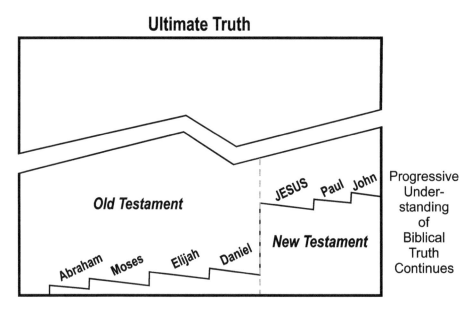

Figure 9: Progressive Revelation of Truth.

God is the author and originator of truth. We may think of "ultimate truth" or "ultimate reality" as the totality of God's knowledge, which is infinite and beyond human comprehension. Look at the adjoining box (Figure 9), where the top line represents the totality of God's knowledge, the Ultimate Truth—what is real about the universe and everything that can ever be known. The bottom line is where human understanding begins. The break I have outlined between the top and bottom of the box represents a vast, immeasurable gap between Ultimate Truth and our diminutive knowledge. There isn't a sheet of paper large enough to show this gap. Please keep the box in your thinking as we proceed.

In the beginning, Adam and Eve were in a perfect relationship with their Creator, each other as equals, and the earth they managed together. In the act of creation, two beautiful things became sacred: the human body and the marriage relationship between a man and a woman (see Gen. 2:21–25). The first act of sin was to destroy the sacredness of both. "Don't you know," cried Paul, "that your body is the temple of the Holy Spirit, who lives in you and was given to you by God? You do not belong to yourself" (1 Cor. 6:19, NLT).

So much has changed since the wall reared its ugly countenance before us. Abandoning the divine parameters of love that graced those original relationships, the human race spiraled downwards into a ruptured and fractured society. Dominance of one over another led to aggression and abuse. Slavery became the portrait of human society. Sex mutated into the selfish use of another's body. In the first act of violence, Cain destroyed his only brother. As a race, we have lost so much. We've inherited a shattered connection with God, twisted relationships with each other, and devastation of our gifted earth. It got so bad that God intervened.

Steps Toward Truth

"The world that then was, being overflowed with water, perished" (2 Peter 3:6, NKJV), but God did not give up on humanity, degenerate as it had become. He meets people where they are. He dispenses some important truths about Himself in very small doses. We may think of it as "progressive revelation." We will explore some truths that God revealed to a few people who were willing to listen. The Old Testament is a record of how God brought ancient Israel step by step toward truth.

> *As a race, we have lost so much. We've inherited a shattered connection with God, twisted relationships with each other, and devastation of our gifted earth. It got so bad that God intervened.*

- In Mesopotamia, He found a man whose family worshipped false gods. "Abram, will you trust me if I ask you to pack up everything and move to another country?" It turned out to be more than a physical journey. Abraham also had a long way to go in learning to trust a God who made promises that were almost unbelievable. It was a long haul to the place where Abraham trusted God enough to obey an appalling command that made absolutely no sense to him: "Take your son, your only son, whom you love—Isaac—and go up to the region of Moriah. Sacrifice him there as a burnt offering on a mountain I will show you" (Gen. 22:2). The journey there was a harrowing experience, but God intervened and taught Abraham a vital truth: that *God is worthy of our complete trust.* We serve a faithful God who keeps His promises. We must learn patience and trust.

- Time passed, and at the exodus, God began again, this time with a demoralized band of slaves who understood authority only by the whip and lash. At Sinai, He came through to them with thunder and smoke. It was the only way they could understand. Speaking through Moses, God taught those ex-slaves that the universe and everything in it operates according to a finely tuned set of laws. With the giving of the law at Sinai, He showed them that society can only be happy and safe by respecting moral and physical laws. He introduced to them the forgotten gift of the Sabbath. Throughout their wilderness wandering, they learned more new truth about *the God who loved and protected them.* We serve a patient God who combines justice with love.

- The learning wasn't always upward. When God called Elijah to be His prophet to the Israelite nation, their religion had deteriorated to the mass worship of Baal. It was time to teach some new truth. One memorable day on Mount Carmel, God moved and acted through His servant in a spectacular showdown between true and false worship (see 1 Kings 18:16–45). The Israelites learned a truth they had long forgotten: that *the false gods they worshipped were powerless against the mighty Jehovah.*

 Elijah learned something else about God soon after that victorious day on the mountain. Paralyzed by fear from a wicked queen's death threat, Elijah fled to the desert of Sinai. God found him there, hiding in a cave, with a chronic case of depression, and the same God who could thunder on Sinai and explode the altar with fire on Carmel, cared enough about His discouraged servant to whisper words of comfort that restored his soul (1 Kings 19:5–18). We serve *a God of dynamic power and quiet peace.*

- Truth took a big step when Daniel was shown amazing motion pictures about the time of the end. The visions overwhelmed the prophet as he pled for an explanation. "While I was speaking in prayer, the man Gabriel…reached me about the time of the evening offering. And he informed me, 'O Daniel, I have now come forth to give you skill to understand'" (Dan. 9:21, 22, NKJV). Among the end-time revelations given to Daniel was the first clear Old Testament truth about the final resurrection day. "At that time Michael, the great prince who protects your people, will arise. There will be a time of distress such as has not happened from the beginning of nations until then. But at that time your people—everyone whose name is found written in the book—will be delivered. Multitudes who sleep in the dust of the earth will awake: some to everlasting life, others to shame and everlasting contempt" (Dan. 12:1, 2). We serve *a gracious God of renewal and resurrection.*

While the wall of fear and distrust blocked the face of the Creator, the prophets of the Old Testament were given progressive revelations of truth. Many of them, like Abraham, Moses, Elijah, and Daniel, had steep learning curves, but they were faithful in communicating what God was showing them. After each step upward, though, the community slipped back into old ways and understandings. Repeatedly, "they forgot God, their savior, who had done such great things" (Psalm 106:21, NLT).

There were some truths that God did not clearly reveal to Israel. They were not ready for them. In a world populated by many gods, Jehovah emphasized His oneness: "Hear, O Israel: The Lord our God, the Lord is one" (Deut. 6:4). That meant that the truth about the Godhead was not understood by ancient Israel. Only by looking back from the New Testament can we discern the evidence of a triune God. However, more astonishing to modern readers is the concealment of Satan in the Old Testament. His name appears there only three times:

- The first two chapters of the Book of Job tell about Satan's uninvited appearance in a heavenly council where he challenges God to remove the hedge of protection around Job. Through the rest of the book, we find Job believing that all of his suffering comes from God. The author of the book was inspired to give us the inside story, but neither Job nor his friends had any knowledge of Satan's existence.

- At the other end of Old Testament history, after the Jewish exiles returned home to Jerusalem, the prophet Zechariah was given a vision of their high priest, Joshua, standing before God, while Satan stood by sneering about his unrighteousness (see Zech. 3:1, 2). This vision finds its ultimate meaning in the clothing of repentant sinners with the righteousness of Christ.
- Writing about the same time as Zechariah, the author of Chronicles mentions Satan, blaming him for inciting King David to take a census of Judah and Israel. He contradicts the earlier historian who thought that *God* was responsible. Compare 2 Samuel 24:1 with 1 Chronicles 21:1.

Who *was* responsible for inciting the king to count Israel? Was it God, or Satan? The best answer is that throughout Israel's history, God took responsibility for many of Satan's actions. Why? In a polytheistic society, Jehovah did not want His people to believe they were ruled by two gods, one to worship for giving them good things, the other luring them to sacrifice their children in order to deflect the bad things. It is interesting and worthwhile to reread the Old Testament with that perspective. Satan made his first undisputed appearance at the three temptations of Christ (see Matt. 4:1–11; Luke 4:1–13).

Then Jesus Came

Truth took a giant step upward when Jesus came. There was a desperate need for it. The once-sacred relationships had become a twisted mess of grave injustices, marred marriages, a male-dominated society, and a slave economy that reached its peak during the Roman Empire.

Jesus lived and taught truth. To some believing Jews, He promised, "You will know the truth, and the truth will set you free" (John 8:32). In the Gethsemane prayer for His disciples: "Make them holy by your truth. Teach them your Word, which is truth" (John 17:17, NLT). In His interrogation before Pilate: "I was born and came into the world to testify to the truth. All who love the truth recognize that what I say is true" (John 18:37, NLT).

In the upper room in Jerusalem, just hours before His death, Jesus gave a glorious promise of truth to the troubled disciples. "Don't let your hearts be troubled," He said. "I am going home to my Father where I will prepare a home for you. Then I will come back and get you." He finished by saying, "And you know the way to where I am going."

Thomas immediately protested, "No, we don't know, Lord. We have no idea where you are going, so how can we know the way?" Jesus answered him by saying, "I am the Way, the Truth, and the Life. No one can come to the Father except through me" (John 14:1–6, NLT). Those words encapsulate the truth about salvation—"except through me." Jesus was the epitome of truth. His death on the cross is the fullest expression of God's character of love.

During that last, long conversation with the disciples before His death, Jesus explained that there was a lot more truth He wanted to share with them, but it was more than they could absorb in those crisis hours. "However," He said, "when the Spirit of Truth has come, He will guide you into all the truth" (John 16:12, 13, NKJV). That promise began its fulfillment with the coming of the Holy Spirit at Pentecost.

The revelation of truth continued through the apostolic age. One day, Peter was visiting at the home of Simon the Tanner at Joppa, overlooking the Mediterranean, when he was given a strange vision. A sheet full of unclean creatures was displayed before him, with instructions to kill and eat. Revolted by the sight and the command, Peter responded that he had never been guilty of eating what the Lord Himself had forbidden centuries ago. The meaning of the vision became clear when three men knocked at the Tanner's gate, asking for Peter to accompany them to the Roman city of Caesarea where a centurion was waiting to hear the good news of Jesus Christ. The Holy Spirit was at work with several Roman citizens at Caesarea, and from the experience Peter learned the great truth of *salvation for everyone, including Gentiles* (see Acts 10).

Peter's testimony presented a problem for the early church leaders. Should the Gentile converts be circumcised? God had given that rite as a command to Abraham and his descendants many centuries before. Soon the issue came before the Church Council at Jerusalem. It was only after some heated debate and careful listening to Peter's account of his experience at Caesarea that church leaders agreed to waive the ancient requirement for Gentile converts (see Acts 15). However, could they lawfully do that? Was circumcision a God-given doctrine or truth that could be abolished by men without the Lord's direct approval?

Pilate's question—"What is truth?"—may be relevant here. We must distinguish between beliefs that are a part of God's eternal truth and symbolic rites or sacraments such as circumcision, baptism, the marriage ceremony, and holy communion. It must be recognized that truth is eternal and unchanging, while rites such as circumcision and baptism may be instituted by God as symbolic ordinances specific to times and cultures.

Other truths that became clear in New Testament times included the doctrine of the Trinity and the existence of Satan. We saw that these were not well understood in the Old Testament era when Israel lived and worshipped within a community of multiple gods that sometimes fought for supremacy among their followers. In such a time, God emphasized His unity and oneness. The Trinity became a clear teaching of the New Testament, especially with the gospel commission to the apostles—"Go and make disciples of all nations, baptizing them in the name of the Father and of the Son and of the Holy Spirit, and teaching them to obey everything I have commanded you" (Matt. 28:19).

Nevertheless, not all truth was understood and practiced in New Testament times. Writing to believers in Galatia, Paul made this bold statement: "There is neither Jew nor Gentile, neither slave nor free, neither male nor female, for you are all one in Christ Jesus" (Gal. 3:28). The first of these was already becoming accepted in Paul's day; the second saw significant progress in the 19th century when slavery was abolished in the United States and other countries; the third awaits acceptance in our time.

Serious errors infiltrated the Christian church through the dark centuries, largely due to Roman and Greek influences. One thinks of Sunday sacredness, belief in an immortal soul, and everlasting torment in hell. Nonetheless, the understanding of truth did not die completely. Martin Luther's study of the Scriptures led him to a rediscovery of the truth of salvation through faith in Jesus and ushered in the Protestant Reformation of the 16th century. Ellen White confirms, "There was a present truth in the days of Luther—a truth at that time of special importance; there is a present truth for the church today."[2] That last phrase leads us into the progressive revelation and understanding of truth in our time.

Truth for Our Time

Was progressive revelation a part of God's purpose in the establishment of the Seventh-day Adventist Church? Gerard Damsteegt, professor of theology at the Seventh-day Adventist Theological Seminary, helps our understanding: "Progressive revelation has played an important role in the development of the Seventh-day Adventist church and its theology. By 'progressive revelation' I mean God's continuous unfolding of *prior revealed truth*. Without such progressive revelation, *the unfolding of inspired truth building on truth previously revealed* and never denying it, the Seventh-day Adventist Church would not exist"[3] (italics mine).

Damsteegt has clarified for us that since New Testament times, we have received, and may continue to receive, clearer *understandings* of truth as revealed in the Holy Scriptures.

We may illustrate this with the truth about the great controversy between Christ and Satan. It finds its foundation in both the Old and New Testament Scriptures, but it was largely lost to the Christian church until 1858, when Ellen White received her vision concerning this cosmic conflict at Lovett's Grove, Ohio. It is a special truth for the end time. "The great controversy between good and evil will increase in intensity to the very close of time. In all ages the wrath of Satan has been manifested against the church of Christ; and God has bestowed His grace and Spirit upon His people to strengthen them to stand against the power of the evil one."[4]

Another foundational truth of Scripture was lost for a time to the majority of Seventh-day Adventists. At the 1888 General Conference session held at Minneapolis, Minnesota, two young preachers, Alonzo Jones and Ellet Waggoner, presented powerful sermons on the topic of righteousness by faith. Ellen White welcomed their presentations as "present truth" for Seventh-day Adventists: "That which God gives His servants to speak today would not perhaps have been present truth twenty years ago, but it is God's message for this time."[5] Later she wrote, "Laborers in the cause of truth should present the righteousness of Christ, not as new light but as precious light that has for a time been lost sight of by the people. We are to accept Christ as our personal Savior, and He imputes unto us the righteousness of God in Christ."[6]

Why had the truth of righteousness by faith "for a time been lost sight of by the people"? We may find the answer by remembering that the Adventist pioneers placed a heavy emphasis on another rediscovered truth about the Sabbath and its place within the Ten Commandments. Excitement about the law and the Sabbath characterized the evangelistic zeal of Joseph Bates, one of the church's founders. It was this emphasis on law-keeping, not justification by faith, that brought thousands of early converts into the Seventh-day Adventist faith. Some of the church leadership in 1888 found it very hard to accept the new emphasis on righteousness by faith, believing that the church was moving away from established truths. Ellen White commented: "There are men among us who profess to understand the truth for these last days, but who will not calmly investigate advanced truth. They are determined to make no advance beyond the stakes which they have set, and will not listen to those who, they say, do not stand by the old landmarks."[7]

In the article just quoted, Ellen White also said, "The truth of God is progressive; it is always onward, going from strength to a greater strength, from light to a greater light. We have every reason to believe that the Lord will send us increased truth, for a great work is yet to be done." Nine years previous to that, she had recorded a similar statement: "The Word of God presents special truths for every age. The dealings of God with His people in the past should receive our careful attention. We should learn the lessons which they are designed to teach us. But we are not to rest content with them. God is leading out His people step by step. *Truth is progressive*"[8] (italics mine).

How should we interpret her statements that "truth is progressive"? Doesn't this contradict what we have already said? Is God in the business of adding to our set of beliefs? Are there indeed new or "special truths for every age"? Should I be expecting "new light"? Are we talking about truth that is not based in Scripture? Is truth indeed progressive?

Gerard Damsteegt again helps us with this clarification: "Throughout their history Seventh-day Adventists have looked forward to discovering or receiving *additional truth that would harmonize with prior truth.* Ellen G. White, one of the principal founders of our church, kept this hope alive with statements such as: 'Truth is an advancing truth' and, 'There are mines of truth yet to be discovered by the earnest seeker.' *In speaking of 'truth' she always meant truth as given by God in His divine Word*"[9] (italics mine).

There are several points to be noted here. First, we cannot really speak about "new truth." All truth is part of God's eternal reality, which is vastly beyond our knowledge and comprehension. It follows, then, that Ellen White is talking about *the progressive understanding of biblical truth* when she refers to "progressive truth." All revealed truth is found in the Bible. We may, however, be given new insights into some of those truths. Following are two clear statements from Ellen White (italics mine in each quote):

"*New light will ever be revealed on the Word of God* to him who is in living connection with the Sun of Righteousness. Let no one come to the conclusion that there is no more truth to be revealed. The diligent, prayerful seeker for truth will find *precious rays of light yet to shine forth from the word of God.*"[10]

"The written testimonies are not to give new light, but to impress vividly upon the heart the *truths of inspiration already revealed.* Man's duty to God and to his fellow man has been distinctly specified in God's word, yet but few of you are obedient to the light given. *Additional truth is not brought out*; but God has through the testimonies simplified the great truths already given."[11]

Of this we can be certain: the truth of God can never originate in the human mind. Peter confirmed that when he wrote that the prophetic word "never came by the will of man" (2 Peter 1:21, NKJV). Solomon understood it too when he declared that "the fear of the Lord is where wisdom begins" (Prov. 9:10, ISV). Another wise man, the patriarch Job, with perplexing questions about God's knowledge and justice, could only conclude his deliberations by admitting, "I am nothing—how could I ever find the answers? I will cover my mouth with my hand. I have said too much already. I have nothing more to say" (Job 40:4, 5, NLT).

To think about:

1. Protestant Christianity holds that the Bible is God's complete revelation of truth to humanity. How shall we respond when an individual or group claims that God is revealing some new and important truth? In considering your response, reference these Scriptures: Jude 3, Isa. 55:8–9, Deut. 13:2, Matt. 24:24, Gal. 1:8–9.

2. In Old Testament times, God seems to have condoned or overlooked some widespread cultural practices such as polygamy, which is still practiced in some parts of the world today. How should the church relate to this or other local, cultural practices?

3. As sin-damaged humans, we cannot comprehend God. Think about Job's reaction to God's greatness (see Job 40:4, 5; 42:3), then read again Timothy Johnson's comment in the third paragraph of this chapter. What is your response to these statements?

References:

[1] Timothy Johnson, *Finding God in the Questions*, 26.

[2] Ellen White, *Great Controversy*, 143.

[3] Gerard Damsteegt, "Seventh-day Adventists and Progressive Revelation", *Journal of the Adventist Theological Society*, 2/1, 1991, 77.

[4] White, *Great Controversy*, ix.

[5] White, Manuscript 8a–1888.6.

[6] White, *Review and Herald*, March20, 1894; also *Selected Messages*, 1:383.

[7] White, *Signs of the Times*, May 26, 1890.

[8]   *Ibid.*, May 26, 1881.

[9]   Damsteegt, 78.

[10]   White, *Sabbath School Worker*, March 1, 1892.

[11]   White, *Testimonies*, 2:605 (1871).

Understanding

Chapter 16—The Hidden Face

The wall that sin built looms in front of us, dark and menacing. We have long forgotten what it was like to walk with our Maker in a breathtaking garden, experience the closeness, joy, and abandon. The prophets reminded us of that time as they peered through small apertures in the wall and gave us some pictures of the One who inhabits space and eternity. However, the pictures are sometimes distorted, portraying an intimidating countenance that induces fear and distrust.

Therefore, God fractured the wall, creating a sizable breach, when the Son of God came to our earth as the Son of Man. It was not always easy, though, to reconcile the loving Stranger of Galilee with some Old Testament images of God. As the disciples sat together with Jesus, Philip was puzzled. The caring face of Jesus he knew and loved, but the face of God? Philip asked, "Lord, show us the Father. That is all we need." Jesus replied, "Philip, I have been with you for a long time. Don't you know who I am? If you have seen me, you have seen the Father. How can you ask me to show you the Father" (John 14:8, 9, CEV)?

The opening verses of John's gospel answer Philip's question: "No one has ever seen God. The only Son, who is truly God and closest to the

Father, has shown us what God is like" (John 1:18, CEV). That is the good news. However, God's opponent, Satan, the self-appointed keeper of the wall, has done his utmost to erase the New Testament picture of Jesus and made the audacious claim that there is no God behind the wall. Turning scientists and philosophers into atheists and agnostics is one of Satan's well-honed skills.

We know about general revelation as one way through which God shows Himself to us. Our beautiful planet is the evidence of a God who made it especially for us. Not everyone sees it that way, of course, but in their observations of the universe or the molecular structure of their own bodies, some scientists find the imprint of a God whose specialty is order and design.

In this chapter, we are going to dive into the realm of science. If you are like me, you have little more than a peripheral understanding of the subject, so we may be venturing into territory where even angels fear to tread. Fortunately, however, there are scientists with the unique ability to converse at our level that are willing to help us enter their world. We will meet some well-respected scientists and philosophers who recognized the existence of God in their observations or studies and are willing to show us what they have found.

One such individual is Gerald Schroeder. He is an Orthodox Jew, educated in America, and now living with his family in Jerusalem. Schroeder did his doctoral work at Massachusetts Institute of Technology (MIT) in the fields of nuclear physics and earth sciences. He served for a while as a member of the U.S. Atomic Energy Commission. A firm believer in a creator God, Schroeder is the author of several notable books, including *The Science of God* and *The Hidden Face of God*. He writes, "In the wonders of nature, we have discovered the imprint of the metaphysical within the physical. As one who sees the wake of a boat that has passed by, so we encounter the hidden face of God....The Eternal said to Moses, and to us today, 'I will make all My goodness (the wonders of creation) pass before you....You shall see My back (as one finds, in the wake left by a boat, evidence of the boat's passage), but My face shall not be seen' (Exod. 33:20, 23). Even in the closest of encounters, the face of God remains hidden."[1]

The Wake of a Boat

Did you notice Schroeder's reference to "the wake left by a boat"? Standing at the lakeshore, we may have missed seeing the boat, but the churning water is evidence that it passed by. We have not been able to see the Creator God—His face is hidden—but in nature we see evidence of His presence and character. In the "wake" of His creation, there are some interesting phenomena that have attracted the attention of scientists and philosophers. They sometimes appear as questions. We will examine four:

- The universe is orderly, operating according to a set of laws. Where did they originate?
- How do we account for the universe? Was it always there?
- How can we explain human consciousness?
- How, when, and where did life originate?

Law and Order in the Universe

One of the most significant and controversial philosophers of our time was Antony Flew. Born in London, Flew studied philosophy at Oxford, and from there launched a remarkable career as a lecturer and writer. Flew was a strong advocate of atheism, known for his scathing attack on religion. Some say his 1950 essay, "Theology and Falsification", became the most widely reprinted philosophical publication of the last half-century. His wide-ranging interests extended to the philosophy of science, including natural law and the origin of life. Flew approached these topics with an open mind and a willingness to follow the evidence wherever it might lead him. He shocked the academic world in 2000 with the announcement that he now believed in the existence of God.

The story of Flew's conversion from atheism to theism is told in his book *There is a God.* "Three domains of scientific inquiry have been especially important to me," he writes. "The first is the question that puzzled and continues to puzzle most reflective scientists: How did the laws of nature come to be? The second is evident to all: How did life as a phenomenon originate from nonlife? And the third is the problem that philosophers handed over to cosmologists: How did the universe, by which we mean all that is physical, come into existence?"[2]

Now meet Owen Gingerich, an American scientist and committed Christian, highly respected in his field of astronomy, and author of more than twenty books. Born to a Mennonite family in Iowa, the young Gingerich studied at Harvard University. Now retired, he is Emeritus Professor of Astronomy and the History of Science at Harvard. He is also Astronomer Emeritus at the Smithsonian Institution and respected worldwide for his contributions to astrophysical research. Observing how the universe functions according to established laws, he says the idea of a universe without God is an oxymoron and self-contradiction. "To me, belief in a final cause, a Creator-God, gives a coherent understanding of why the universe seems so congenially designed for the existence of intelligent, self-reflective life. It would take only small changes in numerous physical constants to render the universe uninhabitable."[3]

Fascination with physics and the operation of laws led Paul Davies from atheism to an understanding of "someone" in charge of the universe. Davies is an English physicist with a doctoral degree from the University of London, followed by post-doctoral research at the University of Cambridge, and chairmanship of the International Academy of Astrophysics. His extensive research earned him the respected Templeton Prize in 1995 and numerous awards in three countries. Two of his more than twenty books express his belief in a Higher Power—*The Mind of God* and *God and the New Physics*. He writes, "Through my scientific work I have come to believe more and more strongly that the physical universe is put together with an ingenuity so astonishing that I cannot accept it merely as brute fact....I cannot believe that our existence in this universe is a mere quirk of fate, an accident of history, an incidental blip in the great cosmic drama. Our involvement is too intimate....We are truly meant to be here."[4] In his 1995 Templeton Prize address, he said, "Science can proceed only if the scientist adopts an essentially theological worldview.... This contrived nature of physical existence is just too fantastic for me to take on board as simply 'given.' It points to a deeper underlying meaning to existence."

Other thinkers also wonder about the laws of nature:

- British philosopher John Foster concluded that "it is God—the God of the theistic account—who created the laws that operate the universe and the world in which we live."[5]
- Canadian philosopher John Leslie is Professor Emeritus at Guelph University. In his book, *Infinite Minds*, he argues that the failure of chance to explain the fundamental laws of the universe "might well be seen as evidence specially favoring belief in God."[6]
- Austrian-born mathematician and philosopher Kurt Goedel argued that "the world is rational, according to which the order of the world reflects the order of the supreme mind governing it."[7]

One of the most popular scientific books ever published—*A Brief History of Time*—topped the British *Sunday Times* best-seller list for a record-breaking 237 weeks. Its author, Stephen Hawking, is renowned for his research and discoveries in theoretical physics and cosmology. Though he is a confirmed atheist, Hawking said this in his 1988 bestseller: "It would be very difficult to explain why the universe should have begun in just this way, except as the act of a God who intended to create beings like us.…In fact, if one considers the possible constants and laws that could have emerged, the odds against a universe that has produced life like ours are immense."[8]

The Mystery of the Universe

For a long time, there was discussion about whether or not the universe had a beginning. Much of it centered around theology and philosophy rather than scientific observation. That began to change with Einstein's theory of relativity, as scientists concluded that the universe is expanding. Then came the "big bang" model which is still widely accepted by physicists and cosmologists. Antony Flew writes, "When I first met the big-bang theory as an atheist, it seemed to me the theory made a big difference because it suggested that the universe had a beginning and that the first sentence in Genesis ('In the beginning God created the heavens and the earth') was related to an event in the universe."[9]

- Owen Gingerich: "I would prefer to accept a universe created with intention and purpose by a loving God, and perhaps created with just enough freedom that conscience and responsibility are part of the mix.…This, for me is God's Universe."[10]
- Erwin Schrodinger, a European physicist highly regarded for his research in quantum physics, received the Nobel Prize for Physics in 1933 for his contributions to quantum and wave mechanics. One of his books, *My View of the World,* states, "The scientific picture of the world around me is very deficient.…It is ghastly silent about all that is really near to our heart, that really matters to us. It knows nothing of beauty and ugly, good or bad, God and eternity. Science sometimes pretends to answers questions in these domains, but the answers are very often so silly that we are not inclined to take them seriously. Science is reticent, too, when it is a question of the great Unity of which we somehow form a part, to which we belong. The most popular name for it in our time is God."[11]
- David Conway, a professor of philosophy, wrote in his book, *The Rediscovery of Wisdom*, "The explanation of the world and its broad form is that it is the creation of a supreme omnipotent and omniscient intelligence, more commonly referred to as God, who created it in order to bring into existence and sustain rational beings."[12]

- Freeman Dyson is a physicist and mathematician. "The more I examine the universe and study the details of its architecture, the more evidence I find that the universe in some sense knew we were coming."[13]

The author of the Book of Hebrews has the last word on the origin of the universe: "By faith we understand that the universe was formed at God's command, so that what is seen was not made out of what was visible" (Heb. 11:3).

Human Consciousness

"How do I know that I exist?" may seem like a silly question, until I figure out that I am something more than a body made up of trillions of tiny cells. Why am I conscious of my existence? Gerald Schroeder concludes that the cells that make up our bodies contain intelligence or "wisdom"— another evidence of the hidden face of God. Marco Biagini, an Italian physicist, draws the same conclusion: "Consciousness transcends the laws of physics and cannot then be considered the product of biological and cerebral processes. This implies that our mind and our brain are not the same entity, but two different yet interacting entities."[14] In other words, I am more than just the sum total of a physical brain and body parts.

Wilder Penfield was a neurosurgeon, famous as a pioneer in brain surgery methods and techniques. In 1967, he was honored with the Order of Canada and subsequently inducted into the Canadian Medical Hall of Fame. Penfield devoted a lot of his thinking to mental processes, including the study of human consciousness. "Through my own scientific career, I, like other scientists, have struggled to prove that the brain accounts for the mind," he wrote in the introduction to his book, *The Mystery of the Mind*, but finally concluded, "To expect the highest brain mechanism or any set of reflexes, however complicated, to carry out what the mind does, and thus perform all the functions of the mind, is quite absurd."[15]

Others have made the same discovery:

- Paul Davies: "Life is more than just complex chemical reactions. The cell is also an information storing, processing and replicating system. We need to explain the origin of this information, and the way in which the information processing machinery came to exist.… The problem of how meaningful or semantic information can emerge spontaneously from a collection of mindless molecules subject to blind and purposeless forces presents a deep conceptual challenge."[16]

- Marilyn Schlitz, social anthropologist: "I am driven by data, not theory. And the data I see tell me that there are ways in which people's experience refutes the physicalist position that the mind is the brain and nothing more. There are solid, concrete data that suggest that our consciousness, our mind, may surpass the boundaries of the brain."[17]

Richard Dawkins, a self-proclaimed atheist and strident critic of creationism and intelligent design, is best known for two of his books—*The Selfish Gene* (1976) and *The God Delusion* (2006). During a 1999 public debate between two atheists, Dawkins (professor of zoology at the University of Oxford) and Steven Pinker (professor of psychology at Harvard University), Dawkins said this during a discussion of human consciousness: "There are aspects of human subjective consciousness that are deeply mysterious. Neither Steve Pinker nor I can explain human subjective consciousness....In *How the Mind Works* Steve elegantly sets out the problem of subjective consciousness and asks where it comes from and what's the explanation. Then he's honest enough to say, 'Beats the heck out of me.' That is an honest thing to say, and I echo it. We don't know. We don't understand it."[18]

The Origin of Life

Another big ripple in the "wake of the boat" relates to the origin of life from non-life. When and how did life originate? Andrew Knoll, Professor of Natural History at Harvard, with accomplishments in geology and paleontology, and author of *Life on a Young Planet*, was a guest on a 2004 PBS Nova program discussing the question, "How Did Life Begin?" Knoll had this response to that question: "The short answer is we don't really know how life originated on this planet. There have been a variety of experiments that tell us some possible roads, but we remain in substantial ignorance. We don't know how life started on this planet. We don't know exactly when it started, we don't know under what circumstances. I think we have to admit that we're looking through a glass darkly here."[19]

Dawkins, author of *The God Delusion*, had this to say: "The origin of life only had to happen once. We can therefore allow it to have been an extremely improbable event, many orders of magnitude more improbable than most people realize....The spontaneous arising by chance of the first hereditary molecule strikes many as improbable. Maybe it is—very, very improbable....We can make the point that, however improbable the origin of life might be, we know it happened on Earth because we are here."[20] In a separate publication, Dawkins writes, "The probability that any particular sequence of, say 100, amino-acids will spontaneously form is, roughly, 1 in 20^{100}. This is an inconceivably large number, far greater than the number of fundamental particles in the entire universe."[21]

Gerald Schroeder expresses his amazement at the complexity of life in our bodies: "The human body acts as a finely tuned machine, a magnificent metropolis in which, as its inhabitants, each of the 75 trillion cells, composed of 10^{27} atoms, moves in symbiotic precision….Ten to the twenty-seventh power—a one followed by twenty-seven zeros, a thousand million million million million atoms—are organized by a single act when a protozoan-like sperm cell adds its message of genetic material into a receptive egg cell. Combined, these two miniscule cells contain all the information needed to produce the entire body at each stage of its growth, from fetus to adult. We are so embedded in the biosphere that the marvel of its organization has become lost within its commonness….A single cell at fertilization contained within it all the potential that you were ever physically to become. And every cell within your body retains that wisdom."[22]

- Francis Crick, a molecular biologist, was co-discoverer, with James Watson, of the DNA molecule and genetic code, for which they were jointly awarded the 1962 Nobel Prize in Physiology and Medicine. Though an atheist, Crick wrote in 1981, "An honest man, armed with all the knowledge available to us now, could only state that in some sense, the origin of life appears at the moment to be almost a miracle, so many are the conditions which would have had to have been satisfied to get it going."[23]
- Lehigh University biochemist Michael Behe, author of *Darwin's Black Box*, has demonstrated that "irreducibly complex" molecular structures cannot be built piece-by-piece through evolutionary processes. "My conclusion can be summed up in a single word: design. I say that based on science. I believe that irreducibly complex systems are strong evidence of a purposeful, intentional design by an intelligent agent."[24]
- Fred Hoyle, famous English astronomer: "The chance that higher life forms might have emerged [by chance] is comparable with the chance that a tornado sweeping through a junk-yard might assemble a Boeing 747 from the material therein."[25]

A Parable and a Paradox

Antony Flew, the atheist-turned-deist, invented a parable with an interesting application. A satellite phone washes up on the beach of a remote island whose inhabitants think they are the only human beings in the universe. The natives play with the strange device and hear different voices as they hit sequences of numbers on the dial pad. They assume it's the device itself that makes the noises—the voices are just properties of the device. However, a sage of the tribe comes up with an alternative theory: that the voices are coming from a communication network somewhere beyond their island world. Everyone laughs and ridicules such a crazy idea. It is preposterous to believe there could be other humans anywhere.

Flew goes on to suggest a more satisfactory ending for his parable. Some "scientists" of the tribe decide to work on their sage's hypothesis that the device is a medium of contact with other humans. They adopt the theory that intelligent beings do exist "out there." By deciphering the sounds that they hear on the phone, they recognize patterns and rhythms that enable them to understand what is being said, and their whole world changes. They discover they are not alone in the universe. Flew makes the point: "The discovery of phenomena like the laws of nature—the communication network of the parable—has led scientists, philosophers, and others to accept the existence of an infinitely intelligent Mind."[26]

A growing number of research scientists and thought leaders are courageous enough to voice their convictions and "follow the argument wherever it leads", using Flew's own words, but many laugh at what they consider to be a crazy hypothesis. Why are they unwilling to consider the possibility that there is a God? Why do so many attack and ridicule people like Flew who change their stance? Is it their commitment to the theory of evolution? Not likely, because there are many deists and Christians who embrace evolution rather than creation. Is it a reluctance to contemplate the supernatural? An unwillingness to follow the evidence wherever it may lead them? Is there a fear of being wrong about something to which they have devoted their lives and livelihood and losing face with their colleagues in research or the students they teach?

There may be another reason why many thinking people discard the God hypothesis. Nothing generates more anger and outrage in us as human beings than the suffering of defenseless children, especially when their suffering is caused by horrendous torture. Richard Rice emphasizes the outrage we feel at such atrocities, yet "there's a striking paradox involved in using them to reject God. For instead of giving us reasons to object to the existence of God, such feelings, when carefully examined, actually support it." Rice asks why we are repelled by such behavior. From where does our moral code come? "Our instinctive condemnation of human cruelty necessarily implies the existence of a supreme moral being....The only way to account for such a standard is to attribute it to a transcendent source of moral obligation, to a supreme lawgiver, in other words, to God."[27] A famous Russian author, Fyodor Dostoyevsky, said it succinctly in one of his equally famous novels, *The Brothers Karamazov*: "If God does not exist, everything is permitted." Witness the murder of tens of millions of people by both Fascist and Communist governments in European countries after the state eliminated religion and took total control of society.[28] History teaches that if you take God away, moral behavior plunges and society self-destructs.

Werner Heisenberg reached a similar conclusion. A world-renowned German physicist and one of the key pioneers of quantum physics, Heisenberg was awarded the Nobel Prize in Physics in 1932. In accepting the Gardini Prize, he said, "Where no guiding ideals are left to point the way, the scale of values disappears and with it the meaning of our deeds and sufferings, and at the end can lie only negation and despair. Religion is therefore the foundation of ethics, and ethics the presupposition of life."[29]

Experiencing God

The face is hidden. We may see evidence of God in the "wake of the boat", but the believing Christian may know through personal encounter that there is a caring God behind the wall. I can know that God is alive and real when I experience His presence through the Holy Spirit in my life. In final encouraging words to the disciples

We may see evidence of God in the "wake of the boat", but the believing Christian may know through personal encounter that there is a caring God behind the wall.

before His crucifixion, Jesus promised them, "I will ask the Father to send you the Holy Spirit who will help you and always be with you. The Spirit will show you what is true. The people of this world cannot accept the Spirit, because they don't see or know him. But you know the Spirit, *who is with you and will keep on living in you*" (John 14:16, 17, CEV). That promise is for us too. The Apostle John remembered that promise from Jesus and confirmed it for us in his letter: "Those who obey his commands live in him, and he in them. *And this is how we know that he lives in us: We know it by the Spirit he gave us*" (1 John 3:24).

Austrian physicist Erwin Schrodinger understood that. He once said, "we know that whenever God is experienced, it is an experience exactly as real as a direct sense impression, as real as one's own personality."[30]

Antony Flew made his discovery of God late in life from the evidence that he saw in the operation of the universe. In the final paragraph of his book, *There is a God*, he reveals an openness to discovering something more. "The discovery of phenomena like the laws of nature…has led scientists, philosophers, and others to accept the existence of an infinitely intelligent Mind. Some claim to have made contact with this Mind. I have not—yet. But who knows what could happen next? Someday I might hear a Voice that says, 'Can you hear me now?'"[31]

To think about:

1. Gerald Schroeder uses the imagery of "the wake of a boat" to illustrate the evidence for God in the natural world. What aspects of nature provide that kind of evidence for you?

2. Some scientists see the existence of laws governing the operation of the universe as evidence for a "divine lawmaker." Discuss how this might also be true for moral law, including the Ten Commandments.

3. Physicist/mathematician Freeman Dyson said, "The more I examine the universe and study the details of its architecture, the more evidence I find that the universe in some sense knew we were coming." Discuss his comment in the context of our solar system and the physical earth we inhabit.

4. In what ways do you experience God?

References:

[1] Gerald Schroeder, *The Hidden Face of God*, 187.

[2] Antony Flew, *There is a God*, 91.

[3] Owen Gingerich, *God's Universe*, 12.

[4] Paul Davies, *The Mind of God*, 16, 232.

[5] John Foster, *The Divine Lawmaker*, 160.

[6] John Leslie, *Infinite Minds*, 213.

7   Kurt Goedel, cited by Palle Yourgrau in *A World Without Time*, 104.

8   Stephen Hawking, *A Brief History of Time*, 126,127.

9   Flew, 136.

10   Gingerich, 96.

11   Erwin Schrodinger, *My View of the World*, 93.

12   David Conway, *The Rediscovery of Wisdom*, 2.

13   Freeman Dyson, *Disturbing the Universe*, 250.

14   Marco Biagini, "Mind and brain," in *The Existence of God*, by John J. Pasquini, 37.

15   Wilder Penfield, *The Mystery of the Mind*, quoted in *The Case for a Creator* by Lee Strobel, 263–264.

16   Paul Davies, *The Origin of Life*, 86,87.

17   Marilyn Schlitz, "Do Brains make Minds?" 'Closer to Truth Roundtable'. (2010).

18   Richard Dawkins, quoted by Philip Higgs in *Rethinking Our World*, 2nd ed., 110.

19   Andrew Knoll, PBS Nova Interview, May 3, 2004.

20   Richard Dawkins, quoted by Peter S. Williams, "The Big Bad Wolf, Theism and the Foundations of Intelligent Design." *Evangelical Philosophical Society* paper.

21   Dawkins, *Climbing Mount Improbable*.

22   Schroeder, 49, 87.

23   Francis Crick, *Life Itself*, 88.

24   Michael Behe, quoted by Lee Strobel in *The Case for a Creator*, 298.

25   Fed Hoyle, "Hoyle on Evolution", *Nature*, November 12, 1981, 105.

26   Flew, 85, 157.

27   Richard Rice, *Suffering and the Search for Meaning*, 131, 133.

28   Barry Kosmin, *One Nation Under God*: Introduction.

29   Werner Heisenberg, *Naturwissenschaftliche und religioese Wahrheit*. Frankfurter Allgemeine Zeitung, March 24, 1974, 7.

30   Erwin Schrodinger, *Mind and Matter*, 68.

31   Flew, 158.

Chapter 17—Creation

In 1859, Charles Darwin published a book entitled *On the Origin of Species.* It proposed that all life evolved from more primitive forms through a process of natural selection. His theory presented a direct challenge to God and the creation story of Genesis. His book ushered in a new and drastically different worldview of the earth and the universe.

Fast forward to 1994. That year, in the course of a debate about Darwinism at Stanford University, William Provine, a professor of biological sciences at Cornell University, an atheist and critic of intelligent design, made this candid statement: "Let me summarize my views on what modern evolutionary biology tells us loud and clear, and I must say that these are basically Darwin's views. There are no gods, no purposeful forces of any kind, no life after death....There is no ultimate foundation for ethics, no ultimate meaning in life, and no free will for humans, either."[1]

In a world dominated by this kind of despair, astronomer Owen Gingerich makes this statement: "I would prefer to accept a universe created with intention and purpose by a loving God, and perhaps created with just enough freedom that conscience and responsibility are part of the mix. They may even be part of the reason that pain and suffering are also present in a world with its own peculiar integrity. This, for me is God's Universe."[2]

Did Darwin ever have "second thoughts" about his theory of evolution? In 1877, five years before his death, Darwin wrote and published his auto-biography, *Recollections of the Development of my Mind and Character.* His book contains this statement: "Reason tells me of the extreme difficulty or rather impossibility of conceiving this immense and wonderful universe, including man with his capability of looking far backwards and far into futurity, as the result of blind chance or necessity. When thus reflecting I feel compelled to look to a First Cause having an intelligent mind in some degree analogous to that of man; and I deserve to be called a Theist."[3]

Much has been learned since Darwin's time. One scientist, Gerald Schroeder, sees the miracle of the human body: "When thinking about sight, think of the symphony of molecular reactions of each optic nerve as the multitude of nerves communicate impulses, analyzing each impulse, deciding whether or not to pass on the impulse to other regions and other nerves. Think wonder. And ponder how a batch of carbon, nitrogen, oxygen, hydrogen, and a few other elements got together to cooperate so very wisely, thousands, even millions of times every second, throughout the brain and body. Had Darwin known of the wisdom hidden within life, I have confidence that he would have proposed a very different theory."[4]

Some Christians who believe in evolution would like to remove the first two chapters of Genesis from the Bible, but the truth of a Creator God is not limited to the Genesis story. It is a theme throughout Scripture, from the first verse of Genesis to the final chapters of Revelation.

Creation and the Scriptures

Some Christians who believe in evolution would like to remove the first two chapters of Genesis from the Bible, but the truth of a Creator God is not limited to the Genesis story. It is a theme throughout Scripture, from the first verse of Genesis to the final chapters of Revelation. We could complete this chapter with just biblical references to the creation. Here are just a few of them.

- *"In the beginning God created the heavens and the earth"* (Gen. 1:1).
- *"You alone are the Lord. You made the heavens, even the highest heavens, and all their starry host, the earth and all that is on it, the seas and all that is in them"* (Neh. 9:6),
- *"Where were you when I founded the earth?…Who laid its cornerstone? When the morning stars rejoiced together, and all the divinities shouted for joy"* (Job 38:4–7, CJB)?
- *"By the word of the Lord the heavens were made, and all the host of them by the breath of His mouth"* (Ps. 33:6, NKJV).
- *"My help comes from the Lord, the maker of heaven and earth"* (Ps. 121:1, 2).
- *"For this is what the Lord says—he who created the heavens, he is God; he who fashioned and made the earth, he founded it; he did not create it to be empty, but formed it to be inhabited"* (Isa. 45:18).
- *"Ah, Sovereign Lord, you have made the heavens and the earth by your great power and outstretched arm. Nothing is too hard for you"* (Jer. 32:17).
- *"Through him all things were made; without him nothing was made that has been made" (John 1:3).*
- *For by Him all things were created that are in heaven and that are on earth"* (Col. 1:16, NKJV).
- *"By faith we understand that the worlds were framed by the word of God"* (Heb. 11:3, NKJV).
- *"You are worthy, our Lord and God, to receive glory and honor and power, for you created all things, and by your will they were created and have their being"* (Rev. 4:11).
- *"Worship him who made the heavens, the earth, the sea and the springs of water"* (Rev. 14:7).
- *"Then I saw a new heaven and a new earth, for the first heaven and the first earth had passed away, and there was no longer any sea"* (Rev. 21:1).

In their study of the earth and universe, many scientists have found convincing evidence of a Creator God. That would not surprise the Apostle Paul. In his letter to the Romans, he points to the natural world as a revelation of divine activity: "For since the creation of the world God's invisible qualities—his eternal power and divine nature—have been clearly seen, being understood from what has been made, so that people are without excuse" (Rom. 1:20).

Gerald Schroeder, a Jewish scientist, agrees: "There is an ancient tradition that when divine revelation comes into the world, only one part is given as prophetic writings. The words are only a part of the message. The other part is placed within nature, the wisdom inherent in the Creation. Only when we understand those hidden wisdoms will we be able to read between the prophetic lines, and fully understand the message. With the help of science we are learning to read between the lines....The text is yielding to us the secrets at which the written words had only hinted."[5]

Ellen White said the same thing: "Since the book of nature and the book of revelation bear the impress of the same master mind, they cannot but speak in harmony. By different methods, and in different languages, they witness to the same great truths...The book of nature and the written word shed light upon each other."[6]

Lee Strobel, in *The Case for a Creator*, marshals convincing evidence from cosmology, physics, astronomy, biology, biochemistry, and mind studies to demonstrate that our earth and the life it supports were created. Then he concludes, "If God so precisely and carefully and lovingly and amazingly constructed a mind-boggling habitat for his creatures, then it would be natural for him to want them to explore it, to measure it, to investigate it, to appreciate it, to be inspired by it—and ultimately, and most importantly, to find him through it."[7]

As He completed His work of creation, God did something unique to commemorate what He had done. The last thing He created was also the first thing He made holy—not an object, place, or person, but a piece of intangible time—the Sabbath. The Sabbath predates Noah, Abraham, and Moses. Only Adam and Eve, the biblical parents of all humanity, predate the Sabbath. It was their first full day together. Think of it as their wedding day, the celebration of an intimate relationship with each other and their Creator. Schroeder acclaims the Sabbath as "the Bible's gift to all humanity, the crown of the six days of creation. It is the undersold super-product of the Bible. The essence of the Sabbath is rest....The Sabbath returns to us a taste of Eden, and helps us spread it through the entire week."[8]

Science and Inspired Writings

The following statement about creation is part of the twenty-eight fundamental beliefs of the Seventh-day Adventist Church, as affirmed in 2015: "God has revealed in Scripture the authentic and historical account of His creative activity. He created the universe, and in a recent six-day creation the Lord made 'the heavens and the earth, the sea, and all that is in them' and rested on the seventh day."[9]

Among Christian scientists, there is a great diversity of views about the biblical story of creation and how Genesis 1 should be interpreted. What follows in this chapter does not necessarily conflict with my church's fundamental belief in a recent six-day creation. Whatever you believe, I invite you to read the rest of this chapter with thoughtful understanding. Many of us struggle to fully understand the record of Genesis 1, but we can be respectful of those who come to it with a background or understanding that is different from our own.

How, for example, may we define "a recent" creation? We cannot precisely determine the age of the earth. Before the 20th century, most Christians believed that creation happened about 6,000 years ago. That was based on the widespread assumption that Bishop Usher's chronology of biblical history was accurate. Usher's dates were printed in every Bible. Thus, in Ellen White's time, it was society's "common knowledge" that 6,000 years had transpired since Creation. If she had given a figure different from "about six thousand years", her respect as an inspired writer would have been seriously undermined.

The Bible is our only source of truth about the creation of the earth and humankind, but is it up-to-date with scientific knowledge? Many Christians ask that question as they read the first chapter of Genesis. What is meant, they ask, by a body of water above the sky? "Then God said, 'Let there be a firmament in the midst of the waters, and let it divide the waters from the waters.'…God divided the waters which were under the firmament from the waters which were above the firmament.…God called the firmament Heaven" (Gen. 1:6–8, NKJV). And doesn't it seem odd that light appeared three days before the sun was created (Gen. 1:3, 14–16)? How does the account of Genesis equate with today's knowledge of the world and universe? Why did God not describe the earth and universe in terms of our 21st-century understanding of science?

These are important questions, but perhaps we can learn from an incident in 1846 involving Captain Joseph Bates. The sea captain had already accepted the Sabbath, but was undecided about the inspirational claims of a poorly educated, nineteen-year-old girl. Bates was present one day when Ellen White went into vision. She began to describe features of our solar system, including Jupiter with four moons and Saturn with rings and seven moons. Her descriptions coincided with what astronomers knew at that time. Bates' knowledge convinced him that her vision was God-given. Today, thanks to advances in astronomy, we know much more about our solar system. We know that both Jupiter and Saturn have more moons than Ellen White described, but God worked within the framework of that time and wisely did not show His messenger the full scientific truth about the things she saw in vision.[10]

We may apply the same understanding to the ancient text of the Bible. There may be a good reason why Moses, under inspiration, did not describe creation in terms of 19th-century science, or 20th-century science, or 21st-century science. Frankly, it would have seemed like nonsense to him and the Israelites. One Christian author explains, "God did not give the Bible's authors any supernatural knowledge of future scientific discoveries. There is no conflict between the Bible and science because the Bible is a book of spiritual and moral guidance; it was never intended to be a book of science or history."[11]

The Bible does not speak to us in terms of modern scientific knowledge, which is dynamic and ever advancing. The knowledge of astronomy has changed very much since Ellen White had her vision of the stars and planets. The Israelites received no revelation to update their understanding of the cosmos. They did not know that stars were suns, earth was spherical and moving through space, or the sun was much farther away than the moon. Therefore, we should not approach the Bible as if it has modern science embedded in it. The Bible is not a textbook of science.

John Walton taught biblical history at the Moody Bible Institute for twenty years and is now professor of Old Testament at Wheaton College in Illinois. A firm believer in the Genesis account of creation, he has authored several books on the topic. He writes, "It is helpful to understand that the Bible was written *for* us and for all human kind. But the Old Testament, in particular, was not written *to* us. It was written to Israel. It is God's revelation of Himself to Israel and secondarily through Israel to everyone else....They [the Hebrews] thought about the cosmos in much the same way that anyone

> *We must begin by understanding that there was no concept of a "natural" world in ancient Near Eastern thinking.*

in the ancient world thought, and not at all like anyone thinks today. And God did not think it important to revise their thinking."[12]

Walton says we must begin by understanding that there was no concept of a "natural" world in ancient Near Eastern thinking. Everything was "supernatural". To the ancients, the universe was populated with gods; gods were everywhere and powerful. They fought with each other over control of the universe. Everything that happened in daily life was caused by one god or another. Everything that happened was "supernatural". For the Israelites, every sunrise, every plant that grew, every drop of rain, and every climatic disaster was an act of their one God. He brought about the seasons. Every baby born was a work of God. David acknowledged, "For you created my inmost being; you knit me together in my mother's womb. I praise you because I am fearfully and wonderfully made" (Psalm 139:13, 14).

In our "enlightened" age, we look for *natural* causes for everything. We have little or no room for God. We limit the supernatural to things we cannot explain, such as miracles, and try to explain miracles as natural events if we can. For the Israelites, the parting of the Red Sea was no more supernatural than the sun rising every morning or finding figs on a fig tree. In their thinking, miracles were not supernatural events, but "signs and wonders" showing God's power and presence.

The ancients believed the heart, not the brain, was the organ where mental processes, emotions, and the will originated. Jeremiah understood it that way: "The heart is deceitful above all things, and desperately wicked; who can know it" (Jer. 17:9, NKJV)?

The account of Jonah being swallowed by a "great fish" may be hard to comprehend if we seek a natural explanation, but if God is all-powerful, we can be confident He made it happen. Jacob's experiment with genetic engineering by breeding "spotted and speckled sheep and goats" has no basis in animal genetics that we know of, but God respected his goal and gave him success (Gen. 30:29–39). Perhaps God honors our simple faith in similar ways. There may be more supernatural events in our lives than we recognize.

Ancient Cosmology and Creation

How did the ancients, including Moses and the Israelites, understand the cosmos? Our knowledge of the ancient past advances with new archaeological finds. From records of Babylonia, we learn of a widespread belief in a three-tiered universe, made up of a flat disc-shaped earth floating on water, with water also above a sky or firmament, and a watery underworld. Figure 10 helps us understand how many people visualized the cosmos from ancient times right through to the Middle Ages. The idea makes no sense to us today, but it was a common belief for thousands of years.[13] It was not until the fourth century B.C. that the Greeks developed the concept of a spherical earth. It was not until the Middle Ages that the spherical earth was accepted by the church, and it was not until the 16th century that Nicholas Copernicus discovered that the earth moves around the sun.

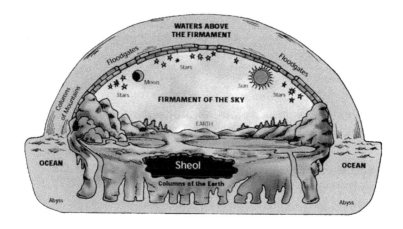

Figure 10: A Common Cosmology of the Ancient World.

The Hebrews may have shared the Babylonian concept of cosmology. We must ever keep in mind that the Bible was not written as a textbook of astronomical knowledge, which continues to advance. This helps us to read parts of the Old Testament in a new way. Notice how David described the daily course of the sun across the sky: "The heavens declare the glory of God....In them He has set a tabernacle for the sun, which is like a bridegroom coming out of his chamber....Its rising is from one end of heaven, and its circuit to the other end" (Ps. 19:1–6, NKJV). Today we know that the earth revolves around the sun.

Day two of creation is described in Genesis. "And God said, 'Let there be a vault between the waters to separate water from water.' So God made the vault and separated the water under the vault from the water above it" (Gen. 1:6, 7). The Psalmist describes the same activity poetically. "You who laid the foundations of the earth, so that it should not be moved forever; you covered it with the deep as with a garment; the waters stood above the mountains. At your rebuke, they fled; at the voice of your thunder they hastened away. They went up over the mountains; they went down into the valleys, to the place which you founded for them. You have set a boundary that they may not pass over, that they may not return to cover the earth" (Ps. 104:5–9, NKJV).

Job declares, "He drew a circular horizon on the face of the waters, at the boundary of light and darkness. The pillars of heaven tremble, and are astonished at his rebuke" (Job 26:10, 11, NKJV). In the thinking of the ancients, rain, snow, wind, and hail were kept in storehouses outside the firmament, which had "windows" to allow them in (see Job 38:22). Scripture describes the waters of the flood entering when the "windows of heaven" were opened (see Gen. 7:11).

By New Testament times, there were some new concepts, including levels of "heaven"—the sky, outer space, and the abode of God. Paul said, "I know a man in Christ who fourteen years ago—whether in the body I do not know, or whether out of the body I do not know, God knows—such a one was caught up to the third heaven. And I know such a man…was caught up into Paradise and heard inexpressible words, which it is not lawful for a man to utter" (2 Cor. 12:2–4, NKJV).

The account of creation in Genesis 1 is difficult to comprehend with today's scientific knowledge, but think about it. Moses grew up in the court of Pharaoh where he must have learned about strange creation myths involving the gods of Egypt; but when, under inspiration, he wrote about the six days of creation, God made certain that some eternal truths were instilled in the Genesis account for Israel and us. In contrast to the sordid creation stories of Egypt and Babylon involving conflict between the gods, the Genesis story comes to us as the sublime account of one supreme God who created the earth "ex nihilo"—out of nothing—with the single and beautiful purpose of making a perfect environment for the humans He placed there as His final act. The Genesis account inspires as we watch the six-day construction of a perfect home for humanity. Two Adventist scholars comment, "Since the Creator, who is none other than Christ… made the cosmos and all that belong to it, since He is the Maker of the forces of nature and the Sustainer of creation, He can use these forces to bring about His will in the drama of ongoing time through mighty acts and powerful deeds in nature and history."[14] We look ahead to a "new earth" creation—a beautiful home for redeemed humanity.

Ellen White and Science

Our understanding of the world and universe has come a long way since Old Testament times. However, science continues to be dynamic, and knowledge has increased vastly since the early 19th century when Ellen White made some observations. She encouraged an education in the sciences: "God is the Author of all true science."[15] She was unsparing in her denunciation of evolutionary theories that cast doubt upon the Scriptures, especially the six days of creation.[16]

In her earliest writings, Ellen White recorded some things about science and medicine that were considered to be correct at that time—part of her society's "common knowledge"—but are no longer supported by scientific and medical knowledge. Examples include the causes of earthquakes and volcanic eruptions[17] and a belief about "amalgamation of man and beast."[18] God did not give her future scientific knowledge, as we saw with her 1846 vision of the stars and planets.

The wall of sin and fear continues to darken our understanding of God and His universe. Among Bible students and scholars, there are different perceptions about creation and science and how we relate to what we find recorded in the Scriptures and writings of Ellen White. I need to be tolerant and accepting of other Bible students as we search for truth together. Just as we look for God's hand in biblical history, instead of getting hung up with strange numbers we can't explain, we must in the same way search for the meaning and purpose of God's creative work and not be side-tracked with exactly how or when He accomplished it.

All this teaches me to be humble. The universe is so vast, my understanding of it is so small, and God is greater than everything. I must place my trust in the One who created, looking beyond the "how" to the "why", tracing God's ultimate purposes throughout the ancient Scriptures.

> *The universe is so vast, my understanding of it is so small, and God is greater than everything.*

To think about:

1. Gerald Schroeder believes that "the Sabbath is the undersold super-product of the Bible." Discuss.

2. John Walton makes the point that the Bible, and particularly the Old Testament, was written *for* us, but not *to* us. Does this help us to better understand some of the difficult passages in the Old Testament?

3. God appears to have allowed Ellen White to include in her writings some 19th century "common knowledge" about science that is totally rejected today. How does that impact your understanding of inspiration?

References:

1   "Darwinism: Science or Naturalistic Philosophy?" The Debate at Stanford University, 1994.

2   Owen Gingerich, *God's Universe*, 96.

3   Charles Darwin, *Recollections of the Development of my Mind and Character*, 92.

4   Gerald Schroeder, *The Hidden Face of God*, 113.

5   *Ibid.*, 173, 187.

6   Ellen White, *Education*, 128.

7   Lee Strobel, *The Case for a Creator*, 202.

8   Schroeder, 181, 182.

9   *Seventh-day Adventists Believe.* General Conference of S.D.A., 2015.

10   Arthur L. White, *Ellen G. White: The Early Years, 1827–1862*, 113, 114; also J. N. Loughborough: *The Great Second Advent Movement*, 258.

11   Cliff Leitch, "Should the Bible be Interpreted Literally?" http://1ref.us/m6 (accessed October 10, 2017).

12   John H. Walton, *The Lost World of Genesis One*, 9, 16.

13   *NIV Cultural Backgrounds Study Bible*, 6, 836.

14   Gerard F. Hasel and Michael G. Hasel, "Unique Cosmology of Genesis 1", in *College and University Dialogue*, 28:1, 11.

15   White, *Fundamentals of Christian Education*, 329.

16   White, *Education*, 128.

17   White, *Spiritual Gifts*, 3:79, 80 (1864).

18   *Ibid.*, 63, 75 (1864).

Chapter 18—Wellness

As the Israelites left Egypt en route to the Promised Land, God gave them a generous promise: "If you diligently heed the voice of the Lord your God and do what is right in His sight…I will put none of the diseases on you which I have brought on the Egyptians. For I am the Lord who heals you" (Exod. 15:26, NKJV).

Sim McMillen was a young medical graduate from the University of Pennsylvania and the London School of Tropical Medicine when he travelled to Africa as a medical missionary in the 1930s. There he quickly discovered that medical science had little to offer for the treatment of leprosy and other tropical diseases, so he began applying biblical remedies, with amazing results. In 1963, he published a book entitled *None of These Diseases*. It became a best-seller and was recently revised and expanded by the author's physician grandson, David Stern.[1]

Medical Science and the Bible

Fascinated by God's conditional promise that He would protect the Israelites from the diseases of the Egyptians, McMillen made a study of

Egyptian medicine during the time of Moses and came up with some surprises. He learned that ancient Egypt was regarded as the medical center of the world, highly advanced for its time. Homer remarked in his *Odyssey*, "In Egypt, the men are more skilled in medicine than any of human kind."[2] The Greek historian, Herodotus, visited Egypt around 440 B.C. and wrote extensively of his observations about their medical practice. He recorded that King Darius of Persia "kept in attendance certain Egyptian doctors" because of their reputation. Ancient Egyptian medical documents, including the Edwin Smith Papyrus, which dates from the time of Moses (circa 1500 B.C.), detail anatomical observations and advanced surgical procedures. Excavations at the Egyptian temple of Kom Ombo uncovered a bas-relief of surgical instruments (see Figure 11).

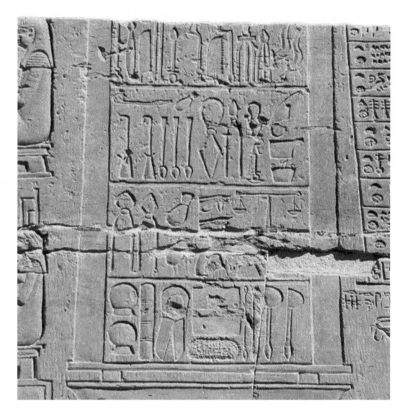

Figure 11: Egyptian Surgical Instruments.

Figure 12: Ebers Papyrus.

However, McMillen found a quite different story when it came to the treatment of illness and disease. He discovered that Egyptian medical practice was a complex blend of reason and superstition. It included medical sorcery and some bizarre treatments. Many of the potions used to treat illness were more toxic than the disease. The Ebers Papyrus (Figure 12) is an outline of herbal knowledge dating to 1550 B.C., the time of Moses. It records prescriptions, magical formulas, incantations, and many foul remedies.[3] Some examples:

- To cure pinkeye, apply the urine of a faithful wife.
- Heal splinters and wounds by applying a salve of worm blood and donkey dung.
- Yellow ochre-clay for intestinal and urological complaints.
- Crocodile dung for contraception.
- For headache, make a poultice of "ass's grease."
- The appearance of pus indicates that healing is taking place.

The widespread application of animal dung to wounds led to the spread of infection and frequent death. Leprosy was rarely recognized as a highly infectious disease in ancient civilizations, so there was no attempt to isolate or quarantine the sufferer.

Moses received his education in Egypt, but a comparison between Egyptian medical remedies and those found in the Pentateuch reveals that Moses did not rely on the wisdom of the Egyptians. The Mosaic health laws exhibit a conspicuous absence of the harmful practices that plagued the Egyptians.

The Mosaic health laws were a long way ahead of their time by focusing on the *prevention* of disease, the choice of *clean foods*, *sanitary practices*, proper *waste disposal*, cleanliness by *frequent washing*, and *quarantine procedures*. In the case of leprosy, "As long as they have the disease they remain unclean. They must live alone; they must live outside the camp" (Lev. 13:46). The Pentateuch exhibits an understanding of germs and disease that much of modern medicine did not grasp for 3,500 years (see Lev. 11–20). God also gave the Israelites moral instruction about sexual practices (see Lev. 18:1–3).

Long before Moses, God commanded Abraham to perform male circumcisions on the eighth day after birth (see Gen. 17:12). McMillen points out that this is the ideal time to carry out the procedure because it ensures that the infant's blood readily clots after bleeding. For the first four days after birth, an infant has a limited amount of vitamin K and clotting factors in its blood. On day five the level of these agents increases, reaching 110 percent of the adult level on day eight.[4]

It is interesting that God did not give His prophet information on every medical practice. Some Mosaic practices may reflect commonly accepted cultural beliefs and practices of his time. The test for a wife's infidelity, recorded in Numbers 5:11–31, makes no sense to us today and would be considered an abuse of a woman's rights.

Medical Science in the 19th Century

Skip ahead 3,000 years. The bubonic plague, known as the Black Death, swept Europe during the 14th century, halving its population. What is astonishing is that European medicine had no idea that the plague was caused by a parasite carried by rats.[5] Five hundred years later, in the mid-19th century, physicians and scientists were struggling to find their way out of a medical wilderness that had gripped the western world for nearly two millennia. In 1864 Louis Pasteur demonstrated the existence of germs for the first time. But medical practice in the 19th century could hardly be called "medical science" by today's standards. Going to a doctor often decreased a sick person's probability of survival and recovery from sickness.[6] Typical medical practices included:

- Blood-letting as a common treatment for health problems.
- Prescription of poisons such as strychnine and arsenic to cure ailments.
- Fresh air, exercise, and use of water were considered unnecessary or even dangerous.
- Medical staff saw no need to wash their hands before, during, or after surgeries and autopsies.

On this last point, McMillen tells about an Austrian physician, Dr. Semmelweis. In 1847 Semmelweis was practicing in the maternity ward of a large hospital in Vienna, where he discovered that the spread of child-birth fever and the death of mothers could be *prevented* if birth attendants simply washed their hands after doing deliveries or autopsies.[7] Yet biblical health laws promoted this practice 3,500 years earlier: "Whoever touches a human corpse will be unclean for seven days." (Num.19:11) A new mother was declared unclean for seven or fourteen days. (Lev.12)

During the 1830s in America, Sylvester Graham led a popular health-reform movement by prescribing a vegetarian diet, pure water, physical exercise, cleanliness, and avoidance of most dairy products. James C. Jackson opened "Our Home on the Hillside" in Dansville, New York, using hydrotherapy and a health model based on ten natural remedies: air, food, water, sunlight, dress, exercise, sleep, rest, social and moral influence. Despite those positive concepts, they and other health reformers of the time had a confused offering of advice, as these examples illustrate:[8]

- By shaving or cutting their hair, men reduce their manly powers and shorten their life.
- Night air is bad for one's health.
- Don't nurse babies at night.
- Babies should not be rocked to sleep.
- Don't heat your house.
- Avoid activities that cause you to perspire.
- Marital sexual activity is dangerous to health.
- Phrenology is scientific.
- Avoid use of soap.
- Overweight people are healthy people.

- Do not sleep in the same bed with someone else.
- When eating meat, eat mostly the fat.
- If you must eat meat, eat it raw.
- Avoid salt.
- Sugar is good for you.
- You can live exclusively on bread.
- Get your liquids from fruit, not water.
- Don't let children eat fruit.
- Avoid most vegetables, except potatoes.
- Children should not be fed potatoes.
- Avoid cucumbers.
- Breakfast may be skipped.

Even James Harvey Kellogg, MD, practicing in the late 19th century, had some peculiar advice:

- Don't indulge in sex more than once a month.
- Women under 30 and men under 25 should not have sex.
- Surgical circumcision before puberty will improve a girl's health.
- Masturbation causes insanity.
- Do not squint or roll your eyes.

Ellen White and Health Science

Ellen White wrote a great deal about health, recognizing that health of the body has a close relationship to mental health. "Anything that lessens physical strength enfeebles the mind and makes it less capable of discriminating between right and wrong. We become less capable of choosing the good and have less strength of will to do that which we know to be right."[9]

As a young mother, Ellen White read widely from the works of the health reformers of her time, and prior to her major health vision of 1863, she supported a number of their health practices. In 1858 she rebuked the Haskell family for telling their Adventist friends that they should abstain from pork: "If God requires His people to abstain from swine's flesh, He will convict them on that matter."[10] That conviction came with the Health Reform vision of 1863.

Ellen's first health vision in 1848 warned against tobacco and stimulants such as coffee; her second in 1854 counseled against use of rich foods. Then, less than one month after the formal organization of the Seventh-day Adventist Church in May 1863, she received her major health reform vision. "It was at the house of Brother A. Hilliard, at Otsego,

Michigan, on June 6, 1863, that the great subject of health reform was opened before me in vision."[11] The vision lasted about 45 minutes. Some of it was counsel given specifically to alleviate James White's deteriorating health; the rest was general counsel for the church. A partial account was written by Ellen shortly after it was received. The full account was published in 1864.[12] That vision paved the way for new understandings about health, including use of a plant-based diet, and established the Seventh-day Adventist emphasis on health and wholeness.

Ellen White said that "health reform is a part of the third angel's message" but emphasized that "it is not the message."[13] Already in the 1860s Adventists were tending toward fanatical extremes in regard to health reform. Some were putting it at the center of the denomination's message. Ellen White had to argue against perversions of her teachings on health for the remainder of her life.

In *Prophetess of Health*, Ronald Numbers argued that virtually all of Ellen White's health principles were based on her reading from the health reformers of her day. Leonard Brand comments, "It is evident that the health-reform movement was well underway long before Mrs. White wrote on the subject. It is also evident that at least some of her health concepts significantly resemble those that other reformers were advocating."[14] This brings an important question: Did Ellen White receive her health messages from God, or from other human sources?

Early this century an Australian physician, Don S. McMahon, conducted a detailed study of Ellen White's stated principles of health for which she claimed inspiration, assessing each one from the findings of 21st century medicine. The research was professionally conducted with co-assessments by other physicians. McMahon identified 46 clear health and medical statements published by Ellen White in 1864, following her health reform vision.[15] Each one was checked against modern medical knowledge. From the study, McMahon was able to find medical support for 44 of those statements, leaving just 2 unverified by modern medicine in 2005.[16] The two 1864 health statements which were not medically verifiable were these: Avoid leaven in bread, and Eat two meals a day usually.

The 44 medically verified statements represents a 96% score—a high level of correctness—as we should expect if they came by way of inspiration. McMahon then looked at dozens of health and medical statements published by four health reformers who were contemporary with Ellen White in the 1850s and 1860s, as well as health statements published by Dr. John Harvey Kellogg in the 1890s. A comparison of the percentage of verifiable health principles enunciated by these reformers with those from Ellen White following her 1863 vision, is quite startling. See Figure 13.

Brand concludes: "Dr. Don McMahon's research reveals a dramatic difference in quality between Mrs. White's health principles and those advanced by other health reformers in the 1800s. . . . This difference indicates that Mrs. White had health information that could not have come from any human source available anywhere at the time she lived and wrote."[17]

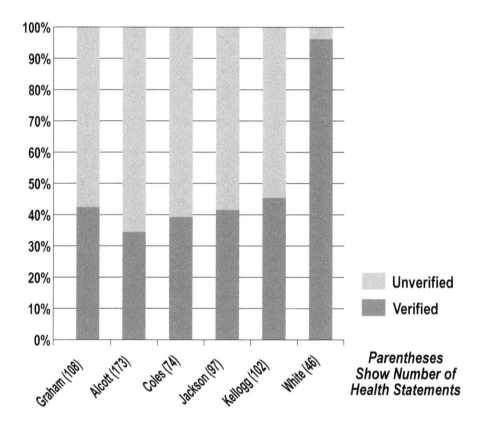

Figure 13: Health Reformers of the 19th Century

McMahon went on to study Ellen White's *Ministry of Healing,* published in 1905, finding 40 new health statements, additional to the 46 principles from her 1863 health reform vision. He found that 31 (78%) of these new statements were medically verifiable in 2005. He noted that her 1864 high level of correctness (96%) declined as she continued reading various health publications. He identified the following health advice in

Ministry of Healing (1905) that could not be verified from medical science in 2005. None of them originated from Ellen White's 1863 health vision.

- Avoid eating both fruit and vegetables at any one meal.
- Cheese is wholly unfit for food.
- Do not eat blood.
- Do not eat very hot or cold food (should be lukewarm).
- Don't allow waste vegetables or heaps of fallen leaves to remain near the house.
- Don't engage in intensive study right after eating.
- Don't engage in violent or excessive exercise immediately before or after eating.
- Don't eat when you are excited, anxious, or hurried.
- The more liquid you take with a meal, the more difficulty you will have digesting the meal.

(McMahon notes that the last two practices do slow digestion, but are not considered medically to be a health hazard.)[18]

Ellen White did not always understand the *reason* for a particular medical or health statement that she received in vision. She emphasized some health principles even when she could not explain why they were given. "I use some salt, and always have, because from the light given me by God, this article, in the place of being deleterious, is actually essential for the blood. The whys and wherefores of this I know not, but I give you the instruction as it is given me."[19]

In most cases, God did not tell Ellen White *why* the health principles He revealed to her were important. She was shown *what* practices were important, but not *why* they were important. So while most of the health principles—the "what's"—are consistent with the findings of modern medicine, the same cannot be said of the reasons—the "why's"—she sometimes gave for following those principles. For example, she was shown that flesh foods should be avoided, but she gave as a reason that use of flesh foods "excites the animal propensities to increased activity, and strengthens the animal passions. . . . The use of flesh of animals tends to cause a grossness of body, and benumbs the fine sensibilities of the mind."[20] Avoiding coffee, she claimed, was important because its use unbalanced the nervous system, made the liver inactive, and injured the mind.[21] Those reasons are not supported by modern medicine.

God did not give Ellen White a complete set of health principles, nor the explanations to support them. After 1863 she continued to read from the popular reformers of her time. She was exposed to many commonly held beliefs and remedies that are no longer verifiable by modern medicine. From her reading, she wrote about the dangers of cosmetics, possible insanity from wearing wigs, leprosy and cancer from eating pork, and severe mental and physical effects of masturbation. She had her sons Edson and Willie examined by a phrenologist.[22]

God gave Ellen White much health information that is only now medically verifiable, but He did not stop her from reading widely and choosing some commonly held ideas of her time. It must have been like that when God gave health regulations to Moses. He was not given information on every medical practice. Some strange pieces of advice in the Mosaic health laws likely came from commonly accepted beliefs and practices of his time. This reminds us again that prophetic writings were not verbally dictated by the Holy Spirit. God's messengers were also exposed to the common knowledge of their times, and did their best to convey truth as they understood it.

My personal response to what we have shared in this chapter is to rejoice that God created me to become a whole person, mentally, spiritually, physically, and socially. I find that truth in the Scriptures, and I find it is strongly supported in the messages God gave to Ellen White.

To think about:

1. Why is health and wellness an important aspect of the life of a Bible-based Christian?

2. Ellen White was not always given reasons for some of the health statements given to her in vision. How might that influence your reading of her writings on health?

3. Neither Moses in Israel's time, nor Ellen White in modern times, were given complete information on health and wellness. Think about this in relation to God's communication with humanity, and His emphasis on human freedom to reason and to make intelligent choices.

References:

[1]   S.I. McMillen and David E. Stern, *None of These Diseases.*
[2]   Ellie Crystal, "Ancient Egyptian Medicine"
[3]   Wikipedia: "Ancient Egyptian Medicine."

4   McMillen, 80–85.

5   Norman Cantor, quoted by Sigve Tonstad, in *The Lost Meaning of the Seventh Day*, 329.

6   Leonard Brand and Don S. McMahon, *The Prophet and Her Critics*, 36.

7   McMillen, 17–26.

8   Brand, 77-79.

9   Ellen White, *Christ's Object Lessons*, 346.

10   White, *Testimonies* 1:206, 207.

11   White, *Review and Herald*, Oct.8, 1867.

12   White, *Spiritual Gifts*, v.2.

13   White, *Testimonies* 1:559.

14   Ronald Numbers, *Prophetess of Health;* Brand, 40.

15   These 46 principles are listed in Brand and McMahon, 76.

16   Brand, 58–63.

17   Brand, 87,88.

18   Brand, 79.

19   Letter from Ellen White to Drs. Daniel and Lauretta Kress, May 29, 1901.

20   White, *Testimonies* 2: 63.

21   White, *Christian Temperance and Bible Hygiene*, 35.

22   Graeme Bradford, *More Than a Prophet*, 132,133.

Understanding

Chapter 19—Crisis

In September 1900, Ellen White disembarked in San Francisco at the end of a long voyage from Sydney, Australia. Back in America, after nine years in Australia, she found a church that had changed very much since her departure in 1891. World membership had doubled to 68,000 in those nine years, and most of the increase had happened in the United States, where there were now 55,000 Seventh-day Adventists. Membership growth had been remarkable ever since 1863 when the church was formally organized with just 3,500 believers. Ellen White saw that a reorganization of church structure was overdue: "What we want now is a reorganization. We want to begin at the foundation and build upon a different principle", she told the leaders.[1] Due to her influence, the 1901 General Conference Session in Battle Creek voted into existence a new church structure of divisions, unions, local conferences, and missions.

Several other issues were bothering the Adventist Church on the threshold of the 20th century. Some believers in Indiana were shouting and praying until they fell prostrate and obtained "holy flesh" by the Spirit. A similarly aberrant concept had taken hold among one or two church leaders and some physicians at the Battle Creek Sanitarium, where Dr. John

Harvey Kellogg was about to publish a book entitled *The Living Temple*. It espoused a pantheistic view in which God was believed to be present in grass, trees, and water. Ellen White came out strongly against these fanatical beliefs.

Battle Creek, Michigan had been the home of the Adventist Church since its birth in 1863. There was now a continual migration to this "Jerusalem" of Seventh-day Adventism. The city was the location of the church's headquarters, Battle Creek College, Battle Creek Sanitarium, and the Review and Herald Publishing Association. Even before she left for Australia in 1891, Ellen warned of the dangers of centering everything in one location. Lethargy prevailed, however, until fire destroyed the Battle Creek Sanitarium in February 1902, and months later the Review and Herald building went up in flames. The college had already been moved to a new site at Berrien Springs, Michigan. At the 1903 General Conference Session, the decision was made to move church headquarters to Washington D.C.

Crisis of Understanding

Because of Ellen White's long absence overseas, more than half of the North American membership had not set eyes on her, though they were acquainted with her books, which were always on sale in Battle Creek and at local camp meetings. People recognized her as their authentic prophet and surrounded her with an aura of infallibility. Most believed her every word was inspired by the Lord.

Why shouldn't they? The 1890s in America saw the rapid growth of the Protestant Fundamentalist Movement as a reaction to higher criticism and Charles Darwin's theory of evolution. At its core, the Fundamentalist Movement emphasized that the Bible was infallible, inerrant (without error), and with every word inspired by the Holy Spirit. The annual Niagara Bible Conference attracted a lot of attention among Protestants. No surprise, then, that Seventh-day Adventist leaders and clergy were increasingly found in the fundamentalist camp with its belief in verbal inspiration of the biblical prophets. Surely Ellen White must also fit that description.

However, Ellen White did *not* support the concept of verbal inspiration. On two occasions before 1900, she had given clear counsel on understanding inspiration of the Scriptures. "The writers of the Bible had to express their ideas in human language. *It was written by human men*. These men were inspired of the Holy Spirit.... *It is not the words of the Bible that are inspired*, but the men that were inspired. Inspiration acts not on the man's words or his expressions but on the man himself, who, under the influence of the Holy Spirit, is imbued with thoughts. But the words receive the impress of the individual mind. The divine mind is diffused. The divine mind and will is combined with the human mind and will; thus the utterances of the man are the word of God"[2] (italics mine).

Unfortunately, these clear words about divine inspiration, penned in 1886, remained unpublished until 1958, when they appeared in *Selected Messages*, Book 1. Meanwhile, the growing influence of the higher criticism movement caused most Seventh-day Adventists to gravitate toward the fundamentalist teaching of inerrancy and verbal dictation for the inspiration of the Bible. That influence extended to Ellen White's own writings, in spite of her denial of this claim. Figure 14 shows the spread of views about Ellen White's inspiration.

Liberal View	Central View	Fundamentalist View
"Divine element" perhaps?	Visions and Inspired Thoughts, not Words	Verbally Inspired
Fraudulent Claims	Points to Bible as the Source of Truth	Source of Truth for Our Time
Her Writings not be taken Seriously	Her Writings to be Read with Understanding	Her Writings to be Understood Literally
Unreliable for Facts of History and Science	Common Knowledge about History and Science not given by Inspiration	Reliable Source of History and Science

Figure 14: Different Understandings of Ellen White's Inspiration.

Unfortunately, several Seventh-day Adventist administrators and pastors went along with the fundamentalist view of inspiration, believing that the biblical prophets wrote the very words given to them by the Holy Spirit. And if that was true of the Bible, would it not also be true of their prophet, Ellen White? They weren't listening to what she was saying and writing about inspiration and her own infallibility. "In regard to infallibility, I never claimed it; God alone is infallible."[3] Unfortunately, some of the church's brightest scholars fell for the flawed fundamentalist concept of inspiration.

Meanwhile, the growing influence of the higher criticism movement caused most Seventh-day Adventists to gravitate toward the fundamentalist teaching of inerrancy and verbal dictation for the inspiration of the Bible. That influence extended to Ellen White's own writings, in spite of her denial of this claim.

- Dudley M. Canright was an Adventist pastor for many years, but by 1900 he had become the foremost critic of the church and Ellen White. His book on the life of Ellen White, published in 1919, reflects what he had believed for a long time: "Every line she wrote, whether in articles, letters, testimonies, or books, she claimed was dictated to her by the Holy Ghost, and hence must be infallible."[4]

- David Paulson, a physician who founded Hinsdale Sanitarium, also misunderstood the nature of inspiration. Writing to her in 1906, he said, "I was led to conclude and most firmly believe that *every* word that you ever spoke in public or private, that *every* letter you wrote under *any* and *all* circumstances, was as inspired as the ten commandments." Ellen White responded: "My brother, you have studied my writings diligently, and you have never found that I have made any such claims."[5]

- Edward Ballenger, a brother of Albion F. Ballenger, was a pastor in southern California when he challenged what Ellen White had written about Paradise Valley Sanitarium. She made reference to forty rooms in the sanitarium, but in fact there were only thirty-eight rooms. Responding to Ballenger, she wrote, "The information given concerning the number of rooms in the Paradise Valley Sanitarium was given, not as a revelation from the Lord, but simply as a human opinion...There are times when common things must be stated. Such words, such information, are not given under the special inspiration of the Spirit of God."[6] Both Ballenger brothers held that Ellen White was verbally inspired in everything that she wrote. Both left the Adventist church and became outspoken critics of the church and Ellen White.

- Stephen Haskell was a prominent evangelist, administrator, and pioneer Adventist missionary to New Zealand. He was disturbed when a new edition of *The Great Controversy* was published in 1911, with corrections to historical details. How, he wondered, could an inspired document be corrected or changed in any way? He received an explanatory letter from W.C. White, which said, in part, "Regarding mother's writings, she has never wished our brethren to treat them as authority on history." Haskell was not satisfied with the explanation, believing that W.C. White used "precisely the same reasoning as the higher critics of the Bible… which destroys the inspiration of the Testimonies."[7]

- Alonzo T. Jones, who preached righteousness by faith at the 1888 General Conference Session, later became entangled with perfectionism and a belief in verbal inspiration. Seizing upon a statement of Ellen White that she did not claim "the title of prophet or prophetess", Jones became openly critical and eventually abandoned the faith.

- Like A.T. Jones, John Harvey Kellogg held to a very literal and rigid view for interpreting Ellen White's writings. Both men were critical of Arthur G. Daniells, the General Conference president at that time. Kellogg's views about pantheism, strongly opposed by Ellen White, finally led him to sever his connection with the church.

Unfortunately, these men of responsibility did not remember an action taken at the 1883 General Conference Session, when a decision was taken to republish the text of Ellen White's early *Testimonies*. She herself said the text needed some work in correction and careful editing, because some of the testimonies had been written "under the most unfavorable circumstances."[8]

The 1883 General Conference Session approved the task, emphasizing that Adventists "believe the light given by God to His servants is by the enlightenment of the mind, thus imparting the thoughts, and *not (except in rare cases) the very words in which the ideas should be expressed*"[9] (italics mine). The editorial work was completed in 1884. The first four volumes of *Testimonies for the Church* resulted from that republication.

Ellen White   David Paulson   Alonzo T Jones   John H Kellogg

Arthur G Daniells   W W Prescott   Stephen Haskell   Dudley Canright

Figure 15: Adventist Persons of the Early 1900s.

Did these men not read or understand Ellen White's own introduction to *The Great Controversy*, a book which they knew well and deeply respected? There she had written when it was first published in 1888: "The Bible points to God as its author; *yet it was written by human hands; and in the varied style of its different books it presents the characteristics of the several writers.* The truths revealed are all 'given by inspiration of God' yet they are *expressed in the words of men....*The truth was entrusted in earthen vessels, yet it is, nonetheless, from Heaven"[10] (italics mine).

Ellen White was continually perplexed and embarrassed by the popular view that every word spoken or recorded by a prophet of God was inspired. Despite her several attempts to clarify her role, the majority of Adventists continued to hold her every word as inspired by the Lord. For her it was a no-win situation. On April 1, 1901, one day before the official beginning of the General Conference Session, she addressed a large group of church leaders in the Battle Creek College Library. Can you sense her frustration as she spoke about their relationship to the Bible and her own writings? *"Do not repeat what I have said, saying 'Sister White said this' and 'Sister White said that.' Find out what the Lord God of Israel says, and then do what He commands. Do not quote my words again as long as you live, until you can obey the Bible"*[11] (italics mine).

Two men who *did* understand the nature of Ellen White's inspiration were W.W. Prescott and Arthur G. Daniells. Prescott stood out among early church leaders as an able administrator, scholar, and educator. He became the first vice-president of the General Conference in 1902 and was a member of the Executive Committee for forty-two years. Prescott had worked closely with Ellen White in preparing some of her books for publication, including *The Desire of Ages* and *Christian Education*. In 1909, he was entrusted with revisions and historical corrections for the 1911 reprint of *The Great Controversy*. According to Gilbert Valentine, who wrote Prescott's biography, "the professor never wavered from his deep conviction that Ellen White exhibited the genuine gift of prophecy, but on the basis of his own intimate acquaintance with the editorial process involved in preparing her publications, he advocated the need for more openness on the part of the White Estate and the church about the dynamics of the editorial process."[12]

The other leader who understood the nature of Ellen White's inspiration was Arthur G. Daniells. Called to New Zealand and Australia in 1886, Daniells spent fourteen years establishing the church in those countries. He had close association with Ellen White throughout her nine years of ministry there (1891 to 1900). Returning to America in 1901, Daniells was immediately elected president of the General Conference. For the next twenty-one years, he guided the church through some turbulent times and continued to communicate regularly with Ellen White until her death in 1915, when he delivered her funeral address in the Battle Creek Tabernacle. He maintained a firm faith in her prophetic ministry, even when he received counsels from her that confronted his mistakes and sometimes harsh administrative style.

Bible Conference Crisis

Ellen White died in 1915. During her lifetime, she saw the Seventh-day Adventist Church develop and grow from a handful of disappointed Millerites in 1844 to a truly worldwide movement. At the time of her death, church membership numbered 136,000. God had guided His special messenger in amazing ways during her seventy years of ministry.

On December 6, 1974, Donald Yost, newly appointed by the General Conference to establish an archives office at church headquarters, made an interesting discovery. In a vault, he found two packages that had been stashed away for a long time. The packages contained 1,200 typewritten pages that were the minutes of a conference of Adventist teachers and administrators held in July and August of 1919. Yost's discovery proved to be a significant one for the traditional Adventist understanding of Ellen White's inspiration.

Confused thinking about inspiration was still very much the case in 1919, four years after Ellen White's death, when the General Conference convened a meeting of the church's leading teachers, writers, and admin-istrators to discuss issues related to the historical fulfillment and inter-pretation of Bible prophecies. Sixty-five participants attended the Bible conference, which dealt with several theological issues.

Of special interest, though, was a concurrent "Bible and History Teachers' Council" attended by twenty-two delegates. It was in this coun-cil that the topic of inspiration came up for discussion. Chairing two days of meetings that deliberated about the inspiration issue was Arthur G. Daniells, who had served as president of the General Conference for the past eighteen years. During the sometimes-heated discussion, Daniells responded to questions regarding Ellen White's use of literary helpers in her writing. Some questioned whether some of her books were inspired. Daniells reported what he had personally witnessed, during his years in Australia, of the writing process for *The Desire of Ages* and *Christ's Object Lessons.* Marian Davis was then Ellen White's assistant in the preparation of both books. What Daniells had observed did not diminish his confi-dence in these books as inspired writings.

Delegates expressed fear because so many Adventists believed that "every word that Sister White has written was to be received as infallible truth." One expressed concern that "our students are being sent out with the idea that the *Testimonies* are verbally inspired, and woe be to the man out there where I am that does not line up to that." Responding, Daniells said, "It is of no use for anybody to stand up and talk about the verbal inspiration of the Testimonies, because everybody who has ever seen the work done knows better, and we might as well dismiss it." Summing up, Daniells said, "Our difficulty lies in two points, especially. One is on infal-libility, and the other is on verbal inspiration."[13]

The 1919 meetings concluded without consensus on the issue of Ellen White and inspiration, but two main views emerged:

- Some (labeled the "progressives") held that Ellen White's writings were not infallible, but many of them believed that the Bible is inerrant, infallible, and verbally inspired.

- Others (the "traditionalists") regarded the writings of Ellen White as infallible and equal to Scripture, both being verbally inspired.

Church leaders, fearing that church members would become "terribly upset" if they discovered that Ellen White was not infallible, tucked the conference proceedings away in the basement of the General Conference building where they lay, forgotten, until Yost found them in 1974, and made them public.[14]

Adventist historian George Knight helps us understand the inspiration issue during the 1920s in America: "That decade saw polarization on the topics of verbalism and inerrancy between the fundamentalists and the liberals. While the liberals explained away the divinity of Scripture, the fundamentalists made their definitions so rigid that they are still warring over them nearly a century later. Adventism found itself caught in the midst of the crisis over inspiration and in the process, unfortunately, lost its balanced position....The loss of Ellen White's and Adventism's moderate stance on inspiration during the 1920s set the church up for decades of difficulties in interpreting the Bible and the writings of Ellen White. The resulting problems have led to extremism, misunderstandings, and bickering in Adventist ranks that exist, unfortunately, until the present."[15]

Merlin Burt adds to Knight's comments: "Certain repetitive patterns appear among Ellen White's opponents. First, those who reject her visions usually reject the idea of modern prophetic special revelation. Second, they hold to a more verbal view of inspiration and reject the idea of progressive or unfolding revelation. They typically do not allow the prophetic messenger to grow in his/her understanding of God's revelation over time and with repetition."[16]

In the final moments of the 1919 discussions, J. N. Anderson, a teacher from Union College, phrased two questions: "*Is it well to let our people in general go on holding to the verbal inspiration of the Testimonies? When we do that, aren't we preparing for a crisis that will be very serious some day?*" No one attempted to answer those questions; but today, nearly a century later, we face a crisis in our understanding of revelation and inspiration:

- A neglect of the Bible as God's primary revelation to us.
- Placing Ellen White on a pedestal and using her writings to interpret the Bible.
- A belief in verbal inspiration for Ellen White.
- At the opposite extreme, abandoning belief in the inspiration and authority of Ellen White as God's special messenger.

A Personal Crisis

A sick, five-year-old boy was taken by ambulance to a distant hospital in 1943. The prognosis: tetanus. For six weeks, his body struggled with disease and pneumonia. At home, the church prayed for his recovery and the parents promised God that if their boy recovered, they would dedicate him for their Lord's service. A report in the regional newspaper said his recovery was a miracle.[17]

I sensed that God had a plan for my life. Twelve years after that trauma, I began four years of study at Avondale College. My major was education, but a required religion course in each year of study instilled a firm faith in my Adventist upbringing and brought spiritual satisfaction. I completed my college education with a certainty that both the Bible and Ellen White were verbally inspired and infallible.

Within a year after graduation, at the urging of the Avondale College president, I began study in librarianship. Returning to the school in 1961 as its first qualified librarian, I found that many things required my attention. The library's Spirit of Prophecy collection needed a fresh approach. As I browsed and cataloged some of Ellen White's books, I came upon some utterances of my beloved prophet that shook me to the core of my being, like the amalgamation of men with animals and unscientific nonsense about earthquakes and volcanoes.

I have already described in my preface to this book what resulted from those discoveries. For twenty-five years, I discarded Ellen White from my reading and serious consideration. The camp-meeting experience of 1967 plumbed the depth of my spiritual discouragement.

However, I praise God that my journey did not end there. God had a plan for me to grow in my understanding of inspiration.

To think about:

1. Throughout this book, we have highlighted different understandings of the way inspiration functioned for biblical prophets and Ellen White in our time. Study Figure 14 carefully before deciding where you presently stand in relation to the inspiration of Ellen White.

2. Jewish leaders seriously misunderstood the role of Jesus Christ when He came. Do you see a parallel between that time and the misunderstandings of Adventist leaders about inspiration around the beginning of the 20th century?

3. Standing before church administrators on the eve of the 1901
    General Conference Session, Ellen White said plainly, "Do not
    quote my words again as long as you live, until you can obey the
    Bible." Could that remark be applicable to us today? Why or why
    not?

References:

1   *General Conference Bulletin*, April 3, 1901.

2   Ellen White, Manuscript 24, 1886; *Selected Messages*, 1:19, 21.

3   White, Letter 10, 1895.

4   Dudley M. Canright, *Life of Ellen White*, Preface.

5   "Correct Views Concerning the Testimonies" published in *Review and Herald,
    August 30, 1906*; also in *Selected Messages*, 1:24.

6   White: Manuscript 107, 1909.

7   Quoted by George R. Knight, "The case of the overlooked postscript,"
    Ministry, August 1997, 9–11.

8   White, *Selected Messages*, 3:96.

9   General Conference Proceedings, *Review and Herald*, November 27, 1883.

10 White, *Great Controversy*, v, vii.

11 White, Manuscript 43, 1901.

12 Gilbert Valentine, article about Prescott in *The Ellen G. White Encyclopedia*,
    495.

13 All quotations from the Bible Conference are taken from "Transcripts of the 1919
    Bible Conference", *Spectrum*, vol. 10, no. 1, May 1979, 21–58.

14 Michael Campbell, *The 1919 Bible Conference and Its Significance for Seventh-
    day Adventist History and Theology* (Andrews University Dissertation).

15 George Knight, *A Brief History of Seventh-day Adventists*, 129, 130.

16 Merlin Burt, "Bibliographic Essay on Publications about Ellen G. White" in *The
    Ellen G. White Encyclopedia*, 149.

17 Keith Clouten, *The Road from Stoney Creek: A Personal Journey* (2014).

PART THREE:
RESTORATION

The wall is still there,

massive and repulsive,

mocking every attempt to peer over it,

to find a way around it,

or to penetrate its stubborn silence.

Am I alone in my despair and doubt?

Does anyone else share my story?

Or a story that is something like mine?

But God is busy.

He had a plan for me to discover,

and He has one for you too!

Stay with me as we explore together

these final chapters.

The wall must go!

We cling to a great hope that promises

the renewal of relationship

with our Creator.

A glorious

Restoration

.

Restoration

Chapter 20—Growing

Growing is also about dying. Molecular biologists inform us that our bodies are composed of trillions of cells, and the bad news is that every second of our lifetime millions of them give up and die. The good news is that they are replaced—every second—by millions of new cells. The life cycle of each cell is carefully controlled; each type of cell in your body has its own defined lifespan. Physically, you have a different body every second because, from creation, God implanted wisdom in our cellular structure.

This wisdom and growth are ceaseless and miraculous. Job recognized it: "In his hand is the life of every creature and the breath of every human being" (Job 12:10). King David exclaimed, "The Lord keeps me alive" (Ps. 54:4, NLT)! Expounding on the miracle of life, God gives this very personal assurance: "I have cared for you since you were born. Yes, I carried you before you were born. I will be your God throughout your lifetime—until your hair is white with age. I made you, and I will care for you" (Isa. 46:3, 4, NLT).

The largest retail establishment in Sydney, Australia, used to be known for its motto, "While I live, I'll grow." To live is to grow, not only physically, but in every other way. Luke says that "as Jesus grew up, he increased in wisdom and in favor with God and people" (Luke 2:52). In this chapter, we will seek evidence of spiritual growth in men and women of the Bible and in our time. So many of God's prophets and kings were broken people. They experienced moral failures, weak faith, a lack of knowledge and understanding, and sometimes their spiritual life suffered decline instead of growth. Nevertheless, God's grace and forgiveness was always ready.

Growing in Grace

Let's begin by looking at two people from the Old Testament. David has always been a favorite Bible character. We remember him for so many of his righteous acts—his courage in defeating Goliath, magnificence in sparing the life of Saul, who was out to get him, determination to rescue the sacred ark from the Philistines, and gifted talents which still bring blessing to millions.

However, there was another side to King David. One biblical scholar characterizes him as ambitious, an outlaw, wife-stealer, polygamist, murderer, and traitor; and all of those things are probably true.[1] The sin of pride led David to show off Israel's military might by ordering a census of his nation's fighting men. His loyal army captain, Joab, tried hard to dissuade the king, and the exercise resulted in the death of several thousand men (see 1 Chron. 21). On another occasion, David displayed an ugly spirit of revenge in an encounter with Nabal, a wealthy and selfish landowner. David ordered the death of Nabal and his entire family; this was prevented only by the kindness of the man's wife, Abigail (see 1 Samuel 25). With that said, the sorriest story of David's life resulted from lust when he remained at home instead of leading his army in battle. He raped Bathsheba, then arranged to have her husband, Uriah, killed (see 2 Sam. 11). David was a sinner in need of salvation.

Despite all that, God said something amazing about David even before he was anointed as king. Hear these words from Samuel to King Saul after he disobeyed a plain command from the Lord: "Now your kingdom will not endure; the Lord has sought out *a man after his own heart* and appointed him ruler of his people, because you have not kept the Lord's command" (1 Sam. 13:14). And just in case we wonder who it was that God had in mind to replace Saul, we find these words of Paul to a congregation of Jews in Asia Minor: "After removing Saul, he [God] made David their king. God testified concerning him, 'I have found David son of Jesse, *a man after my own heart*; he will do everything I want him to do'" (Acts 13:22, italics mine).

How was David "after God's own heart"? How was he in tune with the heart of God? Just look at how David responded when he recognized he had sinned. After ordering Joab to conduct the army census: "I have sinned greatly by doing this" (1 Chron. 21:8). When he sought revenge against Nabal, he listened and responded to Abigail: "Praise be to the Lord, the God of Israel, who has sent you today to meet me. May you be blessed for your good judgment and for keeping me from bloodshed this day" (1 Sam. 25:32, 33). With bitter remorse after his adultery with Bathsheba: "Wash away all my iniquity and cleanse me from my sin. For I know my transgressions, and my sin is always before me….Create in me a pure heart, O God" (Ps. 51:2, 3, 10). Reflecting on this painful experience: "I waited patiently for the Lord; he turned to me and heard my cry. He lifted me out of the slimy pit, out of the mud and mire; he set my feet on a rock and gave me a firm place to stand" (Ps. 40:1, 2). David opened his heart to the impulses of the Holy Spirit. His repentance was deep and he grew in grace.

The story of Rahab provides another glimpse into growth in grace. Rahab was a prostitute. Her house abutted the wall of Jericho, which was probably convenient for some of her guests who could leave the premises by slithering down a rope outside the wall. Was she a common prostitute? One commentator suggests that Rahab may have been a temple prostitute, which in Canaanite eyes was a respectable line of work. It is also likely that her house doubled as an inn, which explains why Joshua's two spies checked in there (see Josh. 2:1, 2).

News of Israel's approaching army brought fear to the inhabitants of Jericho. When Rahab heard that the king was sending his men to interrogate her two guests, she hid the spies under the flax on her rooftop and reported that they had already left the city. Meanwhile, though, she made an agreement with the two spies that if she helped them to safety by way of the wall rope, they in turn would save her and her family from otherwise certain death.

Rahab came to believe that the God of Israel was unlike the Canaanite gods she served. She had heard reports about the miraculous crossing of the Red Sea and the defeat of the powerful Amorite kings. She told the spies, "I know that the Lord has given this land to you….Everyone's courage failed because of you, for the Lord your God is God in heaven above and on the earth below" (Josh. 2:9–11). The spies were faithful in keeping their part of the agreement. Rahab and her family were the only survivors when Jericho was surrounded and completely destroyed.

Rahab cast her lot with the Israelites. She married Salmon, the son of Judah's tribal leader. From their marriage came Boaz, a faithful man of God. Boaz would later marry Ruth the Moabitess, and their son Obed would become the grandfather of King David. The author of Hebrews places Rahab among the great men and women of faith: "By faith the prostitute Rahab, because she welcomed the spies, was not killed with those who were disobedient" (Heb. 11:31). What is even more amazing is that this former Canaanite prostitute is named in Matthew's genealogy of Christ, because she became what every Israelite woman hoped to be—a mother in the line of Jesus the Messiah (see Matt.1:5, 6). Now that's grace!

Growing in Faith

In the cold and dark of an early morning, see Peter warming his hands by a fire in the outer court of the high priest. "After a little while, those standing there went up to Peter and said, 'Surely you are one of them; your accent gives you away.' Then he began to call down curses, and he swore to them, 'I don't know the man'" (Matt. 26:73, 74)! However, Peter changed. Hear him preaching to the Jerusalem crowds at Pentecost: "Let all Israel be assured of this: God has made this Jesus, whom you crucified, both Lord and Messiah" (Acts 2:36).

Twelve men whom Christ selected to be trained for ministry and evangelism were a strange bunch—seven fishermen from Galilee, a tax collector, a religious zealot, a couple of tradesmen perhaps, and a treasurer. Regardless of their occupations or professions, they left everything to follow their Master. Their intentions were good and expectations large.

Twelve men whom Christ selected to be trained for ministry and evangelism were a strange bunch.

However, their faith was small. They had some growing to do. Matthew's gospel illustrates how much their faith needed to grow with two stories that probably happened on the same day. In the Galilean city of Capernaum, Jesus and His disciples were met by a Roman centurion—a gentile—who requested healing for his slave-servant at home. When Jesus said, "Shall I come and heal him", the officer gave an incredible reply: "Lord, I do not deserve to have you come under my roof. But just say the word, and my servant will be healed", which brought this response from Jesus: "I have not found anyone in Israel with such *great faith*" (Matt. 8:5–10).

That same evening, Jesus and the twelve were crossing the lake when a windstorm struck their vessel. Afraid, the men woke Jesus. "Lord, save us! We're going to drown!" Jesus got up and looked into their frightened faces. "You of *little faith*, why are you so afraid" (Matt. 8:25, 26)? Then He calmed the sea.

It was during another nighttime crossing of the lake that Peter was given a faith lesson. Observing his Master walking on the waves, Peter was given an opportunity to do the same. It was an exciting experience while Peter kept his eyes on Jesus, but when he saw the wind-driven waves, he began to sink. "Immediately Jesus reached out his hand and caught him. 'You of little faith,' he said, 'why did you doubt'" (Matt. 14:31)?

During their training, the disciples were given authority to heal diseases and drive out demons (see Matt. 10:1). Success brought confidence in this unique gift, but it was easy to miss the essential connection with the source of power. There was pandemonium one day when Jesus came down from the Mount of Transfiguration. A desperate father had brought his devil-possessed boy to the disciples for healing. Their failed attempt brought ridicule from the crowd. Jesus intervened, healed the boy, and later, when the embarrassed disciples queried, "Why couldn't we drive it out", Jesus responded, "Because you have so little faith" (Matt. 17:19, 20). Those men had to learn that power on God's part must be matched with faith on their part.

The struggling faith of those men took a monumental leap when the power of the Holy Spirit came into their ministry. Listen again to Peter, this time in conversation with a crippled beggar at the gate of the temple in Jerusalem: "Silver or gold I do not have, but what I do have I give you. In the name of Jesus Christ of Nazareth, walk. Taking him by the right hand, he helped him up, and instantly the man's feet and ankles became strong" (Acts 3:6, 7).

What does it mean for me to have faith? The standard biblical definition is found in Hebrews 11: "Now faith is being sure of what we hope for and certain of what we do not see" (Heb. 11:1). From the Scriptures, we can piece together several essential elements of faith:

- It means to trust and obey. "When the Lord sent you out from Kadesh-Barnea, he said, 'Go up and take possession of the land I have given you.' But you rebelled against the command of the Lord your God. You did not trust him or obey him" (Deut. 9:23).
- It means conquering fear with trust. Jesus repeatedly chided the disciples because of their fear. "You of little faith, why are you so afraid?" "Don't be afraid, just believe." "Don't be afraid, you

are worth more than many sparrows." "Do not let your hearts be troubled. Trust in God; trust also in me" (Matt. 8:26, Luke 8:50, Luke 12:7, John 14:1).

- It means claiming power from the Holy Spirit through prayer. Christ's parting words to His disciples were, "You will receive power when the Holy Spirit comes on you; and you will be my witnesses" (Acts 1:8). The Holy Spirit ignites our faith.

- It means placing our complete trust in Jesus to save us. "These are written that you may believe that Jesus is the Messiah, the Son of God, and that by believing you may have life in his name" (John 20:31).

Faith is not a passive thing. It grows and shows in the life of one who follows Jesus. It is the visible evidence of my trust and conviction that Jesus Christ will keep His promises, offering me salvation now and eternal life in the future.

Growing in Knowledge

Paul's prayer for new believers in Colossae is comprehensive and beautiful: "We have not stopped praying for you since we first heard about you. We ask God *to give you complete knowledge of his will and to give you spiritual wisdom and understanding.* Then the way you live will always honor and please the Lord, and your lives will produce every kind of good fruit. All the while, *you will grow as you learn to know God better and better.* We also pray that you will be strengthened with all his glorious power so you will have all the endurance and patience you need. May you be filled with joy, always thanking the Father" (Col. 1:9–11, NLT, italics mine). Paul emphasized growth in the knowledge of God.

Prophets and apostles grew in their knowledge of God and truth. Abraham grew in faith and knowledge, from doubt as he waited long and impatiently for a son to total trust when he laid that very son on a wilderness altar. The patriarchs and their descendants took a long time to learn that multiple wives were not in harmony with God's plan for humanity. From the Old Testament, we learn a great deal about the patience and forgiveness of God.

Christ's disciples had a long way to go in their knowledge about God. James and John believed they should have top places in the kingdom they expected Christ to establish. When John observed someone outside of their group casting out demons, he wanted to stop him (see Luke 9:49, 50). As the group traveled together through Samaria, Jesus sent word ahead, asking for a place to stay. When the Samaritans refused the polite request, James and John quickly asked, "Lord, should we call down fire from heaven and burn them up" (Luke 9:54, NLT)? Was it the same John who talked so much about love in the letters he wrote?

In Gethsemane, when soldiers came to arrest Jesus, Peter promptly grabbed and swung his sword, missing the head of Malchus, the high priest's servant, but taking off his right ear (see John 18:10, 11). Years later, in a vision at Joppa, Peter learned that the gospel was for all people; yet soon afterwards, at Antioch, he took a backward step when he declined to publicly eat with Gentiles during a visit by church leaders. Paul observed Peter's hypocrisy and scolded him in front of everybody (see Gal. 2:11–14). Peter learned that growth is not always in an upward direction, but he concluded his second epistle by saying, "grow in the grace and knowledge of our Lord and Savior Jesus Christ. To him be glory both now and forever! Amen" (2 Peter 3:18).

Did Ellen White grow in her knowledge of God and His truth? Certainly. Reflecting on her teen years, she wrote, "In my mind the justice of God eclipsed His mercy and love. I had been taught to believe in an eternally burning hell, and the horrifying thought was ever before me that my sins were too great to be forgiven....Our heavenly Father was presented before my mind as a tyrant, who delighted in the agonies of the condemned."[2] Much later she came to understand that Jesus did not die to placate a Father's wrath, because they shared the same deep love for humanity: "He whose eyes have been opened by the love of Christ will behold God as full of compassion. He does not appear as a tyrannical, relentless being, but as a father longing to embrace his repenting son."[3]

It took many years for Ellen White to move from the "shut door" belief that salvation was no longer available to the thousands who rejected the Millerite prediction of Christ's coming in 1844. As late as 1883, she wrote, "I was shown in vision, and I still believe, that there was a shut door in 1844. All who saw the light of the first and second angel's messages and rejected that light were left in darkness."[4] Her understanding of the great controversy also grew after her 1858 vision at Lovett's Grove. For a time she shared a view among Adventists that obedience to God's law and observance of the true Sabbath were the qualifications for heaven.[5] Later, she understood that the whole controversy has to do with freedom of choice and serving God from love. In a similar way, her understanding of righteousness by faith grew when she heard presentations on the subject by Alonzo Jones and Ellet Waggoner at the 1888 General Conference.[6]

Merlin Burt, who has given much study to Ellen White's growth of knowledge, says, "A common misconception regarding the gift of prophecy is the belief that prophetic revelation does not allow for correction or growth in understanding on the part of the messenger.…Looking at the biblical model we find that the prophets and apostles did not always have immediate and perfect understanding, and on occasion even misunderstood aspects of what they were shown."[7] Peter's slowness in accepting God's plan to evangelize the gentiles is a case in point. Ellen White acknowledged her process of growth when she wrote in 1906, "For sixty years I have been in communication with heavenly messengers, and I have been constantly learning in reference to divine things."[8]

Our knowledge is so small in comparison to God's eternal truth, but we are challenged to grow daily in our understanding of truth and relationship with God. Like Peter and all the prophets, we will often fail and take a few steps backwards, but to stop growing is to die a spiritual death. Christ's prayer in the garden for His disciples is also for us: "Now this is eternal life: that they know you, the only true God, and Jesus Christ, whom you have sent" (John 17:3). We seek an ever-clearer picture of God behind the wall.

Growing in Understanding

I have already talked about my spiritual journey. Looking back, I can discern how God led me step by step. A new interest and excitement about Seventh-day Adventist history led to my participation in Jim Nix's Adventist history tour in the summer of 1986. It was during a special communion service at the William Miller farm that the Holy Spirit spoke to my heart.

My spiritual journey has not always been upward, but in the past twenty-five years I have developed a passion for the Scriptures and a greater knowledge and understanding about God's revelation of Himself to humanity. When Alden Thompson's book on inspiration appeared in 1991, I grasped a new confidence in the Bible and the ministry of Ellen White.[9] That confidence becomes more firmly rooted as I seek the guidance of the Holy Spirit in my personal study of God's Word. Reflecting on my past, I am humbled and grateful to a God of mercy and grace.

Growing is also about looking backwards. Our past has important things to teach us. We cannot truly understand the present and intelligently choose a path for the future without reviewing and respecting the journey that brought us to where we are. Someone quipped, "Those who fail to learn from history are doomed to repeat it."[10] Ellen White understood those wise words when she wrote, "In reviewing our past history, having traveled over every step of advance to our present standing, I can say, Praise God! As I see what the Lord has wrought, I am filled with astonishment, and with confidence in Christ as leader. We have nothing to fear for the future, except as we shall forget the way the Lord has led us, and His teaching in our past history."[11]

To think about:

1. God chose His prophets, but He gave them the freedom to make mistakes and experience failures. Why do you think He did that, and does it help us to better understand Ellen White as a prophet and person?

2. Fear is a worldwide phenomenon. Why is fear incompatible with faith? Consider the Apostle Peter as an example of one who moved from fear to faith.

3. Prayerfully consider how your spiritual life has reflected growth and, sometimes perhaps, decline. What promoted the growth, and what caused any decline you may have experienced?

References:

[1]   Joel S. Baden, *The Historical David.*

[2]   Ellen White, *Testimonies*, 1: 23,24.

[3]   White, *Christ's Object Lessons*, 204.

[4]   White, Manuscript 4, 1883; *Selected Messages*, 1:63.

[5]   Alden Thompson, "The theology of Ellen White: the great controversy story", *Adventist Review*, December 31, 1981.

[6]   White, Manuscript 8a, 1888.

[7]   Merlin Burt, "Understanding Ellen White and the 'Shut Door'", in *Understanding Ellen White*, 175.

[8]   White, Letter 86, 1906.

[9]   Thompson, *Inspiration: Hard Questions, Honest Answers.*

[10] The famous quote is ascribed to George Santayana.

[11] White, *Life Sketches*, 196.

Restoration

Chapter 21—Reading

The Book of Hebrews describes the penetrating power of God's Word this way: "For the word of God is alive and active. Sharper than any double-edged sword, it penetrates even to dividing soul and spirit, joints and marrow; it judges the thoughts and attitudes of the heart" (Heb.4:12).

Let me put those words alongside these from Ellen White: "The creative energy that called the world into existence is in the Word of God. This Word imparts power; it begets life. Every command is a promise; accepted by the will, received into the soul, it brings with it the life of the Infinite One. It transforms the nature and recreates the soul in the image of God."[1]

Coming from the God of the universe, brought to us by dozens of prophets and messengers over a period of about 1,500 years, is this amazing artifact, the Bible. Some consider it the most controversial book in existence. "Men have been executed for translating it. People have been jailed for reading it. It has been banned and burned, lampooned, ridiculed, denounced and shot down in flames."[2] Yet this book has changed more lives and given more hope than any other book ever published.

Sadly, though, it is a neglected and unread book for countless millions of people who formally acknowledge it as the Word of God.

I wish that last statement was untrue of Seventh-day Adventists, but church leaders and pastors know and say otherwise. That happens in spite of an avalanche of materials that encourage us to read and study our Bibles. We are offered a variety of reading plans and guides.

This chapter is about reading inspired writings. In these troubled times, it is critical for us to maintain a strong and active faith in the Bible. We must know personally the God of the Scriptures. Reading God's Word in dialogue with Him lies at the heart of a living and learning relationship with Him. The Holy Spirit is given to us as a guide to our understanding and application of what we read. This is what we mean by "illumination." The Holy Spirit promises to be our personal guide whenever we read or study the Scriptures. We begin this chapter with the sacred Scriptures and continue with the inspired contributions of Ellen White.

Reading the Old Testament

Some Christians give up on the Old Testament because of the picture of God they find there. Philip Yancey asks, "Is the Old Testament worth the effort it takes to read and understand it?"[3] God sometimes appears angry, arbitrary, and vengeful. Even Christ's disciples found it hard to equate the gentle Jesus with the God of ancient Israel. "Show us the Father," they implored, and were surprised at Christ's response: "If you have seen me, you have seen the Father" (John 14:8, 9). It is hard for us too, because the face of God is hidden behind the formidable wall of our sin and misunderstanding. How can we make our reading of the Old Testament truer to reality? Some suggestions follow:

> *Some Christians give up on the Old Testament because of the picture of God they find there.*

1. Keep in mind that *the Old Testament was written to the Israelite nation.* It was first their book, their Bible, their history. Read it with that in mind, because it helps to explain cultural peculiarities such as the strange and exaggerated numbers we have already observed. Nevertheless, the Old Testament was also written for us, because God communicates to all humanity through all time.

Jesus quoted and referenced all five books of Moses; the historical books of Joshua, Samuel, and Kings; the Psalms; and seven prophetic books, especially Isaiah. He reminded the Jews that their Scriptures testified of Him (see John 5:39). He revealed the prophecies about Himself to two disciples on the road to Emmaus (see Luke 24:44, 45). It is insightful and sometimes amazing to read the Old Testament through the eyes of the New Testament.

2. Read with *an understanding of its cultural background*. What do we know about the context and origin of the passage? Was it written to address a particular event or behavior? It helps to understand the realities of life and death in the ancient world. They were rugged times. Keep in mind that Satan sometimes masquerades as God, as he did with Job. The repeated hardening of Pharaoh's heart at the exodus does not sit well with a God who values human freedom. Satan, though, revels in the use of force and control (see Exod. 9:12; compare 1 Sam. 6:6).

3. Read *to discover God's purposes* in the narratives of the Old Testament. Look for evidence of His active involvement in the world of Israel and its neighbors. Can we learn something positive from the way the Israelites behaved and how God reacted to their behavior? What lessons can you take from these stories?

4. Look for *abundant evidence of grace and forgiveness* in the lives of Old Testament characters and God's dealings with Israel. Expect wonderful surprises as you read with that in mind. *A Strange Place for Grace* is the title of a helpful little book that reveals how we can discover a loving God in the Old Testament.[4]

5. Be aware that *much of the Old Testament is in Hebrew poetic form*. This is true of the prophetic books, along with Job, Psalms, Proverbs, Ecclesiastes, and Song of Solomon. Hebrew poetry is characterized by parallelism, imagery, emotion, and sometimes hyperbole, so it is not always appropriate to interpret it literally. "Poetic license" was not restricted to modern literature. Look for spiritual rather than theological meaning when reading from the Psalms, Proverbs, and Ecclesiastes.

6. *Explore new ways of reading* the Old Testament. Instead of reading sequentially from Genesis to Malachi on a daily plan, try following the story chronologically, bringing prophetic books into their historical settings in Kings and Chronicles,[5] or choose a character

to study. It could be someone well-known like David or Daniel, or a lesser-known character like Jehoshaphat or Judah. You can also adopt your own unique approach to the Scriptures.

Find and cherish your favorite Old Testament passages. I'm sharing three of mine.

- *"Even youths grow tired and weary, and young men stumble and fall; but those who hope in the Lord will renew their strength. They will soar on wings like eagles; they will run and not grow weary, they will walk and not be faint"* (Isa. 40:30, 31).
- *"Because of the Lord's great love we are not consumed, for his compassions never fail. They are new every morning; great is your faithfulness"* (Lam. 3:22, 23).
- *"The Lord your God in your midst, the Mighty One, will save; He will rejoice over you with gladness, He will quiet you with His love, He will rejoice over you with singing"* (Zeph. 3:17, NKJV).

Reading the New Testament

The Old Testament gives us glimpses of a coming Redeemer; the New Testament brings us the wonderful reality. Jesus is here, and the transformation in the lives of men and women is on display. Hear the words of a converted fisherman, Peter, who experienced that transformation: "For we were not making up clever stories when we told you about the powerful coming of our Lord Jesus Christ. We saw his majestic splendor with our own eyes when he received honor and glory from God the Father. The voice from the majestic glory of God said to him, 'This is my dearly loved Son, who brings me great joy.' We ourselves heard that voice from heaven when we were with him on the holy mountain" (2 Peter 1:16–18, NLT).

1. *Immerse yourself in the four gospels.* Here is the best picture we have of the God behind the wall. The Apostle John assures us that "the Word became flesh and made his dwelling among us." Like Peter, John remembers that he was with Jesus on the mount of transfiguration: "We have seen his glory," he exclaims, "the glory of the one and only Son, who came from the Father, full of grace and truth" (John 1:14). The story of Jesus is the best and most magnificent story ever written. Read it with passion and holy joy, especially the scenes of His death and resurrection.

2. *Take your time with the words you are reading.* Try a variety of translations. Each gospel writer takes a different angle on the

life and ministry of Jesus. Be inspired by Luke's stories of what happened all over the empire after Christ's ascension and Pentecost. Connect those missionary stories about Paul, Peter, and John with the letters they wrote to the fledgling Christian Church, not forgetting the revelations given to John on lonely Patmos.

3. *Look for the God who is love* in all your reading and study of the Scriptures.

4. *Make use of the abundance of devotional aids and commentaries* which add value to your study of the New Testament. Use Bible maps of Palestine and the Mediterranean world to locate events and follow journeys. Participating in organized and professionally guided tours of the Holy Land, the journeys of Paul, or the sites of the seven churches of Revelation, adds color and brings life to your reading.

Here are three of my favorite New Testament Scriptures:

• *"I am the resurrection and the life. Anyone who believes in me will live, even though they die; and whoever lives by believing in me will never die"* (John 11:25, 26).

• *"I pray that out of his glorious riches he may strengthen you with power through his Spirit in your inner being, so that Christ may dwell in your hearts through faith. And I pray that you, being rooted and established in love, may have power, together with all the Lord's people, to grasp how wide and long and high and deep is the love of Christ, and to know this love that surpasses knowledge"* (Eph. 3:16–19).

• *"For we are God's masterpiece. He has created us anew in Christ Jesus, so we can do the good things He planned for us long ago"* (Eph. 2:10, NLT).

Reading Ellen White's Writings

Although Ellen White does not have the status of the Bible's canonical prophets, we have ample evidence that she was chosen by the Lord for a particular time in earth's history and received messages through inspiration.

A unique problem in reading Ellen White is the volume of her writings. During sixty years of prophetic ministry, she produced approximately 100,000 pages in books, articles, letters, and manuscripts. By comparison, the five books of Moses total less than 200 pages of print. This raises a question: How much of what Ellen White wrote was inspired by the Holy Spirit? It is not always easy to draw a sharp line between what is inspired counsel and what is personal writing. How shall we make the distinction?

In the case of Moses, all that we have of his utterances is the Pentateuch, an inspired record. We do not have his daily interactions with his wife, father-in-law Jethro, sister Miriam, brother Aaron, or conversations with friends and individual Israelites. However, in the case of Ellen White, a significant proportion of her written output comprises letters to family members and close friends, discussions about a variety of mundane topics, travel diaries, and talks and sermons.

How shall we discern between Ellen White's inspired counsel and what is mere human opinion or the commonly held information and beliefs of her time? She read widely from books and magazines of her day. She incorporated some of that in her writings, as we saw with some statements on science or health that do not make sense today.

Tim Poirier of the White Estate reminds us that Paul and other New Testament apostles wrote letters to churches or individuals, and we correctly regard them as having been written under inspiration. In a similar way, he says, "Ellen White used letters to convey Spirit-inspired instruction she received. At the same time, however, she plainly expressed that she did not expect us to take everything she said or wrote as a revelation from God."[6] It is impossible to lay down a rule that neatly divides what is inspired from what is not inspired, although the distinction is often self-evident.

Her writings fall into several groupings:[7]

> "Conflict of the Ages" Books
>
> Other Devotional Books
>
> Topical Books and Collections
>
> Testimonies for the Church
>
> Periodical Articles
>
> Compilations
>
> Autobiographical Books
>
> Letters and Manuscripts

- **Conflict of the Ages Books**: The five volumes in this series— *Patriarchs and Prophets*, *Prophets and Kings*, *The Desire of Ages*, *The Acts of the Apostles*, and *The Great Controversy*—are her most important books. "Those five volumes provide the theological framework for everything else Ellen White has to say. An understanding of the great themes they highlight is foundational to understanding her other writings."[8]

- **Other Devotional Books**: A classic in this category is *Steps to Christ,* a beautiful introduction to the spiritual life. In 2017, Andrews University Press published a commemorative edition, with notes and other valuable information supplied by Denis Fortin.[9] Other titles in the devotional category include *Christ's Object Lessons* and *Thoughts from the Mount of Blessing.*

- **Topical Books and Collections**: *Ministry of Healing* (1905) and *Education* (1903) are original and significant works in their respective fields. Among topical collections made up from her articles, sermons, and manuscripts are these: *The Sanctified Life* (1889, 1937), *Gospel Workers* (1892, 1915), *Counsels to Teachers* (1913, 1943), *Messages to Young People* (1930), *Counsels on Diet and Foods* (1938), *Counsels on Stewardship* (1940), *Evangelism* (1946), *The Adventist Home* (1952), *Colporteur Ministry* (1953), *Faith and Works* (1979), and *Last Day Events* (1992).

- **Testimonies for the Church**: When Ellen White realized that the counsel God had given her for certain individuals or church situations also applied to many other people and situations, she authorized their publication, starting in 1855. The first four of nine volumes were published in 1883. The value and understanding of the *Testimonies* is greatly enhanced when we know the historical context for a particular testimony.

- **Periodical Articles**: Ellen White published more than 5,000 articles in Seventh-day Adventist periodicals—*Review and Herald*, *Signs of the Times*, *Youth's Instructor*, and *General Conference Bulletin*. Many of her articles have been republished in various topical collections.

- **Compilations**: The first two compilations (*Gospel Workers* and *Counsels to Parents, Teachers, and Students*—more commonly known as *Counsels to Teachers*) were made during Ellen White's lifetime and with her direct involvement. In her will, she gave the White Estate authorization to publish topical compilations, of which there are now many. They typically comprise large numbers of short quotations on a given topic, but without the historical context of each statement. Ellen White gave counsels to many different people in many different situations, and as George Knight observes, "there is no way that any one reader can have all those problems."[10]

- **Autobiographical Books**: One of Ellen White's first books was *A Sketch of the Christian Experience and Views of Ellen G. White* (1851), with descriptions of many of her early visions. This book and a supplement were republished in 1882 as *Early Writings*. The final step in her autobiographical writing came in 1915 with *Life Sketches of Ellen G. White*. It covers the entire span of her life from childhood to her funeral.

- **Letters and Manuscripts**: In addition to her published books and articles, the White Estate houses roughly 50,000 pages of letters and manuscripts, comprising more than 8,000 separate documents. These include letters addressed to people like "My Dear Son Edson" or "My Dear Niece Addie". Most of the documents have been in print in one form or another, but all are now available on the Ellen G. White Estate web site.[11] In 2014, the White Estate commenced a new publication series entitled *The Ellen G. White Letters and Manuscripts with Annotations*. When complete, this series will provide the context of her letters and manuscripts.

In reading Ellen White's letters and manuscripts, it is inevitable that we will find many apparent contradictions of advice, simply because she dealt with so many differing situations at different places and times. Adventist historian George Knight has produced a trilogy of small, readable books which help us understand Ellen White as a person and how to approach her writings.[12] One of those books, *Reading Ellen White,* contains excellent advice for understanding and applying her writings. What follows incorporates some of those suggestions.

1. *Focus on the major themes* in all of her writings:

- *The Love of God*. A theme she repeatedly mentions and discusses in her books. It also provides the context for her telling of the great controversy story.
- *Great Controversy*. The cosmic conflict between God and Satan and how it is played out on this earth.
- *Jesus, His Death, and Heavenly Ministry*. Central to this theme is *The Desire of Ages*, but also *Christ's Object Lessons* and *Mount of Blessing*.
- *The Centrality of the Bible*. Throughout her life, she upheld the Bible as the Word of God.
- *The Second Coming of Christ*.
- *Three Angels' Messages and Adventist Mission*.

- *The Development of Christian Character.*

2. *Approach her writings with a mindset of faith* rather than doubt, as you do with the Scriptures. Ellen herself commented, "God gives sufficient evidence for the candid mind to believe; but he who turns from the weight of evidence because there are a few things he cannot make plain to his finite understanding will be left in the cold, chilling atmosphere of unbelief and questioning doubts, and will make shipwreck of his faith"[13]

3. Ellen White *always directed her readers to the Scriptures*. Follow her counsel by reading her "Conflict of the Ages" books such as *Patriarchs and Prophets*, *The Desire of Ages*, and *Acts of the Apostles,* in tandem with the biblical accounts. Do the same with *Christ's Object Lessons* and *Thoughts from the Mount of Blessing*.

4. *Realize that inspiration, whether of Scripture or Ellen White, is not infallible, inerrant, or verbal.* "The same kind of factual errors can be discovered in Ellen White's writings as are found in the Bible. The writings of God's prophets are infallible as a guide to salvation, but they are not inerrant or without error."[14]

5. *Do not impose an Ellen White interpretation on the Bible.* Every inspired passage of Scripture should remain open for fresh insight and application. No one, not even Ellen White, may claim to have the final interpretation of a Biblical passage or text. "The written testimonies are not to give new light…Additional truth is not brought out, but God has through the Testimonies simplified the great truths already given."[15]

6. *Always consider the context*, especially when Ellen White's counsel comes with forceful words. Here is an example: "Both in public and private worship it is our duty to bow down upon our knees before God when we offer our petitions to Him. This act shows our dependence upon God."[16] This counsel came in the context of a church meeting in which an elder stood to offer public prayer just before Ellen White rose to speak. Some years later she said, "You must be men and women of prayer. Your petitions must not be faint, occasional, and fitful, but earnest, persevering, and constant. It is not always necessary to bow upon your knees in order to pray. Cultivate the habit of talking with the Savior when you are alone, when you are walking, and when you are busy with your daily labor. Let the heart be continually uplifted in silent

petition for help, for light, for strength, for knowledge. Let every breath be a prayer."[17]

7.   Other topics that require a careful, contextual approach include the location of schools in the country[18] and the age when a child should start school.[19] Ellen White's son, W.C. White, hit on the point when he wrote that "when we take what she has written, and publish it without any description, or particular reference to the conditions existing when and where the testimony was given, there is always the possibility that the instruction being used as applying to places and conditions that are very different."[20] Ellen White herself cautioned, "God wants us all to have common sense, and he wants us to reason from common sense. Circumstances alter conditions. Circumstances change the relation of things."

The evidence of divine inspiration in the writings of Ellen White is cumulative as we read and give careful and serious study to her work. George Knight said, "We have a precious gift in the writings of Ellen White. But, unfortunately, those writings have not always been studied as carefully as they should have been. That was true in her lifetime, and it remains so in ours. Fortunately, because of the problems of her day, she has provided us with priceless counsel on how to interpret her writings in our times."[22]

Finally, I'm sharing three of my favorite selections from Ellen White:

"You confess your sins, and give yourself to God....If you believe the promise—believe that you are forgiven and cleansed—God supplies the fact."[23]

"The sinner unites his weakness to Christ's strength, his emptiness to Christ's fullness, his frailty to Christ's enduring might. Then he has the mind of Christ. The humanity of Christ has touched our humanity, and our humanity has touched divinity. Thus through the agency of the Holy Spirit man becomes a partaker of the divine nature. He is accepted in the Beloved."[24]

"To him who is content to receive without deserving, who feels that he can never recompense such love, who lays all doubt and unbelief aside, and comes as a little child to the feet of Jesus, all the treasures of eternal love are a free, everlasting gift."[25]

To think about:

1. Reflect on the time you spend with the Bible. How significant are the Scriptures to your daily activities? Do you find yourself reading or listening to more devotional material *about* the Bible than spending time with the Word itself? What could change that mix?

2. The quantity of material written by Ellen White is overwhelming. What approach could help you glean spiritual insights from her writings as an alternative to extensive reading?

3. Read the Old Testament story of Naomi (Ruth 1). Why does Naomi hold God responsible for the untimely deaths of her husband and two married sons (v. 21)? Does the story of Job help our understanding?

References:

[1] Ellen White, *Signs of the Times*, April 11, 1906.

[2] David Marshall, *The Battle for the Bible*: Introduction.

[3] Philip Yancey, *The Bible Jesus Read*, 19.

[4] Jon Dybdal, *A Strange Place for Grace*.

[5] For an example of this approach, read *The Story: The Bible as One Continuous Story of God and His People*.

[6] Tim Poirier, "Ellen White's Letters and Manuscripts", *Adventist World*, February 2016.

[7] George R. Knight, "Ellen G. White's Writings" in *The Ellen G. White Encyclopedia*, 121–140.

[8] *Ibid.*, 124.

[9] Ellen White, *Steps to Christ: historical introduction and notes by Denis Fortin*.

[10] George Knight, *Reading Ellen White*, 39.

[11] Ellen G. White Internet Web site. http://1ref.us/md (accessed October 10, 2017).

[12] George Knight, *Meeting Ellen White*; *Reading Ellen White*; and *Walking with Ellen White*.

[13] White, *Testimonies*, 4:232.

[14] Knight, *Reading Ellen White*, 111.

[15] White, *Testimonies*, 5:665.

[16] White, Manuscript 84b, 1897; also *Selected Messages*, 2:312.

17   White, *Ministry of Healing*, 510.

18   White, Compare Manuscript 8a, 1894, with Manuscript 152, 1902.

19   White, Compare *Testimonies*, 3:137 (1872), with Manuscript 7, 1904.

20   W.C. White, Letter to C.W. Irwin, February 18, 1913.

21   Ellen G. White, *Selected Messages*, 3:217.

22   Knight, *Reading Ellen White*, 139.

23   White, *Steps to Christ*, 51.

24   White, *Desire of Ages*, 675.

25   White, *Signs of the Times*, February 28, 1906.

Chapter 22—Restoring

You Can't Go Home Again is the title of a novel by Thomas Wolfe, an American writer of the early 20th century. "You can't go back home to your family, back home to your childhood…back home to the old forms and systems of things which once seemed everlasting but which are changing all the time."[1]

I discovered for myself the truth of those words when I returned to Australia for a short visit in 2015. Thirty-five years had passed since our family of four packed our worldly belongings, said a tearful goodbye to Sally, our golden retriever, and migrated to a job and new home in Alberta, Canada. Driving around my former home community of Cooranbong, New South Wales, I observed some old and familiar landmarks, but the village I had known and loved was no longer the place we had left. More than three decades of change had wrought such a makeover that I hardly recognized or identified it as the community where I had studied, lived, and worked for thirty years. Cooranbong didn't look or feel like home anymore.

However, something strange happened while I was there. I began to meet people whom I recognized. Yes, they had changed, as I had, but as we looked into each other's faces, we began conversations that were draped in remembrance and celebration of our common heritage. We recounted familiar stories and shared laughter and tears. Then the truth suddenly hit me—you *can* go home again! *Relationships* make all the difference.

The Longing

A longing for relationship is the key to understanding why God bothered to break through the wall after sin entered the world. Why else did He choose to create our human parents the way He did? With His voice He spoke everything else into existence. That included the ochre soil from which He carefully and lovingly, with His

> *We recounted familiar stories and shared laughter and tears. Then the truth suddenly hit me—you can go home again! Relationships make all the difference.*

own hands, formed the body of Adam, then, taking a rib from the man's side, used the same care and love in forming Eve. What more wonderful way could there be to create and define relationship?

We began this book with a captivating picture of relationship, perfect and holy, in a faraway garden home. Then we watched as sin invaded our planet. A sinister wall materialized, shutting out the face and presence of God. We found ourselves in a cold, dark world, separated from our original home, refugees in a war zone, but then a miracle happened. God came to us.

Just days before He was executed on a Roman cross, Jesus poured out His soul for the people of a city He loved: "Jerusalem, Jerusalem, you who kill the prophets and stone those sent to you, how often I have longed to gather your children together, as a hen gathers her chicks under her wings, and you were not willing" (Matt. 23:37). During the triumphal entry in that same week, the procession paused on the slopes of Olivet while Jesus wept over the city (see Luke 19:41).

The longing of God for a restored relationship is a powerful theme throughout the Bible. We see it first in the Garden when He comes in search of a frightened couple: "Where are you?" Later, He comes with mercy to Cain after he angrily killed his brother, Abel (see Gen.4:15). Time after time, we find God seeking friendship among people in rebellion.

- He found and placed His trust in Abraham: "Abraham believed

God, and it was credited to him as righteousness, and he was called God's friend" (James 2:23).

- In the hot Arabian desert, He came to a sobbing, castaway mother, alone with a thirsty little boy, and led them to a spring of water (Gen. 21:15–19).

- He came to Jacob, a scared runaway, with a precious promise: "I am with you and will watch over you wherever you go, and I will bring you back to this land. I will not leave you until I have done what I have promised you" (Gen. 28:15).

- He enjoyed face-to-face conversation with Moses: "The Lord would speak to Moses face to face, as one speaks to a friend" (Exod. 33:11).

- In spite of the many mistakes and sins of David, God gave the prophet Nathan a message for him: "My love will never be taken away from him" (2 Sam. 7:15).

- Isaiah painted this beautiful picture of a God who identified with His people:

> "I will tell of the kindnesses of the Lord,
> the deeds for which he is to be praised, according to all
>   the Lord has done for us—
> yes, the many good things he has done for the house of Israel,
> according to his compassion and many kindnesses.
> He said, 'Surely they are my people, children who will be
>   true to me';
> and so he became their Savior.
> In all their distress he too was distressed, and the angel of
>   his presence saved them.
> In his love and mercy he redeemed them; he lifted them up
> and carried them all the days of old" (Isa. 63:7–9).

In the prophetic books, God uses two beautiful symbols to illustrate His relationship with His often-rebellious people. In the last line of the Isaiah passage above, as well as in other places, God is pictured as a heavenly parent—a mother even—with loving concern for a wayward child: "When Israel was a child, I loved him, and out of Egypt I called my son.... It was I who taught Ephraim to walk, taking them by the arms; but they did not realize it was I who healed them. I led them with cords of human kindness, with ties of love. To them I was like one who lifts a little child to the cheek, and I bent down to feed them" (Hosea 11:1–4). The prophet Zephaniah depicts the heavenly parent singing a lullaby to His child: "The

Lord your God is with you, he is mighty to save. He will take great delight in you, he will quiet you with his love, he will rejoice over you with singing" (Zeph. 3:17, NIV).

God is also pictured as the divine Lover, looking for a reciprocal response from His often-wayward spouse. The prophet Hosea was given the task of representing the heavenly Lover in His yearning for adulterous Israel: "Go, show your love to your wife again, though she is loved by another....Love her as the Lord loves the Israelites, though they turn to other gods" (Hosea 3:1). The entire Song of Solomon is a poetic celebration of the kind of intimacy God wanted with His chosen people. Through Jeremiah, God declared, "I have loved you with an everlasting love; therefore I have continued my faithfulness to you. Again I will build you, and you shall be built, O virgin Israel! Again you shall adorn yourself with timbrels, and shall go forth in the dance of the merrymakers" (Jer. 31:3, 4 RSV).

Is it possible to visualize this heartfelt longing of God in the Ten Commandments? They were given to a motley band of abused and dysfunctional slaves. Commands don't readily lend themselves to loving invitations, so are you surprised when you read this from the pen of Ellen White?—"That law of ten precepts of the greatest love that can be presented to man is the voice of God from heaven speaking to the soul in promise....*There is not a negative in that law*, although it may appear thus"[2] (italics mine).

Richard Davidson, an Old Testament scholar, looked closely at the original Hebrew of the Decalogue and discovered that eight commandments that begin with "Thou shalt not" can be translated either as negative commands *or* emphatic promises.[3] Thus, one may translate the first commandment this way: "I promise you, you will not have any other gods before Me" and so on with the commands that follow. The Holy Spirit must have given Ellen White this insight when she wrote, "The ten commandments, Thou shalt, and Thou shalt not, are *ten promises*, assured to us if we render obedience to the law governing the universe"[4] (italics mine).

Let's follow that concept through the first four commandments—our love to God—drawing some insights from David Asscherick, a Bible teacher with ARISE.[5] We are surprised to discover a God longing for a personal relationship with us. Read and understand each command as a conditional promise.

- "You will have no other gods before me" (Exod. 20:3). *I want to be first in your life, the primary recipient of your love and affection. You won't want to share that love with other "gods" of this world that will always want to control and manipulate you.*

- "You will not make for yourself an idol in the form of anything in heaven or on earth" (Exod. 20:4). *Just like I formed the body of Adam long ago, I have made you unique and different from any other human person who has ever lived. Your body is a sacred thing. You won't want to surrender or sacrifice your body to any object or individual that wants to abuse it for sinful pleasure or lust. Your body is my temple* (see 1 Cor. 6:19).

- "You will not misuse the name of the Lord your God" (Exod. 20:7). *My Name represents my character. The words you use when you speak about Me will reflect your thinking about Me. They will show to other people that we have a love relationship.*

- "You will remember the Sabbath day by keeping it holy" (Exod. 20:8). *You will give me your time. Our love relationship can endure only as we spend time together. That was the way My relationship began with your first parents.*

The New Testament continues the same longing of God for relationship. Writing to the believers in Ephesus, Paul compares the love between a man and his wife with Christ's love for the church: "Husbands, love your wives, just as Christ loved the church and gave himself up for her to make her holy, cleansing her by the washing with water through the word" (Eph. 5:25). Revelation carries the same image to the end of time: "Let us rejoice and be glad and give him glory! For the wedding of the Lamb has come, and his bride has made herself ready. Fine linen, bright and clean, was given her to wear" (Rev. 19:7, 8). And in vision, John saw "the Holy City, the new Jerusalem, coming down out of heaven from God, prepared as a bride beautifully dressed for her husband" (Rev. 21:2).

The very last invitation in the Bible echoes the relationship that began so wonderfully in the Garden of Eden: "The Spirit and the bride say 'Come!' And let those who hear say, 'Come!' Let those who are thirsty come; and let all who wish take the free gift of the water of life" (Rev. 22:17).

The Returning

Thinking about relationship, I'm reminded of these words from Timothy Johnson, an American physician who lost God as a young man, but found Him again: "This relational drive manifests itself not just in a horizontal dimension but in a vertical one as well—even more suggestive of a divine source. Virtually all religions and mythologies share a common sense that human beings are in relationship to someone or something suprahuman....This sense is heightened by indications from brain researchers that we are, in casual terms, 'hard-wired for God.'"[6]

The Apostle Paul confirms Johnson's words: "The god of this age has blinded the minds of unbelievers, so that they cannot see the light of the gospel that displays the glory of Christ, who is the image of God....For God, who said, 'Let light shine out of darkness,' made his light shine in our hearts to give us the light of the knowledge of God's glory in the face of Christ." Then he adds, "But we have this treasure in jars of clay to show that this all-surpassing power is from God and not from us" (2 Cor. 4: 4, 6, 7).

Like humans throughout all time, we have a deep hunger for God. Separation from Him leaves us perplexed and empty. However, God's love for relationship has a drawing power. He also seeks our longing for Him. He yearns for our returning. The Scriptures are filled with calls to return. First, a sampling from the Old Testament, then a story from Luke's gospel.

- God had this message of encouragement for unfaithful Israel about to be taken into captivity: "I will give them a heart to know me, that I am the Lord. They will be my people, and I will be their God, for they will return to me with all their heart" (Jer. 24:7).
- Isaiah proclaims this powerful invitation: "Let the wicked forsake their ways and the unrighteous their thoughts. Let them turn to the Lord, and he will have mercy on them, and to our God, for he will freely pardon" (Isa. 55:7).
- A message comes from the divine Surgeon who sometimes has to deal painfully with the sin problem in our lives: "Come, let us return to the Lord. He has torn us to pieces, but he will heal us; he has injured us but he will bind up our wounds" (Hosea 6:1).
- Joel makes this appeal: "Return to the Lord your God, for he is gracious and compassionate, slow to anger and abounding in love" (Joel 2:13).
- Jesus invites: "Come to me, all you who are weary and burdened, and I will give you rest." (Matt.11:28)

One day, Jesus stood before an audience that comprised a motley company of people. At the front were unrighteous tax collectors and other sinners. Behind them were a few Scribes and Pharisees—the upper echelons of Jewish society—muttering among themselves because Jesus deliberately associated and even ate with those they considered to be the dregs of society—the crowd sitting in the front row.

Jesus told them about a father who had two sons.[7] One day the younger son asks dad for his share of the family inheritance. Receiving that, he abandons home, traveling to a distant country. There he wastes everything he owns on wild living. Soon, though, a severe famine hits that country, and the boy finds himself broke and hungry. After a while, he finds a job looking after pigs. He is so hungry he wishes he could eat the slop the pigs are eating. He feels sick, alone, and abandoned.

Finally, he says to himself, "What am I doing here? Back home, my dad's hired servants have plenty to eat. Why am I here starving to death?" So, the boy sets out toward home. During the long walk, he is thinking about what he will say to his father: "Dad, I have done wrong. I've forfeited my right to be treated like your son, but I'm just wondering if you would take me on as an employee?"

The boy's father sees his young son coming in the distance and runs to meet him, giving him a big embrace and kisses. The boy starts to tell what he'd planned to say, but his father interrupts, calling to his servants, "Quick! Bring the best robe we have and put it on him. Put a ring on his finger and sandals on his feet. And go get the fattest calf and butcher it. We will have a big party, because my son was dead and is alive again. He was lost and has been found." Everyone is celebrating, except the boy's older brother, who feels insulted and angry, a fitting representation of those muttering Pharisees in Christ's audience.

One afternoon, the anxious father is looking down the road and sees not one, but two boys coming home, and one has his arm around the other. "Look, Dad, I found him, and I've brought him home!" That is how the story was supposed to end.

The story presents a beautiful picture of a God who values our freedom to run away, but looks and longs for us to come home. Yet the story wasn't supposed to happen the way it did. Let's imagine a different ending. The father's older son is concerned about his lost brother. He sees the distress of his grieving dad and volunteers to go out in search of his brother. He goes all the way to the distant country, finds his brother feeding the pigs, assures him that his father still loves him, and brings him home.

One afternoon, the anxious father is looking down the road and sees not one, but two boys coming home, and one has his arm around the other. "Look, Dad, I found him, and I've brought him home!" That is how the story was supposed to end. That is how the gospel works when we return to our Father, bringing lost ones along with us. That is how God seeks to heal broken relationships.

The Arriving

Almost exactly halfway through my Bible, between Genesis 1 and Revelation 22, King David is looking back to creation and then ahead to a re-created planet awaiting our arrival.

> "Long ago you laid the foundation of the earth
>
> and made the heavens with your hands.
>
> They will perish, but you remain forever;
>
> they will wear out like old clothing.
>
> You will change them like a garment and discard them.
>
> But you are always the same;
>
> you will live forever. . . .
>
> For the Lord will rebuild Jerusalem.
>
> He will appear in his glory.
>
> Let this be recorded for future generations,
>
> so that a people not yet born will praise the Lord."
>
> (Ps. 102: 25–27, 16, 18, NLT)

It was Passover Eve, just hours before the trial and crucifixion of Jesus. The Master was with His disciples in the upper room in Jerusalem. Those men wore fear on their faces because Jesus said He would soon go away. Looking around at their anxious faces, He told them not to be troubled. Yes, He would leave them and return to His Father, but He would also be preparing homes for them in heaven. When everything was ready, He would come back and take them home to live with Him. "When everything is ready, I will come and get you, so that you will always be with me, where I am" (John 14:1–3, NLT).

For those troubled disciples, Jesus' promise was full of meaning. They knew about wedding customs in their society. They knew that a prospective bridegroom, after the engagement or betrothal, would return to his parents' home and there prepare a place for his bride. When the house was ready, the bridegroom would come back for his bride and escort her to their new home. A joyful wedding celebration would follow. In the same way, the disciples' loving Master, their Bridegroom, was going away to prepare a home for them. He would return one day to take them home with Him for a great, celestial wedding celebration. They would be with Him forever.[8]

The promise is for us too. Life on planet earth is temporary. We are pilgrims and refugees here. We may enjoy the friendships along the way, but deep down we have hearts longing for home—a place where we will belong forever. That is why Jesus' promise is also for us. "I will come again," He says, "and take you home."

The future that awaits is beyond our dreams. The apostle John tries to describe it for us: "Then I saw 'a new heaven and a new earth', for the first heaven and the first earth had passed away, and there was no longer any sea....And I heard a loud voice from the throne saying, 'Look! God's dwelling place is now among the people, and he will dwell with them. They will be his people, and God himself will be with them and be their God. He will wipe every tear from their eyes. There will be no more death or mourning or crying or pain, for the old order of things has passed away'" (Rev. 21:1–4).

The Apostle John captured the memorable words from God Himself: "I am making everything new!" Then an instruction, "Write this down, for these words are trustworthy and true" (Rev. 21:5).

*   *   *   *   *   *   *

Have you ever tried to imagine your arrival in the courts of heaven? How could so much be happening all at once?

Let's pretend that you are met on arrival by your guardian angel—someone who knows and understands you better than you have ever known yourself. A big hug and "Welcome home" are the first words, full of smiles, that greet you.

Of course, there is the excitement of having a brand-new body. You could do somersaults and cartwheels, but there's more to learn and think about right now. In just moments, you will be led to a special place reserved for your family reunion. However, your angel is bursting to say something: "Please come with me. I want you to meet Jesus."

To think about:

1. We maintain relationships with friends and family in a variety of ways, including social media. Think about some ways you may grow and maintain a strong relationship with Jesus Christ.

2. Arriving in heaven, you have just met your guardian angel. Imagine the conversation between you two. What questions might you ask, and what questions might be asked of you?

References:

[1]   Thomas Wolfe, *You Can't Go Home Again*.

[2]   Ellen White, Letter 89, 1898.14.

[3]   Richard Davidson, "Ellen White's insights into Scripture in light of the original biblical languages", in *The Gift of Prophecy in Scripture and History*, 164,165.

[4]   White, Comment in *The Seventh-day Adventist Bible Commentary*, 1:1105.

[5]   David Asscherick, "Does God Have Time?" *God?* Episode 8, Hope Channel, 2013.

[6]   Timothy Johnson, *Finding God in the Questions*, 67.

[7]   The story comes from Luke 15:11–32. I have adapted parts of the story from the *Voice* Bible.

[8]   Keith Clouten, *Journeys: Devotions for Travelers*, 206.

The Wall: An Epilogue

During my brief visit to Berlin, Germany in 2003, I spent an hour or two wandering along the line of the wall that had divided a city and nation. Most of the wall had now disappeared, but there were one or two isolated fragments, preserved as a reminder of those years of repression. On one remaining piece that is now covered with graffiti art, someone who believed in the values of life and liberty had splashed these words: "The world is too small for walls."

The universe also is too small for walls. The wall that sin created has been an ugly blot on the landscape of the universe for much too long. The time is rapidly approaching when it will be torn down, never to be rebuilt.

The drama of the ages is approaching its climax. The play will soon be over. Something like the massive stone seen by King Nebuchadnezzar in his dream will come hurtling through space and smash the wall into a trillion pieces. It will signal the end of a divided universe.

"And I heard a loud voice from the throne saying, 'Now the dwelling of God is with men, and he will live with them. They will be His people, and God Himself will be with them, and be their God'" (Rev. 21:3).

"And the years of eternity, as they roll, will bring richer and still more glorious revelations of God and of Christ....The great controversy is ended. Sin and sinners are no more. The entire universe is clean. One pulse of harmony and gladness beats through the vast creation. From Him who created all flow life and light and gladness throughout the realms of illimitable space. From the minutest atom to the greatest world, all things, animate and inanimate, in their unshadowed beauty and perfect joy, declare that God is love" (*Great Controversy*, 678).

Bibliography

Andrews, Evan. "Remembering New England's Dark Day." *History.* http://1ref.us/ma (accessed October 10, 2017).

Baden, Joel S. *The Historical David.* New York: Harper Collins, 2013.

Ball, Bryan. *Can We Still Believe the Bible?* Warburton, Victoria: Signs Publishing, 2007.

Benner, Jeff A. "How many came out of the exodus of Egypt?" *Ancient Hebrew Research Center.* http://1ref.us/mh (accessed October 10, 2017).

Biblical Research Institute. "The Inspiration and Authority of the Ellen G. White Writings." *Ministry*, Feb. 1983.

Black, James R. *The Instruction of Amenemope, a critical edition and commentary.* Madison, WI: Univ. of Wisconsin, 2002.

Boston Public Library. *Report of the Examining Committee.* (1875).

Bradford, Graeme. *More Than a Prophet.* Berrien Springs, MI: Biblical Perspectives, 2006.

Brand, Leonard and Don S. McMahon. *The Prophet and Her Critics.* Nampa, ID: Pacific Press, 2005.

Briggs, Peter. "Testing the Factuality of the Conquest of Ai Narrative in the Book of Joshua." http://1ref.us/me (accessed October 10, 2017).

Bruce, F. F. *The Books and the Parchments.* Westwood, NJ: Revell, 1984.

Burt, Merlin D. "Bibliographic Essay on Publications about Ellen G. White." *The Ellen G. White Encyclopedia*, pp.148–213.

Burt, Merlin D., editor. *Understanding Ellen White*. Nampa, ID: Pacific Press, 2015.

Burt, Merlin D. "Understanding Ellen White and the 'Shut Door'." Chap. 12 in *Understanding Ellen White.* Nampa, ID: Pacific Press, 2015.

Butler, George I. "Inspiration: its Nature and Manner of Communication." *Review and Herald*, Jan. 8 through June 3, 1884.

Campbell, Michael. *The 1919 Bible Conference and Its Significance for Seventh-day Adventist History and Theology.* (Andrews Univ. Dissertation).

Canright, Dudley M. *Life of Mrs. E.G. White, Seventh-day Adventist Prophet.* Cincinnati, OH: Standard Publishing Co., 1919.

Clouten, Keith. "Ellen White and Fiction, a Closer Look." *Journal of Adventist Education*, April 2014.

Clouten, Keith. *Journeys: Devotions for Travelers.* Enumclaw, WA: Wine Press, 2011.

Clouten, Keith. *The Road from Stoney Creek: a personal journey.* Lacombe, AB: Mile Post Press, 2014.

Comstock, Anthony. *Traps for the Young.* Cambridge, MA: Harvard Univ. Press, 1967.

Conway, David. *The Rediscovery of Wisdom*. London: Macmillan, 2000.

Coon, Roger W. "Inspiration / Revelation: what it is and how it works." *Journal of Adventist Education*, 44:1–3, 1981–2.

Crick, Francis. *Life Itself*. New York: Simon & Schuster, 1981.

Crystal, Ellie. "Ancient Egyptian Medicine." http://1ref.us/mc (accessed October 10, 2017).

Damsteegt, Gerard. "Seventh-day Adventist Doctrines and Progressive Revelation." *Journal of the Adventist Theological Society,* Spring, 1991.

Darwin, Charles. "Recollections of the Development of my Mind and Character" in *The Life and Letters of Charles Darwin.* London: John Murray, 1887.

Darwinism: Science or Naturalistic Philosophy? The Debate at Stanford University between William B. Provine and Phillip E. Johnson. (1994).

Davidson, Richard. "Ellen White's Insights Into Scripture in Light of the Original Biblical Languages." Chap. 7 in *The Gift of Prophecy in Scripture and History*. Silver Spring, MD: Review and Herald, 2015.

Davies, Paul. *The Mind of God.* New York: Simon & Schuster, 1992.

Davies, Paul. *The Origin of Life*. London: Penguin, 2003.

Dawkins, Richard. *Climbing Mount Improbable.* New York: Norton, 1996.

Dederen, Raoul. "Ellen White's Doctrine of Scripture." *Ministry* supplement, July 1977.

De Souza, Elias Brasil. "The Hebrew Prophets and the Literature of the Ancient Near East." Chap. 5 in *The Gift of Prophecy in Scripture and History.* Silver Spring, MD: Review and Herald, 2015.

Douglass, Herbert E. *Dramatic Prophecies of Ellen White*. Nampa, ID: Pacific Press, 2006.

Douthat, Ross. "Can Liberal Christianity be saved?" *New York Times*, July 16, 2012.

Dybdal, Jon. *A Strange Place for Grace*. Nampa, ID: Pacific Press, 2006.

Dyson, Freeman. *Disturbing the Universe*. New York: Basic Books, 1979.

The Ellen G. White 1888 Materials. Washington, DC: Ellen G. White Estate, 1987.

The Ellen G. White Encyclopedia. Editors, Denis Fortin, Jerry Moon. Hagerstown, MD: Review and Herald, 2013.

Ellul, Jacques. *The Politics of God and the Politics of Man.* Grand Rapids, MI: Eerdmans, 1972.

"The Exodus and Ancient Egyptian Records." *Jewish Action*, Spring, 1995.

Flew, Antony. *There is a God.* New York: Harper, 2007.

Fortin, Denis. "Plagiarism." *The Ellen G. White Encyclopedia*, p.1034.

Foster, John. *The Divine Lawmaker.* Oxford: Clarendon Press, 2004.

Gingerich, Owen. *God's Universe*. Cambridge, MA: Harvard Univ. Press, 2006.

"The God who provides: Logistics of the Exodus."

Gray, James M. "The Inspiration of the Bible." *The Fundamentals*, vol.2, chap.1, 1917.

Harrison, Everett. "The Phenomena of Scripture." Chap. 15 in *Revelation and the Bible*, edited by C.F.H. Henry. Grand Rapids, MI: Baker, 1958.

Hasel, Gerard F. and Michael G. Hasel. "Unique Cosmology of Genesis 1." *College and University Dialogue*, 28:1, 2016.

Hawking, Stephen. *A Brief History of Time.* London: Bantam Dell, 1988.

Heisenberg, Werner. "Naturwissenschaftliche und religioese Wahrheit." *Physikalische Blatter*, 29:8, August 1973.

Higgs, Philip and Jane Smith. *Rethinking Our World.* 2nd ed. Cape Town: Juta, 2007.

Houdmann, S. Michael, editor. *Questions about the Bible.* Bloomington, IN: WestBow Press, 2015.

Johnson. Timothy. *Finding God in the Questions.* Downers Grove, IL: Inter Varsity Press, 2004.

Kenyon, Frederic G. *The Bible and Modern Scholarship.* London: John Murray, 1948.

Kitchen, K. A., *On the Reliability of the Old Testament*. Grand Rapids, MI: Eerdmans, 2003.

Kite, William. "Fiction in Public Libraries." *American Library Journal,* 1:8 (1876), pp. 277–279.

Knight, George R. *A Brief History of Seventh-day Adventists*. 3rd ed. Hagerstown, MD: Review and Herald, 2012.

Knight, George R. "The Case of the Overlooked Postscript." *Ministry,* Aug. 1997.

Knight, George R. "Ellen G. White's Writings." *The Ellen G. White Encyclopedia*, pp.121–140.

Knight, George R. *Meeting Ellen White*. Hagerstown, MD: Review and Herald, 1999.

Knight, George R. *Reading Ellen White.* Hagerstown, MD: Review and Herald, 1997.

Knight, George R. *Walking with Ellen White*. Hagerstown, MD: Review & Herald, 1999.

Knoll, Andrew. "How did Life Begin?" *PBS Nova Interview*, May 3, 2004.

Kosmin, Barry. *One Nation Under God*. New York: Crown Publishers, 1993.

Lake, Jud and Jerry Moon, "Current Science and Ellen White." *The Ellen G. White Encyclopedia,* pp.214–240.

Lake, Jud. "Ellen White's Use of Extrabiblical Sources." Chap. 17 in *The Gift of Prophecy in Scripture and History.* Silver Springs, MD: Review and Herald, 2015.

Leitch, Cliff. "Should the Bible be Interpreted Literally?"

Levterov, Theodore N., *Accepting Ellen White*. Nampa, ID: Pacific Press, 2016.

Leslie, John. *Infinite Minds.* New York: Oxford Univ. Press, 2001.

Marshall, David. *The Battle for the Bible.* Grantham, England: Autumn House, 2004.

McAdams, Don. "Shifting Views on Inspiration." *Spectrum*, 4:4, 1972.

McMillen, S.I. and David E. Stern. *None of These Diseases.* 3rd ed. Grand Rapids, MI: Revell, 2000.

Metzger, Bruce. *The Canon of the New Testament*. New York: Oxford Univ. Press, 1987.

Moon, Jerry and Denis Kaiser. "For Jesus and Scripture: The Life of Ellen G. White." *The Ellen G. White Encyclopedia*, pp.18–111.

Morrison, Michael. *The Purpose and Authority of the Bible.* Grace Communion International, 2005. Accessed June 2017. http://1ref.us/mf (accessed October 10, 2017).

Moule, C.F.D. *The Phenomenon of the New Testament.* London, SCM Press, 1967.

The NIV Cultural Backgrounds Study Bible. Grand Rapids, MI: Zondervan, 2016.

Numbers, Ronald L. *Prophetess of Health: A Study of Ellen G. White.* 3rd ed. Grand Rapids, MI: Eerdmans, 2008.

Olson, Robert W. "Ellen White's Denials." *Ministry*, Feb. 1991.

Olson, Robert W. *One Hundred and One Questions on the Sanctuary and on Ellen White.* Silver Spring, MD: Ellen G. White Estate, 1981.

Pasquini, John J. *The Existence of God.* Lanham, MD: University Press of America, 2010.

Paulien, Jon. "The Gift of Prophecy in Scripture." Chap. 1 in *Understanding Ellen White*. Nampa, ID: Pacific Press, 2015.

Phillips, J.B. *Ring of Truth, a Translator's Testimony*. London: Hodder & Stoughton, 1967.

Poirier, Tim. "Ellen White and Sources: The Plagiarism Debate." Chap. 11 in *Understanding Ellen White.* Nampa, ID: Pacific Press, 2015.

Poirier, Tim. "Ellen White's Letters and Manuscripts." *Adventist World*, Feb. 2016.

Poole, William F. "Some Popular Objections to Public Libraries." *American Library Journal,* 1:2, 1876, pp. 45–51.

Rebok, Denton E. *Believe His Prophets*. Washington, D.C.: Review and Herald, 1956.

"Report on Sacred Scripture: Southern Baptist - Roman Catholic Conversation", September 10, 1999.

Rice, George E. *Luke, a Plagiarist?* Mountain View, CA: Pacific Press, 1973.

Rice, Richard. *Suffering and the Search for Meaning*. Downers Grove, IL: IVP Academic, 2014.

Rodriguez, Angel M. "Revelation, Inspiration and the Witness of Scripture." Chap. 3 in *The Gift of Prophecy in Scripture and History.* Hagerstown, MD: Review and Herald, 2015.

Schlitz, Marilyn. "Do Brains make Minds?" in *Closer to Truth: Challenging Current Belief*, by Robert L. Kuhn. New York: McGraw-Hill, 2000.

Schrodinger, Erwin. *Mind and Matter*. Cambridge, England: Cambridge Univ. Press, 1958.

Schrodinger, Erwin. *My View of the World*. Cambridge, England: Cambridge Univ. Press, 1964.

Schroeder, Gerald. *The Hidden Face of God*. New York: Simon & Schuster, 2001.

Schultz, Richard. *Out of Context*. Grand Rapids, MI: Baker, 2012.

Seventh-day Adventists Believe. Silver Spring, MD: General Conference of Seventh-day Adventists.

Spicer, W.A. *Certainties of the Advent Movement*. Washington: Review and Herald, 1929.

Stowe, Calvin E. *Origin and History of the Books of the Bible*. Hartford, WI: Hartford Publishing, 1867.

Strobel, Lee. *The Case for a Creator*. Grand Rapids, MI: Zondervan, 2004.

Strobel, Lee. *The Case for Christ*. Grand Rapids, MI: Zondervan, 1998.

Thompson, Alden. "The Theology of Ellen White: The Great Controversy Story." *Adventist Review*, December 31, 1981.

Thompson, Alden. *Inspiration: Hard Questions, Honest Answers*. Hagerstown, MD: Review and Herald, 1991.

Thompson, Alden. *Who's Afraid of the Old Testament God?* Grand Rapids, MI: Zondervan, 1989.

Tidwell, Charles H. "Literature and Reading" in *The Ellen G. White Encyclopedia*, pp.943–946.

Timm, Alberto R. and Dwain N. Esmond, editors. *The Gift of Prophecy in Scripture and History*. Silver Spring, MD: Review and Herald, 2015.

Tonstad, Sigve K. *The Lost Meaning of the Seventh Day*. Berrien Springs, MI: Andrews Univ. Press, 2009.

Torrey, R. A., editor. *The Fundamentals: a Testimony to the Truth.* First published 1910–1915. Grand Rapids, MI: Baker, 1994.

"Transcripts of the 1919 Bible Conference." *Spectrum*, 10:1, May 1979, pp.21–58.

Valentine, Gilbert. *W.W. Prescott.* Hagerstown, MD., Review and Herald, 2005.

Veltman, Fred. "The Desire of Ages Project: The Data." *Ministry*, October 1990.

Von Rad, Gerhard. *Old Testament Theology*, v.2. Edinburgh: Oliver & Boyd, 1962.

Walton, John H. *The Lost World of Genesis One*. Downers Grove, IL: IVP Academic, 2009.

Wesley, John. *Explanatory Notes Upon the New Testament.* New York: Soule and Mason, 1818.

White, Arthur L. *Ellen G. White:* 6 volumes. Washington: Review and Herald, 1981–82.

White, Ellen G. *Steps to Christ*, with historical introduction and notes by Denis Fortin. Berrien Springs, MI: Andrews Univ. Press, 2017.

White, James. *A Word to the Little Flock.* Brunswick, ME: 1847.

Williams, Peter S. "The Big Bad Wolf, Theism and the Foundations of Intelligent Design." Paper of the *Evangelical Philosophical Society.* http://1ref.us/mg (accessed October 10, 2017).

Wolfe, Thomas. *You Can't Go Home Again.* New York: Scribner, 1940.

Wood, John. "The Trashy Novel Revisited: Popular Fiction in the Age of Ellen White." *Spectrum,* April 1976, pp.16–21.

Yancey, Philip. *The Bible Jesus Read.* Grand Rapids, MI: Zondervan, 1999.

Yourgrau, Palle. *A World Without Time.* New York: Basic Books, 2005.

TEACH Services, Inc.
PUBLISHING

We invite you to view the complete
selection of titles we publish at:
www.TEACHServices.com

We encourage you to write us
with your thoughts about this,
or any other book we publish at:
info@TEACHServices.com

TEACH Services' titles may be purchased in
bulk quantities for educational, fund-raising,
business, or promotional use.
bulksales@TEACHServices.com

Finally, if you are interested in seeing
your own book in print, please contact us at:
publishing@TEACHServices.com
We are happy to review your manuscript at no charge.

CPSIA information can be obtained
at www.ICGtesting.com
Printed in the USA
LVHW02s1353040118
561783LV00008B/63/P